ASVAB

DeMYSTiFieD®

DeMYSTiFieD® Series

The DeMystified series publishes more than 125 titles in all areas of academic study. For a complete list of titles, please visit www.mhprofessional.com.

ASVAB
DeMYSTiFieD®

Cynthia Johnson and Chris Womack

New York   Chicago   San Francisco   Lisbon   London   Madrid   Mexico City
Milan   New Delhi   San Juan   Seoul   Singapore   Sydney   Toronto

The **McGraw·Hill** *Companies*

Copyright © 2013 by The McGraw-Hill Companies, Inc. All rights reserved. Printed in the United States of America. Except as permitted under the United States Copyright Act of 1976, no part of this publication may be reproduced or distributed in any form or by any means, or stored in a database or retrieval system, without the prior written permission of the publisher.

1 2 3 4 5 6 7 8 9 10   QFR/QFR   1 9 8 7 6 5 4 3 2

ISBN   978-0-07-177835-0
MHID   0-07-177835-7

e-ISBN   978-0-07-177836-7
e-MHID   0-07-177836-5

Library of Congress Control Number   2012938187

McGraw-Hill, the McGraw-Hill Publishing logo, Demystified, and related trade dress are trademarks or registered trademarks of The McGraw-Hill Companies and/or its affiliates in the United States and other countries and may not be used without written permission. All other trademarks are the property of their respective owners. The McGraw-Hill Companies is not associated with any product or vendor mentioned in this book.

McGraw-Hill products are available at special quantity discounts to use as premiums and sales promotions or for use in corporate training programs. To contact a representative, please e-mail us at bulksales@mcgraw-hill.com.

This book is printed on acid-free paper.

Contents

ASVAB

DeMYSTiFieD®

Part I

All About the ASVAB

1

Deciding on Military Service

From the time they are quite young, most children dream about what they want to be when they grow up. Some know from an early age exactly what career paths interest them. Others change their minds repeatedly until entering college, or even beyond. One honorable path which is chosen by thousands each and every day is U.S. military service.

The benefits of military service are many. Training, honor, travel, discipline, and service to our country are but a few of the advantages. In addition, the Post-9/11 GI Bill provides those serving in the military with all in-state tuition and fees for higher education. But, along with these rewards come the requirements of self-discipline, sacrifice, and commitment. Deciding to join the military is a tremendous decision, which requires careful consideration and the support of family and friends.

When considering military service, one major decision is selecting active duty or reserves. Active duty means serving full time during the entire length of service, in a way which is similar to having a full-time job. Being part of a reserve unit is similar to having a part-time job—it gives you the opportunity to continue a civilian life and career and then serve your country during times when your experiences are needed. Either option includes the possibility of deployment.

Another decision is selecting which branch of the Armed Forces to join. The Army, Navy, Air Force, Marines, and Coast Guard each offer different opportunities and benefits. Let's take a look at each of these choices.

Army

The U.S. Army was founded in 1775 and is the oldest branch of military service in the United States. Currently, more than 571,000 soldiers serve full time in this branch of our military by defending and serving our country by land, as well as by sea and by air. The Army offers opportunities for specialized training and to join elite groups, including the Army Rangers and Special Forces, and has permanent bases in Asia, Europe, and the Middle East, in addition to those within the United States. When enlisting, the commitment may be for as little as two years.

The minimum age requirement to enlist in the Army is 18, or 17 with the consent of your parents. The maximum age to enlist is 42. Other requirements include being a U.S. citizen or resident alien and having a high school diploma, although the GED or other equivalent certificate may be acceptable. A physical fitness test and a passing score on the ASVAB are also required. Benefits of enlisting in the Army include

- Educational opportunities
- Training and experience in more than 150 career choices
- Competitive salary
- Health care
- Housing allowance
- Food allowance
- Opportunities for special pay
- Retirement after 20 years of service

Navy

Also founded in 1775, the Navy was begun under the authority of our nation's first president, George Washington, in order to stop British supply ships as they approached Massachusetts. Although successful in several battles during the American Revolution, the expense of having permanent naval forces was considered too great. It was not until 1794, following pirate attacks and other international conflicts, that a standing Navy was established. Today, more than 328,600 men and women serve in this branch of the military, defending our country both above and below the surface of the sea, on the ground and from the air. Opportunities are available to join the elite Navy SEALs and Navy Divers, following specialized training. Generally, those enlisting in the Navy serve a minimum of four years, although it is possible to make a commitment for a shorter time period.

The minimum age for enlisting in the Navy is also 18, or 17 with a parent's permission, and the maximum age to enlist is 34 years old. A high school diploma is also necessary, although an equivalent may be acceptable. Benefits of joining this branch of the military include

- Regular salary
- Additional pay for specialists
- Health care
- Educational support
- Occupational training
- More than 60 career path opportunities
- 30 days of vacation time

Air Force

In 1920, the U.S. Air Force was formed as a division of the Army: it was recognized as its own branch of the military in 1947, following World War II. The vision of the Air Force is global vigilance, reach, and power. Today, more than 333,700 men and women serve in this branch.

To enlist in the Air Force, you must be between the ages of 18 and 27, although 17-year-olds may enlist with their parent's permission. A high school diploma is generally required, although an equivalent, such as a GED credential, may be accepted. Benefits of serving in the Air Force include

- Good salary
- Full health benefits
- Hands-on training
- Career options including pilots, flight crew positions, air traffic controllers, mechanics, electronics technicians, and medical personnel

Marine Corps

Like the Army, the U.S. Marine Corps was also founded in 1775. The core values of this branch of service include honor, courage, and commitment. Those selecting to become Marines are expected to demonstrate exceptional character, and to successfully endure approximately three months of intense mental and physical training. Today, there are more than 202,000 Marines serving our country from their stations around the world. These elite men and women are generally the first to deploy in a conflict, as they are considered warriors. The minimum commitment for those enlisting is four years.

In order to become a Marine, you must be at least 18 years old, 17 with a parent's permission, and no more than 29 years old. A high school diploma is generally required, although a GED credential may be accepted with a strong ASVAB score. Benefits of serving in the Marine Corps are the same as those offered by other branches of service, although the focus is on the intangible benefits reaped by serving as a Marine.

Coast Guard

Originally, the U.S. Lighthouse Service, the Revenue Cutter Service, the Steamboat Inspection Service, the Bureau of Navigation, and the U.S. Life-Saving Service were individual federal services. In 1915, a congressional act combined these organizations to form the U.S. Coast Guard, which was controlled by the Treasury Department for several decades, until it was transferred to the control of the newly created Department of Transportation in 1967. Currently, the Coast Guard serves under the U.S. Navy during times of war and under the Department of Homeland Security during times of peace. Today, more than 43,000 men and women are on active duty with the Coast Guard, making it the smallest branch of our military. They protect our waterways, undertake search-and-rescue missions, enforce laws, and perform environmental cleanup missions.

In order to enlist in the Coast Guard, you must be between the ages of 18 and 27, although with parental consent you may join at age 17. As with the other military branches, a high school diploma is required; however, GED credentials may be accepted. All military branches require physical fitness drills during basic training; in addition, Coast Guard training requires daily swimming drills. Some of the benefits for those joining this branch of service include

- Salary
- Full health benefits
- Tuition reimbursement
- Career training in marine and environmental sciences, law enforcement, and mechanical engineering

Making the Choice

Are you unsure of which career path to choose? Deciding whether or not to join the military, and selecting which branch is the best match for you, are major decisions. Believe it or not, most students change their major at least one time during college, and people average three career changes in their lifetime. You may be considering the military as a career, or as a stepping stone toward a college education. Either way, here are a few suggestions for making the choice that is best for you.

- **Think about your reasons for considering the military.** Are you interested in taking advantage of the educational benefits? Are you looking for a career in the service? Are you excited about the opportunity to travel and live abroad? Once you know *why* you want to enlist, you will be able to focus your decision on finding which options are best for you.

- **Identify your own strengths and interests.** You might think that a life at sea would be amazing, in which case the Navy could be a great choice. On the other hand, you could be someone who lives for physical challenges, and always push yourself. If that's the case, you might feel that the Marines are a good fit. Be honest about what you want to do, what career options you are interested in training for, and what hopes you have for your own future.

- **Make comparisons.** Check out the websites for each branch of our military and compare the options and advantages of each. The information listed in this chapter is just the tip of the iceberg when it comes to fully understanding the benefits, challenges, and opportunities offered. Also, discover the advantages and disadvantages of active duty versus reserve duty.

- **Talk with your family and friends.** Joining the military is a huge decision that impacts not only you but your family and friends as well. Having their support and input can make this decision much easier for you.

chapter 2

Introducing the ASVAB

Anyone who chooses to join any branch of the military will go through several evaluations, both physical and mental. One of these is taking the **Armed Services Vocational Aptitude Battery (ASVAB).** The ASVAB is not an IQ test, but does assess knowledge and ability in a number of areas. The test is used to help determine the qualifications and eligibility for military enlistment and identify strengths and weakness in order to determine the career for which the test-taker is best suited. Administered to more than one million people each year, this multiple-aptitude battery has been proven to accurately predict success in a range of occupations. Since its development, the ASVAB has been taken by more than 40 million military applicants and students.

Developed by the Department of Defense (DOD) in 1968, the ASVAB is one of the most widely used around the word, and is given to students in more than half of the high schools in the United States. The Air Force began using the ASVAB in 1973, and the Marine Corps began using it the following year. In 1974, the DOD decided that all branches of military service should use the assessment to screen those wishing to join and to determine the occupation to which enlistees should be assigned. By using a single test to accomplish both of these tasks, the testing process became more efficient and the matching of individuals to positions was improved.

The ASVAB may be taken as part of the Enlistment Testing Program for those planning to use the scores to join the military. It may also be taken as part of the Career Exploration Program, also known as the Student Testing Program. The test is the same for both programs, with the exception of the Assembling Objects subtest, which is found only in the Enlistment Testing Program. Composite scores do vary, however. The Student Testing Program provides Verbal Skills, Math Skills, and Science and Technical Skills composite scores. The Enlistment Testing Program provides an Armed Forces Qualification Test (AFQT) score and Service composite scores.

When you enlist in the military, your ASVAB scores will be used in several ways. First, these scores are used to determine eligibility for entrance into the armed forces. Later, the scores help servicemen and women to qualify for certain military occupations. As you might expect, the higher the score, the more options you will have when it comes to training. Once you have enlisted, you may retake the test in order to be reclassified for training purposes.

The ASVAB takes about three hours to complete, and includes several tests.

- General Science
- Arithmetic Reasoning
- Word Knowledge
- Paragraph Comprehension
- Mathematics Knowledge
- Electronics Information
- Auto and Shop Information
- Mechanical Comprehension
- Assembling Objects

Separate scores are reported for each of these tests. Let's take a closer look at each of the test areas of the ASVAB.

ASVAB Test Areas

As you know, the ASVAB consists of several separate tests. The number of questions varies by subject. Here, you will learn a little more about what to expect from each of the tests. Although some of the topics may look similar to those found on other assessments, such as the SAT or ACT, the ASVAB serves a different purpose; therefore, the content is very different. The SAT and ACT are designed to predict college success, whereas the ASVAB is designed to predict success in the military.

The ASVAB is offered as both a computer-based assessment, and as a paper-and-pencil assessment. The time limits mentioned in this section apply to the paper-and-pencil version. Specific details related to the computerized assessment will be discussed in a later chapter of this book.

Below, each of the tests is introduced. You will get a basic idea of the types of information found on each, as well as the number of questions and time limits for the paper-and-pencil versions of the tests.

General Science (GS)

You will have 11 minutes to complete the 25 questions on the general science test, which test your knowledge of physical and biological sciences. Specific areas of science that are assessed include

- Life science
- Earth and space science
- Physical science

Arithmetic Reasoning (AR)

This test includes 30 questions, and assesses basic arithmetic skills and the ability to solve basic arithmetic word problems. The time limit for this test is 36 minutes.

Word Knowledge (WK)

Thirty-five questions are found on the word knowledge test. This test uses synonyms to assess ability to understand word meanings, and you will be given 11 minutes to answer the questions. You will be expected to choose the correct meaning of a word presented in context, and to identify a word that has the same meaning or similar meaning as a given word.

Paragraph Comprehension (PC)

As you probably know, comprehension is the ability to understand what you have read. The paragraph comprehension test measures exactly that. You will read a passage, then answer questions showing that you were able to obtain information from the text. This test includes a total of 15 questions, which you will be given 13 minutes to complete.

Mathematics Knowledge (MK)

The mathematics knowledge test assesses mathematical abilities different from those on the arithmetic reasoning test. This 25-question test addresses your knowledge of high school mathematical concepts, principles, and applications, rather than basic math skills. This test has a time limit of 24 minutes.

Electronics Information (EI)

As the name suggests, the electronics information test assesses your knowledge of electronics and electricity. There are 20 questions on this test; you will be given nine minutes to complete the test. These items assess knowledge in the following areas:

- Electrical current
- Circuits
- Devices
- Electronic systems

Auto and Shop Information (AS)

The auto and shop information test includes 25 items. These assess knowledge of

- Automobile technology
- Automotive maintenance and repair
- Tools
- Wood and metal shop practices
- Shop terminology

This test has a time limit of 11 minutes.

Mechanical Comprehension (MC)

There are 25 questions on the mechanical comprehension test, which assesses your knowledge of mechanical and physical principles. You will be allowed 19 minutes to complete these questions. The specific areas of knowledge assessed include

- Principles of mechanical devices
- Properties of materials
- Structural support

Assembling Objects (AO)

The assembling objects test is included for those taking the test as part of the Enlistment Testing Program, but is not included in the Student Testing Program. This test has a time limit of 15 minutes, during which you will answer a total of 25 questions. These questions assess your ability to determine how an object will look after all of its parts have been put together. You will rely on your spatial awareness to complete this test.

Taking the Test

For those wishing to join the military, the ASVAB test is given at one of 65 Military Entrance Processing Stations (MEPS) around the United States and Puerto Rico, although it can be given at Military Entrance Test (MET) sites in other locations if there is not an MEPS located near where you live. MET sites are generally located in government buildings, National Guard armories, or military Reserve centers. Many students taking the test are able to do so at their own high schools. These student scores can be used to enlist in the military for up to two years after taking the test.

On test day, you will need to arrive on time, with valid identification. If you plan to take the ASVAB at an MEPS, the test will be computer based. If you plan to take the ASVAB at an MET site, you can expect to take the paper-and-pencil version of the test at most locations.

As you complete each of the paper-and-pencil tests, you will be allowed to go back and check your work in that test only; you may not return to a previously completed test and you may not work ahead.

Your scores on each of the tests are used to measure your verbal, math, science and technical, and spatial aptitude. The tests that assess each of these domains are listed below.

- **Verbal:** Word Knowledge and Paragraph Comprehension
- **Math:** Arithmetic Reasoning and Math Knowledge
- **Science and Technical:** General Science, Electronics Information, Auto and Shop Information, and Mechanical Comprehension
- **Spatial:** Assembling Objects

As we mentioned earlier, composite scores for the student test will be provided for these domains. Composite scores required for military enlistment will be discussed in a later chapter.

chapter 3

ASVAB Scores and Score Reports

The ASVAB is what is known as a *norm-referenced* test. As such, the scores are reported as *standard scores*. So, what exactly does this mean? Let's find out.

Norm-Referenced Testing and Standard Scores

Scores on each of the subtests of the ASVAB are reported as **standard scores**, meaning that the scores are relative to the performance of a sample of test-takers. The sample, or reference group, includes people between the ages of 18 and 23 years old who represent the people who typically take this test. **Norms** are developed based on the scores of the reference group, and give a summary of the group's performance. These norms are then used as a reference to which individual scores are compared.

National norms are calculated based on the performance of a group of nationally represented test-takers who are similar in age and have a similar level of education as the people expected to take the test. National norms for the ASVAB are calculated about every 15 or 20 years, and are based on the performance of about 6,000 18- to 23-year-old Americans. Your score on the ASVAB will compare your performance to that of the norm group for this test.

In other words, your score on the ASVAB will not necessary be based on the number of questions you answered correctly, but rather how your score compares to the scores of the norm group. To give you an idea of what this means, approximately half of test-takers earn a score of 50 or above, and approximately 16% of test takers earn a score of 60 or above. So, if you receive a score of 50, it does not mean you answered only 50 questions correctly, or that you earned a 50%. It simply means that your score is comparable to that of about half of the other test-takers. And, earning a score of 60 does not mean that you earned a 60%. It actually indicates that your score is comparable to that of the top 16% of the norm group.

Scores

Not all questions on the ASVAB are created equal. In other words, some questions are considered to be more difficult than others. Also, the paper-and-pencil version of the test is not identical to the computerized version, or CAT-ASVAB. For this reason, a formula is used to determine your score. This formula takes into consideration the difficulty of each question and the correctness of each answer. This process, known as *equating*, provides comparable scores for both versions of the test.

Some people may consider one version of the test to be easier or more difficult than the other. However, as a result of equating, the scores on both versions of the test are equivalent.

On both tests, the difficulty of each question is considered in determining the score. Another factor that is considered for each question is how well that question discriminates between test-takers with different ability levels. In other words, would the question separate high-ability test-takers from low-ability test-takers? A third factor that is included in the formula for scoring each item is the likelihood of a low-ability test-taker being able to correctly select the correct answer simply by guessing. These factors are then used to determine an ability estimate for the test-taker.

The ability estimate is then used to determine the standard score. On the ASVAB subtests, the mean, or average, is 50. The standard deviation is 10. So, a standard score of 60 indicates that the test-taker scored one standard deviation above the mean. A standard score of 70 indicates a score that is two standard deviations above the mean. Remember, these scores are reported as a comparison to the scores earned by the norm group.

Keep in mind that on the ASVAB, any question which is left blank is considered to be incorrect, and will negatively impact your score. In order to earn the highest possible score, regardless of how the scores are determined, it is in your best interest to answer every single question.

Receiving Your Score

The big question on everyone's mind following any test is usually, *How did I do?* One advantage of taking the CAT-ASVAB is that an unverified score report is computed automatically, so test-takers receive a printed report as soon as the test is complete. The report lists standard scores for each of the subtests, and composite scores for each service composite for the military. This includes the AFQT score, which will be discussed in a later chapter of this book. Keep in mind that the scores mean exactly the same thing as they would on a score report for the paper-and-pencil version of the test.

If you take the paper-and-pencil test at your school, the score report will be sent to your guidance counselor about one month after taking the test.

Retaking the Test

What happens if you determine that you want to take the ASVAB again? You will need to wait at least one calendar month before retaking the test. If you choose to retake it a second time, you will need to wait another calendar month. However, after that, you will need to wait at least six calendar months to retake it again. You will be able to use your ASVAB scores to enlist in the Armed Forces for up to two years after taking the test.

chapter 4

The ASVAB and Military Entrance AFQT Scores and Eligibility for Enlistment

The ASVAB is an enlistment requirement for each branch of the United States military. Scores are used not only to determine eligibility, but also to determine aptitude for certain jobs. In this chapter, we will further discuss exactly how your ASVAB scores will be used.

AFQT Score

As you know, the ASVAB consists of a number of separate subtests, each with its own standard score. The subtest scores for the math and verbal subtests (Arithmetic Reasoning, Mathematics Knowledge, Paragraph Comprehension, and Word Knowledge) are computed to provide what is called the **Armed Forces Qualification Test (AFQT) score**. It indicates general cognitive ability and training potential, and it predicts job performance.

AFQT scores are reported as percentiles, ranging from 1–99. Percentile scores indicate the percentage of test-takers in a reference group who earned a score at or above that percentile. For example, a percentile score of 50 would indicate that you scored as well as or better than 50% of the test-takers in the reference group. It does not mean that you answered 50% of the questions correctly. Likewise, a percentile score of 80 indicates that you scored as well as or better than 80% of the test-takers in the reference group, not that you answered 80% of the questions correctly.

AFQT scores are grouped into eight categories. Take a look at the categories shown in the table.

AFQT Category	Score Range
I	93–99
II	65–92
IIIA	50–64
IIIB	31–49
IVA	21–30
IVB	16–20
IVC	10–15
V	1–9

All branches of the United States military use the AFQT score to determine eligibility for enlistment. The required score for enlistment varies between the branches. A score in category IIIA or higher could qualify the applicant for enlistment incentives.

Recruiters prefer to enlist those with scores in the higher AFQT categories, I and II, as they are above average as far as trainability potential, meaning that they will be able to be trained quickly, and will perform well in their jobs. In fact, it is required that a minimum of 60 percent of recruits come from categories IIIA and above. Applicants in category III are generally average as far as trainability, and those in category IV are considered to be below average. No more than four percent of recruits can be from category IV. By law, applicants in category V are not eligible for military service.

Educational Requirements for Enlistment

AFQT scores and level of education are considered to be strong indicators of how likely a candidate is to complete his or her first term of military service.

For this reason, it is required that at least 90% of new military recruits have at least a high school diploma. Sometimes these requirements may be closer to 100%. In fact, candidates are categorized into three tiers, according to their level of education.

- **Tier 1:** regular high school graduates, adult diploma holders, and non-graduates who have earned a minimum of 15 hours of college credit
- **Tier 2:** alternative credential holders, including those with GED credentials or other high school equivalency certificates
- **Tier 3:** no educational credentials

The AFQT scoring standards vary at each tier. For the Air Force and Marine Corps, candidates at tier 3 must earn a higher score on the AFQT than those at tier 2. Likewise, those at tier 2 must earn a higher score on the AFQT than those at tier 1. Basically, those without a high school diploma who want to enlist in the military will need to earn a high score on the AFQT. For the Army and the Navy, candidates at tiers 2 and 3 must meet the same standard on the AFQT, which is much higher than the standard required for high school graduates at tier 1.

Eligibility for Enlistment

As we mentioned, the required AFQT score varies among the different branches of our Armed Forces. The Air Force, for example, has the most stringent requirements. In order to enlist in this branch of service, high school seniors and those with a high school diploma must have a minimum AFQT score of 36; those with a GED credential must have a minimum AFQT score of 65. Only about 1% of those enlisting in the Air Force hold a GED rather than high school diploma. In rare cases, the minimum AFQT score can be lowered from 36 to 31 if the applicant holds a special skill that is considered to be critical, such as being able to speak a particular foreign language.

The minimum AFQT scores required to enlist in each branch of service are shown below. Please be aware that these requirements may change at any time.

- Army: 31
- Navy: 35
- Air Force: 36
- Marines: 31
- Coast Guard: 45

Job Eligibility

In addition to being used to determine eligibility to enlist in the military, ASVAB scores are also used to determine eligibility for specific jobs. So, the higher your score, the more choices you have regarding your military occupation or career field. And, enlistment bonuses are generally associated with the occupation chosen. As you can see, a strong ASVAB score is important for many reasons.

The ASVAB is divided into mechanical, administrative, general, and electronics categories. All career fields in the military have minimum score requirements in each of these categories, depending on the requirements of the job. By matching ASVAB scores to job options, an applicant is assigned a job that best corresponds with his or her capabilities.

Take a look at the formulas below, which are used by the Air Force to determine mechanical, administrative, general, and electronics scores. Remember, the subtests on the ASVAB are General Science (GS), Arithmetic Reasoning (AR), Word Knowledge (WK), Paragraph Comprehension (PC), Mathematics Knowledge (MK), Electronics Information (EI), Auto and Shop Information (AS), Mechanical Comprehension (MC), and Assembling Objects (AO).

- Mechanical Aptitude Score = AR + 2 (PC + WK) + MC + AO
- Administrative Aptitude Score = 2 (PC + WK) + MK
- General Aptitude Score = 2 (PC + WK) + AR
- Electronics Aptitude Score = AR + MK + EI + GS

Other branches of the Armed Forces have formulas for determining composite scores as well. The composite scores used to determine job eligibility vary among the branches.

Each composite score is determined by ASVAB subtest scores. For example, the Army's Surveillance and Communications composite score is based on the ASVAB Verbal Expression, Arithmetic Reasoning, Auto and Shop, and Mechanical Comprehension subtest scores. The Field Artillery composite score is based on Arithmetic Reasoning, Mathematics Knowledge, and Mechanical Comprehension scores.

As you can see, ASVAB scores have a major influence not only on ability to enlist in the military, but also on the branch in which one will serve, and the career options available after joining. These scores will help to ensure that the job to which you are assigned is a good match to your abilities and interests, which will not only increase the probability of success, but also the likelihood that you will be given the chance to do something that you will enjoy.

chapter **5**

Taking the CAT-ASVAB

In an earlier chapter, you learned that the ASVAB is offered in a computerized form, as well as in a paper-and-pencil format. Because the computerized test is administered in a **computerized adaptive format**, it is known as the **CAT-ASVAB**. An adaptive test adapts to the ability level of the individual taking the test. In other words, the test tailors itself to the ability level of each individual test-taker. So, the questions you are given could vary from those of the examinee sitting beside you.

Although the questions themselves may be different from those which would be asked on the paper-and-pencil test, keep in mind that a formula is used to equalize the scores. So, the score you receive on the CAT-ASVAB is similar to the one you would receive had you taken the alternative format of the test.

What to Expect on the CAT-ASVAB

The subtests on the CAT-ASVAB are the same as those on the ASVAB. The only difference is that on the CAT-ASVAB, the Automotive and Shop Information subtest is actually divided into two separate tests. The number of questions and the time limit for each subtest are shown in the following table.

Subtest	Number of Questions	Time Limit (in Minutes)
General Science (GS)	16	8
Arithmetic Reasoning (AR)	16	39
Word Knowledge (WK)	16	8
Paragraph Comprehension (PC)	11	22
Mathematics Knowledge (MK)	16	20
Electronics Information (EI)	16	8
Auto Information (AI)	11	7
Shop Information (SI)	11	6
Mechanical Comprehension (MC)	16	20
Assembling Objects (AO)	16	16
Total	145	154

Prior to beginning the CAT-ASVAB, training will be provided on how to use the keyboard and mouse, answering questions on the test, and getting help if needed, although the test is designed in such a way that computer experience is not necessary. In fact, the keyboard of the computer is modified so that the only keys that are labeled are those which are needed to answer the questions. Test-takers can choose whether to use the keyboard or the mouse to select their answers. The keyboard also includes a HELP key. Pressing this key causes the timer on the subtest to stop until the examinee returns to the questions. The HELP key should be used when help is needed, such as needing to get another pencil or requesting additional scrap paper.

Each subtest will have its own set of directions, as well as a practice question. As you work on the CAT-ASVAB, a display in the lower right hand corner of the screen will indicate how much time and the number of remaining questions for each subtest.

Because this is an adaptive test, not everyone will be given the same questions. The difficulty level of each question will be based on your response to the previous item. This matches the difficulty of the items to the ability level of the test-taker. The advantage of this is that no one has to answer questions which are too easy, because these would certainly be answered correctly and provide little information about his or her ability level. Likewise, no one has to answer questions which are too difficult, because they would likely answer these incorrectly, providing little useful information.

Let's use an extreme example to explain this a little further. Suppose a twelfth-grade student were to take a first-grade math test. We would expect that the student would answer every question correctly, and we would not learn anything about his or her ability level through this assessment. Now, suppose a first-grade student were to take a twelfth-grade math test. Again, we would expect that the student would *not* answer any question correctly, and we would not learn anything about his or her ability level. By matching the assessment to the individual, the CAT-ASVAB provides useful information.

So, how does this work? The CAT-ASVAB includes a pool of questions ranging in difficulty level from very easy to very difficult. After the test-taker answers the first question, which is of medium difficulty, his or her answer is evaluated by the computer. Based on this information, a question is selected that best matches his or her ability level. Basically, if the first question is answered correctly, the next question is more difficult. If the first question is answered incorrectly, the next question is less difficult. This pattern continues throughout the test, making sure the questions administered are appropriate for each individual. The chart below shows how each question is selected.

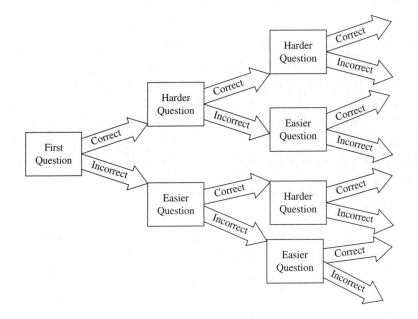

This process continues until all questions have been answered, or the time limit is reached. There is a penalty for questions not answered before time runs out; however, there is usually plenty of time to finish all test items.

Comparing the CAT-ASVAB to the ASVAB

The main difference between the two formats of the test is the fact that questions on the CAT-ASVAB adapt to the ability level of the examinee. The questions on the paper-and-pencil format of the test range in difficulty level from very easy to very difficult. All examinees answer all of the questions, regardless of whether the questions are essentially too easy or too hard for that individual. This is necessary in order to accurately measure each test-taker's ability level.

Although some of the questions on the paper-and-pencil version of the ASVAB are simple and some are hard, the majority are of average difficulty. Test-takers with high ability levels may feel that the CAT-ASVAB is more difficult because they will be given mostly questions which are of above-average difficulty. Test-takers with lower ability levels may feel that the CAT-ASVAB is easier than the paper-and-pencil test because they will be given mostly questions which are of below-average difficulty. Remember, the difficulty level of the questions is taken into account when the test is scored, so regardless of which version of the test you take, or which you feel was more or less difficult, your score will be about the same.

Because the question set is adaptive to the individual examinee, the CAT-ASVAB is actually shorter than the paper-and-pencil version of the ASVAB. As you know, the ASVAB takes approximately three hours to finish. Most people are able to complete the CAT-ASVAB in about an hour and a half. Questions which are too simple or too difficult are eliminated, so the CAT-ASVAB requires fewer questions, and less time.

Another difference between the two forms of the test is that test-takers are able to work at their own pace on the CAT-ASVAB, so when one subtest is completed, they may immediately move on to the next, without having to wait for a proctor to announce that it is time for everyone to move on. Like the ASVAB, each subtest on the CAT-ASVAB does have a time limit; however, the majority of people complete the tests with time to spare.

An additional way that the two test forms vary is that those taking the paper-and-pencil form of the ASVAB have the opportunity to review and change their answers before moving on to a new subtest. This is not the case with the CAT-ASVAB. Once an answer has been submitted, it cannot be reviewed or changed. With that in mind, be sure you are confident in your answer choice before submitting it and moving on to the next question.

Finally, those taking the CAT-ASVAB have the advantage of seeing their test results immediately. Scores are available right away, meaning that test-takers do not have to wait and wonder about how well they did on the ASVAB. They can walk out of the testing center knowing how well they did on the CAT-ASVAB.

chapter **6**

Steps to Acing the ASVAB

The road to doing well on any test begins long before you pick up your pencil (or sit at the keyboard) to fill in the first answer. Acing the ASVAB is no different. To do your best on this exam, there are things you will need to do in the weeks and months ahead of time, on the day of the test, and during the test itself.

Preparing for the Test

Over the years, you have probably learned that cramming for a test on the night before is not the best way to study. In order to do your best, it is important to begin preparing far in advance. Research has shown that the best way to learn any material is to study it repeatedly over a period of time. That means you should start studying for the ASVAB early, and review the information often.

One way to prepare is to know what types of information will be on the test. The good news is that you can find that information in this book! Read the explanations of what skills will be assessed on each of the subtests, and study those with which you are not completely comfortable.

Another way to prepare is to understand the types of questions that will be asked. Again, the practice questions in this book will be a great help for that. Although the format of the questions will resemble the paper-and-pencil version of the test, you will become familiar with the types of questions that will be on the CAT-ASVAB as well. Being comfortable with the style of the questions will help you to feel more confident as you take the test.

One advantage of preparing early for the ASVAB is that you will be able to identify your own strengths and weaknesses in regard to the testing information. Suppose that while reading the chapters and answering the sample questions, you find that the Word Knowledge questions are a snap! That's great! Now you know that you do not need to spend hours and hours studying vocabulary and synonyms. On the other hand, suppose you find that the General Science questions are a little bit tricky. Well, believe it or not, that's good to know, too. Now you can focus your study time on brushing up on science facts. It is better to find out your strengths and weaknesses now and do something about it, than to open up the test and wish you had reviewed some of the skills a little more thoroughly. Take advantage of the opportunity to find out what you need to study, and do it.

Make flash cards of the information, facts, formulas, and definitions that you need to review. That way, you can pick these up and review them throughout the day as you have a few minutes. Take them with you in the car and study them as you wait in line at the bank, while you wait for a doctor appointment, or any other time when you have a few seconds to spare. Also, have family or friends use the cards to quiz you. The more you study, the more comfortable you will become with the material.

Also, before test day arrives, make sure you know which version of the test you will be taking, the paper-and-pencil ASVAB or the CAT-ASVAB. It is important to know what to expect when you enter the testing center. As you know, the information itself will be similar, so you will study the same material, regardless of which version of the test you will be taking. However, you will use different strategies to answer these questions, depending if you will do so with a pencil or a keyboard.

After you have studied and studied and studied, take a break the day before the test. It is important to relax and be well-rested on the big day. The ASVAB is an important test, and you are more likely to do your best if you are not too stressed out. Make sure you have everything ready that you will need to take with you, such as your identification and any other materials that you have been instructed to bring. Spend some time the day before the test doing something you enjoy. Plan your day so that you are ready for bed a little bit earlier than usual so that you can be awake, refreshed, and energetic as you approach the ASVAB.

Test Day

There are several things you can do before you even leave home on test day that will help you to do well on the ASVAB. First, allow yourself plenty of time to avoid feeling rushed. Set the alarm clock a few minutes earlier than you think will be necessary. This will provide a cushion of time in case of emergency, such as traffic or bad weather.

Second, get moving. A great way to relieve stress and anxiety is exercise. While there may not be time to hit the gym before taking the test, at least do some jumping jacks, swim a few laps, jump on the exercise bike, or jog in place for a couple of minutes.

Next, start the day with a decent breakfast. It is important to have plenty of energy and be able to think clearly as you work. You want to be able to hear the wheels turning in your head, not the growling sound in your stomach. Think about what types of food help you to feel good and stay with you the longest. A full four-course meal leaves some people feeling sluggish and ready for a nap, while leaving others ready to take on the world. A cup of coffee wakes some people up, yet causes others to become jittery. Plan a breakfast that will keep you going for several hours.

Finally, dress for success. Wear something that makes you feel confident and comfortable. Consider dressing in layers so you can adjust your clothes according to the temperature of the testing center. You do not want to be distracted by shoes which are too tight, or a room which is too cold. Be prepared to stay focused and to feel good throughout the test.

Taking the Test

Regardless of which version of the test you take, there are a few tips which can help you to do your best. Some of the tips can be used for either the paper-and-pencil ASVAB or the CAT-ASVAB. Others are specific to the format of the test.

Tips for Either Version of the Test

- **Read everything carefully.** This includes directions, passages, diagrams, captions, graphs, questions, or any other test material. The only way to correctly answer any question is to fully understand the material.
- **Think about what you are reading.** Focus on key facts, dates, names, and definitions. Mentally classify information as fact or opinion, and identify

the main idea and supporting details. Actively reading will improve your comprehension and ability to recall the material.

- **Read the questions first.** Some people find it helpful to first read the question, then read the passage. This alerts them to which information in the passage is important, and helps them to focus their attention when reading. If this strategy works for you, be sure to use it.

- **Do not look at the answer choices yet.** Try to answer the questions before you look at the answer choices. Then, once you know what the correct answer should be, look for your answer among the choices listed. If it is there, great! If not, reread the question and the information, and try again.

- **Read every answer choice before selecting the best one.** Do this even if your answer is on the list. There may be more than one answer choice which is at least partially correct. Do not stop reading when one of the choices sounds good, because the next one may be even better. Carefully and completely read each option before selecting the one best answer.

- **Remember that even some of the incorrect answers look good.** On a multiple-choice test, the incorrect answers are there for a reason. Their purpose is to assess how well you are able to distinguish between the correct answer and plausible incorrect answers. That means even the wrong answers may be tempting. Keep this in mind as you make your selection.

- **Keep your eye on the time.** Remember, the subtests on both the ASVAB and the CAT-ASVAB are timed tests. Be aware of how much time is left and pace yourself accordingly. It is important to complete the tests, but working too quickly can lead to making careless mistakes. Work quickly, but most importantly, work carefully.

- **Keep moving.** If you are stumped on one tricky question, take your best guess and move on. Spending too much time on a single question could cause you to run out of time to answer other questions that might come easily to you.

- **Eliminate incorrect answer choices.** There may be times when you truly have no idea which is the correct answer. In that case, figure out which answers are incorrect, and eliminate these choices. Often, answers that stand out from the rest are incorrect and can be eliminated. Also, answers which are not logical can be eliminated. For example, try to estimate approximately what the answer should be to a math problem, and disqualify any choices which are too far off from the estimate.

- **Be wary of extremes**. If an answer choice includes words such as *always*, *never*, or *every*, be careful. There are very few things in the world which always happen, never take place, or occur every single time. While it is possible that an answer with one of these absolutes is correct, make sure you are certain before selecting that answer.

- **Make your best guess.** After eliminating as many incorrect answer choices as possible to a tricky question, guess between those which remain. Keep in mind that the more options you can eliminate, the better your chances are of guessing correctly.

- **Do not look for patterns in the answer choices.** If you happen to notice a pattern in the correct answer choices, it is probably a coincidence. For example, if the odd numbered questions seem to have mostly A's for answers, and the even numbers seem to have mostly B's, do not use this as a basis for selecting your answer. Tests are not generally written to purposely create a pattern in the answers. Usually, answer choices are arranged in an order such as shortest to longest, or least to greatest in math, or they could be arranged completely randomly. That being said, any patterns which appear on your answer sheet were probably not intentional and should not be used as a clue to which answers are correct.

- **Take a few deep breaths.** It is completely normal to feel a little bit of anxiety during a test. Stopping to take a few deep breaths can help you stay calm and focused.

Tips for the Paper-and-Pencil ASVAB

- **Skip the questions you do not know**. Do not waste too much time on any single item. Remember, you can come back later if there is extra time and take another look at any questions you are unsure about.

- **Answer everything.** On this version of the test, any question which is left unanswered is counted as being incorrect. So, mark something for every single item, even if you have to guess randomly. There is no penalty for guessing. If an answer is left blank, it will definitely be wrong. At least by guessing there is some chance of getting it right. If you notice that time is running out, and there is no way you will be able to finish the test, spend the final few seconds randomly filling in answers.

- **Mark your answers carefully.** As you mark you answers on the answer sheet, be sure to do two things. First, make sure that the answer space you are filling in corresponds to the correct question on the test. In other words, make sure the answer to question number 1 is marked in the answer space for question number 1. Second, make sure there is only one answer marked for each question. If you change an answer, be sure to completely erase your original response.

- **Check your work.** If there is time left at the end of a subtest, go back and review your answers. Make sure you have answered every question, and that you are happy with the answers you have chosen. Do not change any answers unless you are confident that your original answer is incorrect. Research has shown that your first answer is usually right. So, unless there is a compelling reason to do so, it may be best not to change an answer.

Tips for the CAT-ASVAB

- **Read the instructions carefully.** During this test, time spent reading the directions is not counted against you. In other words, the clock will not have started yet. Take your time and make sure you completely understand what you are being instructed to do before beginning the test.

- **Ask for HELP.** Remember that the HELP button on the computer keyboard is there for a reason. Use it if there is something you need, or if you have a question.

- **Select your answers wisely.** Make sure you are completely comfortable with your answer choice before selecting it. Once you have chosen an answer, you will not be allowed to go back and change it. Read carefully and remember that you have one shot at answering each question correctly.

- **When time is running out, do not start guessing.** Spend your final few minutes carefully answering the questions you are able to complete. Remember, there *is* a penalty for incorrect answers on the CAT-ASVAB. This penalty is especially large when there are several wrong answers at the end of a subtest. Go ahead and answer a few correctly, rather than guessing and answering a couple incorrectly.

A Final Word

Now that you know a little bit about the ASVAB and the CAT-ASVAB, what will be on the tests, how they will be scored, and what to do to ace the test, you are ready to review the material which will be questioned. You know that the first step to doing well is to be prepared. Read the material carefully, and study anything which you are unfamiliar with. Complete the practice questions to become familiar with the testing format. And, give yourself the best possible chance of acing the ASVAB. Good luck!

Part II

ASVAB Practice Diagnostic Tests

chapter 7

Practice Diagnostic Tests

General Science Diagnostic Test

1. Animal cells do not have
   A. chloroplasts
   B. mitochondria
   C. ribosomes
   D. DNA

2. Ribosomes use the genetic information encoded on RNA to construct
   A. DNA
   B. plasma membranes
   C. triglycerides
   D. proteins

3. All of the following kingdoms feature organisms that have cell walls EXCEPT
   A. Animalia
   B. Plantae
   C. Bacteria
   D. Fungi

4. Oil and natural gas are composed of hydrocarbons that form
   A. over several hundred years
   B. from dead organisms
   C. from igneous rock
   D. after long exposure to seawater

5. Which of the following layers is closest to the earth's center?
   A. The asthenosphere
   B. The mantle
   C. The upper mantle
   D. The outer core

6. When water in the atmosphere precipitates, it
   A. disperses
   B. collects in a central location
   C. falls back to the surface
   D. escapes as a gas from the surface of a body of water

7. The clouds that produce heavy rain are usually
    A. cirrus clouds
    B. cumulus clouds
    C. stratus clouds
    D. altocirrus clouds

8. As a result of the Coriolis effect, hurricanes in the Northern Hemisphere
    and the Southern Hemisphere
    A. turn in opposite directions
    B. turn in the same direction
    C. move from west to east
    D. move from east to west

9. When a warm and a cold air mass meet, the warm air usually passes
    A. above the cold air
    B. below the cold air
    C. at the same altitude as the cold air
    D. alongside the cold air, rather than through

10. Igneous rocks are formed by
    A. cooling of magma or lava
    B. intense pressure
    C. erosion
    D. colliding tectonic plates

11. The outermost planet in our solar system is
    A. Neptune
    B. Jupiter
    C. Pluto
    D. Uranus

12. Most comets consist largely of
    A. metal and rock
    B. rock and dust
    C. ice and dust
    D. metal and ice

13. Of the following components of the earth, tidal forces most affect
    A. the atmosphere
    B. the oceans
    C. the continental crust
    D. the mantle

14. Hair and fingernails are composed of the protein known as
    A. collagen
    B. myelin
    C. keratin
    D. cellulose

15. Oxygen-rich hemoglobin will release its oxygen when it experiences
    A. acidic pH
    B. basic pH
    C. neutral pH
    D. rapidly rising pH

16. The sense of balance is technically known as
    A. proprioception
    B. myopia
    C. equilibrioception
    D. aural perception

17. When the velocity of a rotating object changes, its centripetal acceleration is always directed
    A. toward the center of rotation
    B. away from the center of rotation
    C. tangential to the center of rotation
    D. against the direction of rotation

18. When a change in speed causes a wave to change direction, it has experienced
    A. diffusion
    B. refraction
    C. absorption
    D. convection

19. The force that resists the relative motion of two objects in contact with each other is called
    A. the weak force
    B. the strong force
    C. suction
    D. friction

20. The following elements are located in the right-most column of the periodic table: helium, neon, argon, krypton, xenon, and radon. As a group, they have low chemical reactivity and are collectively known as
    A. halogens
    B. noble gases
    C. natural gases
    D. atmospheric gases

21. The boiling point of water is 100°C at sea-level. The boiling point of water at the top of Mt. Everest—which is at 8,848 meters above sea-level—is most likely
    A. 100°C
    B. 69°C
    C. 150°C
    D. 99°C

22. Which of the following answers shows the three primary forms of matter in order by lowest density to greatest?
    A. Solid, liquid, gas
    B. Liquid, gas, solid
    C. Gas, liquid, solid
    D. Gas, solid, liquid

23. In the human body, the femur is located in the
    A. foot
    B. hand
    C. head
    D. leg

24. The flow of energy among organisms in a particular area is can be understood in terms of a model known as
    A. an ecosystem
    B. a biosphere
    C. a food web
    D. a habitat

25. Herbivores eat
    A. carnivores
    B. other herbivores
    C. plants
    D. decomposers

Arithmetic Reasoning Diagnostic Test

1. A team can carpet a floor at a rate of 100 square feet every 2 hours. If a home has three bedrooms which are 220 square feet each, how long will it take the team to carpet the three bedrooms?
    A. 4 hours 4 minutes
    B. 4 hours 24 minutes
    C. 13 hours 2 minutes
    D. 13 hours 12 minutes

2. Which of the following is a factor of 24?
    A. 3
    B. 5
    C. 18
    D. 48

3. A shipment arrives on 4 pallets weighing 20 pounds each. The weight of the shipment with the pallets included is 800 pounds. How much does the shipment weigh if the pallets are not included?
    A. 700 pounds
    B. 720 pounds
    C. 740 pounds
    D. 780 pounds

4. An individual pen costs $1.75 while a box of 12 pens costs $18.90. What is the percentage discount given when 12 pens are purchased?
    A. 1%
    B. 10%
    C. 17%
    D. 21%

5. If a quart is ¼ of a gallon, how many quarts are in a 280-gallon tank?
    A. 40 quarts
    B. 70 quarts
    C. 1,120 quarts
    D. 1,290 quarts

6. Over the past month of training, Craig has increased the amount he can bench press by 15%. If he could originally bench press 200 pounds, how much can he bench press now?
   A. 203 pounds
   B. 215 pounds
   C. 230 pounds
   D. 300 pounds

7. On Monday, the high temperature was 35 degrees. On Tuesday, it was 5 degrees warmer than on Monday and on Wednesday it was 10 degrees colder than on Tuesday. What was the high temperature on Thursday if it was 5 degrees colder than on Wednesday?
   A. 25 degrees
   B. 30 degrees
   C. 35 degrees
   D. 40 degrees

8. A tree is 3 times as tall as a nearby pole. If the tree is 14 feet 9 inches tall, how tall is the pole?
   A. 4 feet 9 inches
   B. 4 feet 11 inches
   C. 44 feet 3 inches
   D. 44 feet 7 inches

9. A crate is designed to hold 45 boxes of golf balls where each box contains 12 golf balls. How many crates would be necessary to store 810 boxes of golf balls?
   A. 12
   B. 14
   C. 16
   D. 18

10. Robert's initial weekly pay was $520. After his first year, this was increased by 4%. At the end of his second year, this salary was increased by 2%. What was his weekly pay after this second raise?
    A. $524.16
    B. $540.80
    C. $551.62
    D. $561.60

11. An airline maintenance crew performs 4 basic checks before performing a full inspection on any plane. If this crew has to inspect 107 planes, how many basic checks will they perform?
    A. 111
    B. 147
    C. 428
    D. 474

12. In a large meeting, ⅔ of the attendees are women. If 500 attendees are men, how many people in total are attending the meeting?
    A. 333
    B. 750
    C. 1,500
    D. 3,000

13. On the screen of a GPS unit, 1,000 yards is represented by ½ of an inch. If two objectives are ¾ inches apart on the GPS screen, how far apart are they in yards?
    A. 1,500 yards
    B. 1,750 yards
    C. 2,000 yards
    D. 2,250 yards

14. A large cylindrical storage container is 15 feet tall with a diameter of 12 feet. What is the capacity of this container in cubic feet?
    A. 75.36 cubic feet
    B. 180.00 cubic feet
    C. 565.20 cubic feet
    D. 1,695.60 cubic feet

15. What is the next number in the sequence: 14, 21, 28,
    A. 29
    B. 32
    C. 35
    D. 44

16. What is the perimeter of a square with width 5 units?
    A. 10 units
    B. 20 units
    C. 25 units
    D. 30 units

Word Knowledge Diagnostic Test

This test is about the meanings of words. Each question has an underlined word. You may be asked to decide which one of the four words in the choices is a synonym or most nearly means the same thing as the underlined word. It may ask which one of the four words means the *opposite*. Some of the underlined words are used in sentences. In this case, decide which of the four choices most nearly means the same thing as the underlined word, as used in the context of the sentence.

1. Fallible most nearly means
   A. energized
   B. moody
   C. imperfect
   D. personable

2. Moot most nearly means
   A. confused
   B. mysterious
   C. exhausted
   D. arguable

3. Her friends did not understand her tendency to malinger while on the job.
   A. shirk
   B. complain
   C. steal
   D. gamble

4. Levity most nearly means
   A. frivolity
   B. layer
   C. strip
   D. assembly

5. Quixotic most nearly means
   A. uncertain
   B. idealistic
   C. excited
   D. realistic

6. <u>Execrate</u> most nearly means
    A. blame
    B. eyeball
    C. denounce
    D. renovate

7. Warren felt that meeting his nephew was quite <u>fortuitous</u>.
    A. accidental
    B. foolhardy
    C. unnecessary
    D. ominous

8. Angela's face showed a veritable <u>gamut</u> of emotions.
    A. groove
    B. power
    C. delicacy
    D. extent

9. The group was left with a <u>finite</u> number of choices.
    A. full
    B. limited
    C. useless
    D. unlikely

10. <u>Neophyte</u> most nearly means
    A. novice
    B. layer
    C. origin
    D. angle

11. <u>Nondescript</u> most nearly means
    A. orderly
    B. heavy
    C. featureless
    D. hesitant

12. <u>Raiment</u> most nearly means
     A. edging
     B. fool
     C. charge
     D. garment

13. <u>Redress</u> most nearly means
     A. package
     B. finance
     C. remedy
     D. clothe

14. They all found Eric's speech to be <u>sententious</u>.
     A. pompous
     B. repetitive
     C. second-rate
     D. direct

15. As a group they voted to <u>demur</u>.
     A. oblige
     B. object
     C. decline
     D. ratify

16. He found it difficult to believe his friends called him <u>corpulent</u> behind his back.
     A. inaccurate
     B. broad-minded
     C. competitive
     D. stout

17. Martina had been particularly <u>laconic</u> all day.
     A. alert
     B. concise
     C. joyous
     D. cold

18. The <u>litigation</u> was proceeding according to their plan and a decision was expected shortly.
    A. prosecution
    B. printing
    C. liquidation
    D. delay

19. <u>Nefarious</u> most nearly means
    A. instinctive
    B. close
    C. nonexistent
    D. evil

20. <u>Pandemic</u> most nearly means
    A. contradictory
    B. symptomatic
    C. widespread
    D. parasitic

21. Rebecca was <u>culpable</u> of leaving the food out of the refrigerator all night.
    A. violent
    B. confused
    C. blameworthy
    D. beautiful

22. The <u>deleterious</u> results were just now becoming clear.
    A. injurious
    B. toughening
    C. hapless
    D. mediocre

23. <u>Defray</u> most nearly means
    A. amuse
    B. defile
    C. lose
    D. pay

24. <u>Baleful</u> most nearly means
     A. sick
     B. ominous
     C. cheery
     D. wise

25. <u>Amity</u> most nearly means
     A. intention
     B. desire
     C. friendship
     D. approval

26. The soothing sauna provided a <u>palliative</u> for Jessica.
     A. foundation
     B. relief
     C. disappointment
     D. surprise

27. The word most opposite in meaning to <u>demise</u> is
     A. eloquence
     B. illusion
     C. beginning
     D. order

28. <u>Gregarious</u> most nearly means
     A. sociable
     B. habitual
     C. right
     D. truthful

29. As a little girl she loved to watch the cows <u>masticate</u>.
     A. disagree
     B. chew
     C. joke
     D. consent

30. There certainly is an air of <u>hauteur</u> about him.
    A. weakness
    B. flattery
    C. clumsiness
    D. arrogance

31. <u>Garish</u> most nearly means
    A. showy
    B. feminine
    C. flowing
    D. willing

32. <u>Tacit</u> most nearly means
    A. cruel
    B. inferred
    C. urgent
    D. commonplace

33. <u>Supine</u> most nearly means
    A. approving
    B. remedial
    C. flat
    D. arguable

34. <u>Ubiquitous</u> most nearly means
    A. omnipresent
    B. unfailing
    C. capsized
    D. imperfect

35. He told stories of the Medieval Crusades that were especially <u>macabre</u>.
    A. vague
    B. militant
    C. disappointing
    D. gruesome

Paragraph Comprehension Diagnostic Test

1. In 1858 Abraham Lincoln and Stephen A. Douglas ran against each other for the United States Senate. Douglas was running for re-election to a third term. They met in a series of debates throughout the state of Illinois. These were the most important political dialogues in American history. The main topic was the extension of slavery into new U.S. territories. Lincoln lost the election, but two years later he ran against Douglas for President. This time he won.

   Which of the following statements isn't true?

   A. Lincoln lost to Douglas when they were running for United States Senate.
   B. Lincoln and Douglas debated about allowing slavery in new states.
   C. Lincoln was elected President of the United States.
   D. All of the above statements are true.

2. More and more doctors warn against the dangers of too much sun exposure. Although people need a certain amount of sunshine to get enough vitamin D, the sun can do a lot of damage to frail human skin. Too much sun damage in youth, by tanning or being sunburned, can produce skin cancer later in life. Also, it has become clear that the wrinkles that appear on aged skin are not necessarily a part of growing older. Most wrinkling is produced by overexposure to the sun. People who, for some reason or another, have spent little time outside look younger and have younger looking skin. If a person wants to stay young looking and prevent skin cancer, it is best to take care at an early age. Wear sunscreen and cover up when spending long periods of time outside.

   Doctors are advising people to

   A. get vitamin D from sources other than the sun
   B. not use tanning machines
   C. avoid being in the sun for long periods
   D. protect skin by using sunscreen

3. Sojourner Truth was one of the most remarkable women leaders America has produced. Although there are no records of her birth, historians believe that Sojourner was probably born in 1797. We do know that this

African American was born a slave named Isabella Baumfree. She was sold away from her parents when she was only nine years old. She took the name of Sojourner Truth after she was freed by the New York State Emancipation Act of 1827. Her new name represented the ideals for which she lived and fought. Sojourner moved to New York City where she began to work with organizations that helped women. Later, she became a leading abolitionist who fought against slavery. Fighting for freedom and for women's rights, Sojourner Truth became a leader in these struggles.

Which of the following statements isn't supported by the above passage?

A. Sojourner Truth's original name was Isabella Baumfree.
B. Sojourner Truth took her name while she was a slave.
C. Truth was at the forefront of the struggle for rights for women.
D. The Emancipation Act was passed in 1827.

4. The Smart Truck III is a true mobile command and control center with advanced communications, detection and deterrent capabilities. Some of its multiple applications include a command-and-control center with the ability to detect the movement of personnel or vehicles in remote areas, and the power to monitor both bio-threats and personnel movements. It brings state-of-the-art communications and detection systems as well as offering armored protection to withstand terrorist and insurgent roadside attacks. The Smart Truck III was built for the NAC, the Army's official link to developing collaborative technologies with commercial and academic partners.

The Smart Truck III provides

A. capability to avoid detection
B. the ability to launch a biological attack
C. defense against explosive devices
D. collaboration with the Army

Questions 5 and 6 refer to the following passage:

If a person carries on a trade or business as a sole proprietor or an independent contractor, he or she is generally a self-employed person. The same is true if you are a member of a partnership that carries on a trade or business. A self-employed individual is generally required to file an annual tax return and pay estimated tax quarterly. This is because no employer is withholding taxes from a paycheck. In addition to income tax, self-employed people generally must pay self-employment (SE) tax. SE tax consists of a Social Security and Medicare tax, which people who are employed have deducted automatically from their pay. In order to determine if you need to pay a self-employment tax and income tax, you need to figure your net profit or net loss from your business. This is done by subtracting your business expense from your business income. If you have more income than expenses, you have a net profit.

5. A sole proprietor must pay an SE tax because:
   A. He or she has to make quarterly estimated tax payments.
   B. He or she has to pay Social Security and Medicare taxes.
   C. He or she is a member of a partnership.
   D. all of the above

6. A self-employed individual each year needs to
   A. pay income taxes
   B. file a quarterly return
   C. withhold taxes from a paycheck
   D. figure his or her net profit

7. FengShui is an ancient Chinese philosophy that teaches how an environment can assure people live in good health and good fortune. A house is no more than the extension of the person. And rather like a person's clothes, the house must fit correctly. The practice of FengShui ensures that a house is designed to fit the body and be orientated to allow the body to take in a vital energy, called chi, so that it can function effectively. Chi is a natural energy source that is constantly flowing, rather like the wind. Although it cannot be seen, its presence is known by the way it affects the landscape and physical matter. Chi is also like water because it can be diverted to where it is needed in order to be more beneficial. Chi cycles endlessly and if the cycle is broken or interrupted, everything that depends on the cycle will be affected adversely.

   Which of the following statements isn't supported by the above passage?

   A. FengShui is a natural energy source.
   B. The Chinese have practiced FengShui for centuries.

C. Chi is like the wind and water.

D. One's environment can affect how one feels.

8. The first cowboys in North America were the Mexican vaqueros. Vaquero means "cattle driver" in Spanish. Texas was once part of Mexico. After it became independent of Mexico in 1836, many Anglos, or English speaking pioneers, moved into Texas and took over the ranches that the Mexican owners left behind. They hired vaqueros to teach them the cattle business. These vaqueros trained Anglo cowboys. They also gave the English language new names for cowboys' equipment and activities. The leather pants called "chaps" that cowboys wore to protect their legs while riding got their name from the Spanish word *chaparajos*. The lariat that cowboys used to rope cattle got its name from the Spanish *la reata*.

Anglos hired vaqueros because

A. They couldn't speak Spanish.

B. Texas won its independence from Mexico.

C. They didn't know how to use chaps.

D. They had to learn how to operate a ranch.

Questions 9 and 10 are based on the following passage:

The losing party in a decision by a federal trial court can appeal the decision in a federal court of appeals. Likewise, a litigant who is not satisfied with a decision made by a federal administrative agency can file a petition for review of the agency decision by a court of appeals. Judicial review in cases which involve federal agencies or programs, as in a dispute over Social Security benefits, may be obtained first in a district court rather than a court of appeals. In a civil case either side may appeal the verdict. In a criminal case, the defendant may appeal a guilty verdict, but the government cannot appeal if a defendant is found not guilty. Either side in a criminal case may appeal with respect to a sentence that is imposed after a guilty verdict.

9. A good title for the above paragraph would be

A. How to Go to Court

B. Civil vs. Criminal Law

C. The Appeals Process

D. The Insider's Guide to Law

10. A party engaged in a lawsuit who is unsatisfied with a decision may
    A. petition for review of the decision in a federal court of appeals
    B. appeal a sentence that is imposed
    C. appeal a guilty verdict
    D. all of the above

Questions 11 and 12 are based on the following passage:

In 1970 Congress passed the Occupational Safety and Health Act, creating the Occupational Safety and Health Administration (OSHA) to assure safe and healthful working conditions for working men and women. OSHA sets and enforces standards, and provides training, outreach, education, and assistance. OSHA is part of the United States Department of Labor. OSHA offers a wide selection of training courses and educational programs to help workers and employers recognize, avoid, and prevent safety and health hazards in their workplaces. OSHA offers training and educational brochures that help businesses train their workers to comply with the guidelines. Workers are entitled to working conditions that do not pose a risk of serious harm. Workers have the right to ask OSHA to inspect their workplace. They must receive information and training about hazards, methods to prevent harm, and the OSHA standards that apply to their workplace.

11. Under OSHA, workers are entitled to
    A. workplace inspections
    B. hazard avoidance training
    C. OSHA standards updates
    D. all of the above

12. Which of the following statements isn't true?
    A. OSHA standards are enforced by the U.S. Congress.
    B. OSHA can inspect an employer's business.
    C. Workers can ask OSHA about training.
    D. Preventing health hazards in the workplace is a primary function of OSHA.

Questions 13 through 15 are based on the following passage:

One hundred and fifty million years ago, gigantic dinosaurs roamed the western United States. The area was hot and moist then, dotted with many lakes and swamps and the dinosaur inhabitants were many and variegated. Ultimately, these areas became the repository of many fossils found in the mid to late 1800s. Fossils are the remains of plants or animals that died and were buried and then mineralized and preserved. Some fossil remnants provide a clear picture of life long ago. That is why they are so important to scientists.

In 1877, a great discovery of seven miles of dinosaur fossils was made in Como Bluff, Wyoming. The fossils were shipped to museums to be studied, but, unfortunately, not many bones arrived at their destinations unbroken. The fossils were too fragile to transport.

Finally, scientists kept the fossils in place and sent back carefully constructed casts of them to enable museum scientists to study them. At first, dinosaur bones were seen only by scientists who analyzed them. But the public was fascinated then, as they are now, by these gigantic creatures. So by the 1890s, museums were putting models of dinosaurs on display. The Carnegie Museum in Pittsburgh had one of the best displays. In 1898, a brontosaurus, a huge plant-eater with a long neck, was displayed there. Dinosaur displays continue to be the most popular exhibits in natural history museums all over the world.

13. A fossil can best be described as
    A. a discovery made in Como Bluff, Wyoming
    B. mineralized remains
    C. a display in a museum
    D. variegated inhabitants of swamps

14. Casts were made of the fossils because
    A. The casts were heavier than the fossils.
    B. The casts did not break during shipment.
    C. The casts were better looking than the original fossils.
    D. The casts made it easier to dig up the fossils.

15. The author of the above passage would agree that
    A. People are intrigued with dinosaurs.
    B. The climate was different during the Age of the Dinosaurs.
    C. The study of fossils allows scientists to re-create what dinosaurs were like.
    D. all of the above

Mathematical Knowledge Diagnostic Test

1. A right triangle has a hypotenuse of 25 and one of the legs has a measure of 15. What is the measure of the remaining leg?
    A. 10
    B. 20
    C. 25
    D. 35

2. $3^2 - 4(2 - 3)^2 =$
    A. 1
    B. 5
    C. 41
    D. 65

3. Which of the following represents the statement "the product of a number and 4 is 9"?
    A. $4x = 9$
    B. $9x = 4$
    C. $x + 4 = 9$
    D. $x + 9 = 4$

4. Find the product of x^2 and $x^2 - 7$.
    A. 7
    B. $-6x^2$
    C. $2x^2 - 7$
    D. $x^4 - 7x^2$

5. The perimeter of a square garden is 20 feet. What is the area of this garden, in square feet?
    A. 5 square feet
    B. 25 square feet
    C. 50 square feet
    D. 100 square feet

6. 75% of a number is 150. What is the number?
    A. 112.5
    B. 150.0
    C. 200.0
    D. 207.5

7. The probability a particular machine will fail is 20%. The probability a different machine will fail is 35%. What is the probability both machines will fail?
    A. 7%
    B. 15%
    C. 48%
    D. 55%

8. In an equilateral triangle, at least one of the angles must measure
    A. 30°
    B. 45°
    C. 60°
    D. 90°

9. Solve for w: $\dfrac{7}{2w} = \dfrac{1}{4}$

    A. 4
    B. 7
    C. 14
    D. 28

10. $(x + 1) + (-2x - 5) =$
    A. $-x - 4$
    B. $-3x + 6$
    C. $x - 4$
    D. $-3x - 4$

11. If $x \leq -1$, which of the following equations must be true?
    A. $-3x \leq 3$
    B. $-3x \geq 3$
    C. $2x \leq 2$
    D. $2x \geq 2$

12. $\sqrt{25} \cdot 16$
    A. 0
    B. 1
    C. 3
    D. 5

13. In terms of π, the circumference of a circle is 16π. What is the area of this circle?
    A. 4π
    B. 8π
    C. 16π
    D. 64π

14. Terrance has saved four times as much money as his friend Robbie. Robbie has saved twice as much as Sarah who has been saving $50 every week for the past six weeks. How much has Terrance saved?
    A. $300
    B. $600
    C. $1,200
    D. $2,400

15. Which of the following is equivalent to $x^3 + 4x^2 + 4x$?
    A. $(x + 2)^2$
    B. $(x^2 + 2x)^2$
    C. $x(x + 2)^2$
    D. $x^2(x + 2)$

16. The smallest angle in a triangle measures $20°$. The largest angle in this triangle is 3 times the measure of the remaining angle. What is the measure of the largest angle?
    A. $40°$
    B. $120°$
    C. $160°$
    D. $180°$

Electronics Questions Diagnostic Test

Use the wiring diagram below to answer questions 1 through 6.

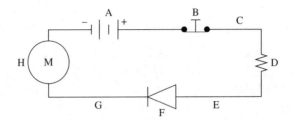

1. The symbol at letter A represents
   A. a generator
   B. a battery
   C. a wattmeter
   D. AC voltage

2. Which symbol represents a switching device?
   A. B
   B. D
   C. F
   D. H

3. How many electrical consumers are in the circuit depicted in the diagram?
   A. None
   B. One
   C. Two
   D. Three

4. The voltage reading at point C compared to point E would be
   A. the same
   B. lower
   C. higher
   D. undetermined

5. The diagram depicts which type of circuit?
   A. Parallel
   B. Zener
   C. Inductive
   D. Series

6. The function of component F is to
   A. allow current flow in one direction only
   B. reduce voltage
   C. switch DC current to AC current
   D. protect the circuit in the case of a short

7. The best way to measure energy usage is with a
   A. voltmeter
   B. ampmeter
   C. wattmeter
   D. ohmmeter

8. A generator performs the following work
   A. stores electrical power
   B. converts mechanical power to electrical power
   C. increases the voltage on high tension wires
   D. changes the amplitude of electricity

9. With AC wiring, the black wire indicates which type of connection?
   A. Hot
   B. Neutral
   C. Ground
   D. Negative

10. Which two values must be known to calculate resistance in a circuit?
    A. Watts and amplitude
    B. Capacity and voltage
    C. Frequency and amp
    D. Voltage and current

11. Which of the following acronyms has to do with memory storage in computers?
    A. ASCII, CPU, and ISP
    B. IPO, PCI, and ASCII
    C. RAM, ROM, and SIM
    D. DOS, IP, and MEM

12. A 120V system with a 12 amp current would have a resistance of
    A. 1 ohms
    B. 1.2 ohms
    C. 10 ohms
    D. 60 ohms

13. Typical household voltage in the United States is
    A. 120V DC
    B. 120V AC
    C. 240V DC
    D. 240V AC

14. Frequency is measured in
    A. hertz
    B. watts
    C. ohms
    D. amps

15. How much power is in a 12 volt system with a current of 10 amps?
    A. 60 hertz
    B. 120 hertz
    C. 60 watts
    D. 120 watts

16. Most automotive electrical systems are
    A. 12V DC
    B. 12V AC
    C. 120V DC
    D. 120V AC

Automotive Questions Diagnostic Test

1. Low tire pressure will cause the following issues:
   A. A drop in fuel economy
   B. Poor handling while driving
   C. Uneven tire wear
   D. All of the above

2. When a "check engine" warning light comes on, it primarily indicates that
   A. The amount of oil in the engine is low and needs topping up.
   B. It is time for the engine to be checked and serviced.
   C. There is an emissions fault code stored in the system.
   D. The driver needs to check with the dealership for recalls on the engine.

3. While driving on a winding, hilly road, you notice a squealing sound when you use the brakes. When you go to your mechanic, which of the following should be performed?
   A. The brake linings should be inspected for wear.
   B. The brake fluid should be refilled.
   C. The engine belts should be tightened.
   D. The muffler bearings need to be replaced.

4. A loss of power steering could be caused by any of the following EXCEPT
   A. a loose belt
   B. low steering fluid
   C. a bad master cylinder
   D. a weak pump

5. A stoichiometric ration of 13.7:1 indicates
   A. the need for more fuel in the mixture
   B. the need for more oxygen in the mixture
   C. a lean mixture
   D. an ideal mixture

6. A diesel engine won't run. Which of the following would not be a cause?
   A. Bad spark plugs
   B. Low compression
   C. A blocked fuel filter
   D. A faulty control module

7. Which of the following is considered to be high voltage in an automobile?
    A. The charging system
    B. The primary ignition system
    C. The secondary ignition system
    D. The electronics system

8. Jack stands are necessary to
    A. extend the height a floor jack can lift
    B. secure a vehicle while working underneath
    C. store the jack securely in a shop
    D. lift heavy duty vehicles

9. Which of the following is an example of an electrical circuit protection device?
    A. Fuse
    B. Switch
    C. Alternator
    D. All of the above

10. On a four-stroke engine, which valves are open on the power stroke?
    A. Intake
    B. Exhaust
    C. Both A and B
    D. Neither A nor B

11. An illuminated airbag warning light indicates
    A. a fault in the secondary restraint system
    B. a failed compressor
    C. the reserve air tank needs to be refilled
    D. a leak in the system

Shop Questions Diagnostic Test

1. Upon walking into a workshop, you see a rivet gun, a welding torch, and a shear. Which of the following items do you suspect is constructed there?
    A. Livestock pens
    B. Guitars and drums
    C. Brick pizza ovens
    D. Stained glass windows

2. What is one advantage of using a drill with a keyless chuck?
    A. The bit will rotate faster because there is less friction.
    B. The drill is more portable because it has no cord.
    C. There is one less tool to keep track of.
    D. A wider range of bits can be used with the drill.

3. How many board feet of 1 × 2 lumber will be required to build a bench top measuring 18 inches by 4 feet?
    A. 22'
    B. 36'
    C. 48'
    D. 72'

4. Which of the following tools would a plumber use most often?
    A. Plumb bob
    B. Countersink
    C. Pipe wrench
    D. Ball peen

5. To achieve a fine, smooth finish on a well-crafted piece of furniture, which tools, and in which order would give the best results?
    A. Lathe, file, and rasp
    B. Rasp, sander, and steel wool
    C. Belt sander, planer, and grinder
    D. Sander, rasp, and planer

6. The primary purpose of a welding mask is
    A. to protect the work from burning by masking it
    B. to help the metals blend properly
    C. to protect the welder from fumes
    D. to prevent permanent vision damage

7. MDF stands for
   A. Managed Deciduous Framing
   B. Medium Density Fiberboard
   C. Manufactured Deck Flooring
   D. Mature Dado Finish

8. In an auto shop, spills
   A. should be cleaned up quickly before the supervisor notices
   B. can be ignored until later when the clean-up crew comes in
   C. need to be contained immediately and disposed of properly
   D. are to be expected and don't really cause a problem

9. All of the following are tools used to work with concrete, EXCEPT
   A. a lathe
   B. a float
   C. a trowel
   D. a straightedge

10. If you become a certified welder, the certification means you
    A. are able to perform all types of welding
    B. have gone to classes with certified instructors
    C. have passed a written exam and been given a certificate
    D. are approved to competently perform a specific type of welding

11. A screw should <u>always</u> be installed
    A. by drilling a pilot hole first
    B. in a direction in agreement to its threads
    C. with a clockwise motion
    D. with a counter-clockwise motion

Mechanical Comprehension Diagnostic Test

1. Which has both a magnitude and direction?
   A. Speed
   B. Displacement
   C. Distance
   D. Work

2. A man walks away from you. He moves 100 m in 50 s. What is his velocity?
   A. +2 m/s
   B. +50 m/s
   C. +150 m/s
   D. −2 m/s

3. A plane moves horizontally at a constant velocity of 100 m/s. The engines put out +100,000 N of thrust. What is the force of the air resistance?
   A. −100,000 N
   B. −100 N
   C. +100 N
   D. + 100,000 N

4. Which happens when you apply the brakes on a moving car to bring it to a stop?
   A. The brakes apply a positive acceleration and the speed increases to zero.
   B. The brakes apply a negative acceleration and the speed decreases to zero.
   C. The brakes apply a negative acceleration and the speed increases to zero.
   D. The brakes apply a positive acceleration and the speed decreases to zero.

5. Four soldiers have masses of 20 kg, 40 kg, 50 kg, and 80 kg. Which one has a weight of approximately 800 N?
   A. 20-kg soldier
   B. 40-kg soldier
   C. 50-kg soldier
   D. 80-kg soldier

6. A soldier fires a bullet from his rifle at a target. Which is the reaction force?
   A. The firing of the bullet
   B. The bullet traveling through the air

C. The impact of the bullet on the target

D. The recoil of the rifle

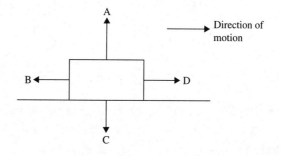

7. A box is moving along the floor as shown in the diagram. Which arrow represents the force of friction?

A. A

B. B

C. C

D. D

8. A relief package canister is parachuted from a plane from a height of 1000 m. Which explains what happens to the package?

A. The kinetic energy of the package decreases to zero while its potential energy increases to maximum.

B. Both the potential energy and kinetic energy of the package decrease to zero.

C. The kinetic energy of the package increases to maximum while its potential energy decreases to zero.

D. Both the potential and kinetic energy of the package increase to maximum.

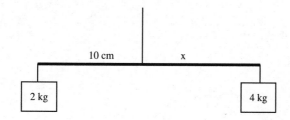

9. Two masses are balanced from a rod attached to a wire as shown in the diagram. The distances from the center of rotation are shown. What is the value of x?
    A. 2 cm
    B. 5 cm
    C. 10 cm
    D. 20 cm

10. In a competition, four soldiers push a 50-kg crate 10 m across a wooden floor. Soldier A does it in 15 s. Soldier B does it in 30 s. Soldier C does it in 45 s. Soldier D does it in 60 s. Which soldier exhibited the most power?
    A. Soldier A
    B. Soldier B
    C. Soldier C
    D. Soldier D

11. A man wants to use a lever to lift his car out of a ditch. He has a pipe that he will use as the lever arm and a rock that he will use as a fulcrum. Where should he place the rock?
    A. Close to the end where he will apply the force
    B. About one-third of the way away from the end where he will apply the force
    C. About half way along the pipe
    D. As close to the car as possible

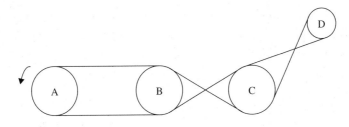

12. A belt-and-pulley system is shown in the diagram. Pulley A is the driving pulley and is spinning in the direction indicated by the arrow. Relative to Pulley A, which is true?
    A. Pulley B will turn in the same direction, but at a slower rate.
    B. Pulley C will turn in the opposite direction, but at a faster rate.
    C. Pulley D will turn in the same direction, but at a faster rate.
    D. All the pulleys will turn in the same direction at the same rate.

13. Which is similar to an inclined plane?
    A. A wheel and axle
    B. A lever
    C. A single pulley
    D. A screw

14. A machine has a mechanical advantage that is less than one. Which is true?
    A. The output force is greater than the input force.
    B. The output distance is greater than the input distance.
    C. The input distance is greater than the output distance.
    D. The input force equals the output force.

15. The movement of water across a hydrofoil generates lift. Which must be true?
    A. The curvature of the upper surface must be less than that of the lower surface and the water must move faster across the lower surface.
    B. The curvature of the upper surface must be greater than that of the lower surface and the water must move faster across the lower surface.
    C. The curvature of the upper surface must be less than that of the lower surface and the water must move faster across the upper surface.
    D. The curvature of the upper surface must be greater than that of the lower surface and the water must move faster across the upper surface.

16. Which machine does not have a mechanical advantage?
    A. A Class 1 lever
    B. A wheel and axle with weight attached to axle by rope
    C. A single fixed pulley
    D. A 10-m long ramp attached to a 2-m high loading dock

Assembling Objects Diagnostic Test

In each of the following questions, the picture at the left shows a group of parts. Answer choices A–D show objects made from assembled parts. Choose the one that is made from the parts shown at the left.

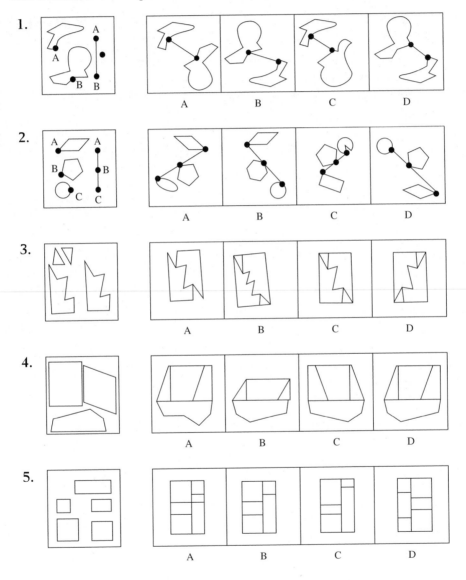

6.

7.

8.

9.

10.

11.

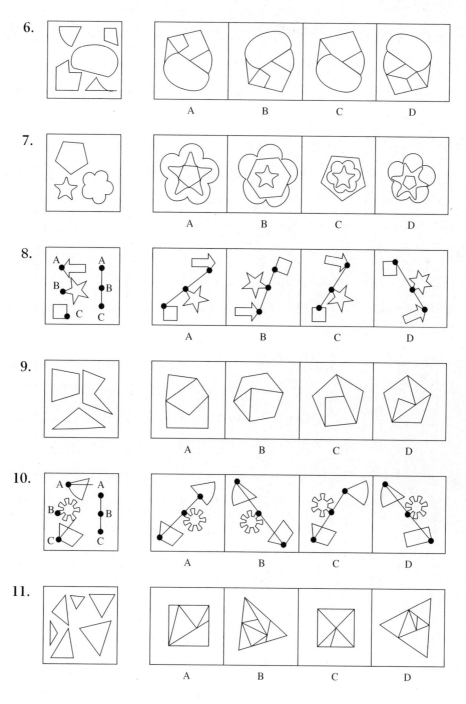

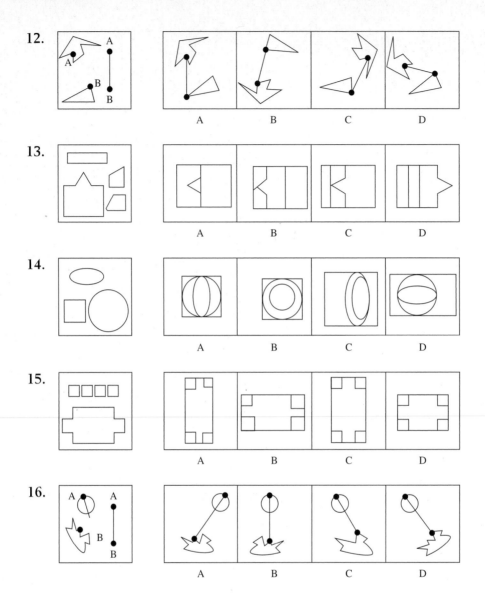

Practice Diagnostic Test Answers

General Science Answers

1. **A.** Chloroplasts. Only plants carry these organelles.

2. **D.** Proteins. Based on the information encoded on RNA, ribosomes string a specific sequence of amino acids together, a process that creates specific proteins.

3. **A.** Members of Kingdom Animalia do have cell membranes, but they do not have cell walls, which are tougher and more rigid.

4. **B.** Over millions of years, hydrogen and carbon from dead organisms combine under intense pressure and heat to form a mixture of hydrocarbons, such as those in oil and natural gas.

5. **D.** The core, including the outer core, is a liquid layer nearest the inner core, which is a solid sphere at the center of the earth.

6. **C.** When water precipitates, it falls back to the surface as rain, snow, or hail, for example.

7. **B.** The fluffy, full cumulus clouds are most likely to produce heavy rain.

8. **A.** Turn in opposite directions. The Coriolis effect encourages hurricanes in the Northern Hemisphere to turn counter-clockwise, while Southern Hemisphere hurricanes turn the opposite way.

9. **A.** Warm air rises, so a warm air mass usually passes above a cold air mass when they meet.

10. **A.** Igneous rocks are formed when magma below the earth's surface, or lava on the surface cools to become a solid.

11. **A.** Neptune is the planet furthest from the sun, because Pluto is no longer considered a planet.

12. **C.** Most comets are made of ice and dust.

13. **A.** Tidal forces—caused by the gravitational influence of the moon and the earth's rotation—affect the entire planet. But the atmosphere experiences the greatest impact because it is most fluid and compressible.

14. **C.** Hair and fingernails are made of the protein called keratin.

15. **A.** Carbon dioxide-rich areas of the body have a lower, more acidic pH, which triggers hemoglobin to release oxygen.

16. **C.** Equilibrioception is the technical name for the sense of balance.

17. **A.** Centripetal acceleration is directed toward the center of rotation.

18. **B.** Refraction. For example, a straight pole will appear to be bent below the surface when it's partially submerged in water. Light waves reflecting off of the pole underwater change direction as they cross from water to air.

19. **D.** Friction. Charged particles on the surfaces of each object interact, resisting the relative motion between objects at the point of contact.

20. **B.** Noble gases. These six elements are found in group 18 of the periodic table. They participate in few chemical reactions because all of their available electron shells are occupied.

21. **B.** 69°C. The lower pressure at high altitudes causes the boiling point of water to decrease.

22. **C.** The molecules of a gas are furthest apart for a given mass. The same mass of a liquid takes up much less volume. The molecules or atoms of solids have even less space between them. Liquids and solids are highly resistant to compression, unlike gases.

23. **D.** The femur, or thigh bone, is located in the upper part of the leg.

24. **C.** A food web describes the relationships between species, showing where each obtains its energy.

25. **C.** Herbivores mostly eat plants. Cows, giraffes, and buffalo are examples of herbivores.

Arithmetic Reasoning Answers

1. **B.** The team can carpet 100 square feet in 2 hours. The three rooms have a total of $3 \times 220 = 660$ square feet to be carpeted which will take $660 \div 100 = 6.6$ times as long. In other words, it will take $6.6 \times 2 = 13.2$ hours which is 13 hours and $0.2 \times 60 = 12$ minutes.

2. **A.** A factor is a number that divides the original number without any remainder.

3. **B.** The pallets weigh a total of $4 \times 20 = 80$ pounds. Without them, the shipment weighs $800 - 80 = 720$ pounds.

4. **B.** Without the discount, 12 pens would cost $12 \times 1.75 = \$21$. The difference is $21 - 18.90 = 2.10$. To find the percentage discount divide this number by 21 to get 0.10 or 10%.

5. **C.** Saying a quart is $\frac{1}{4}$ of a gallon is the same as saying there are 4 quarts to every gallon. Therefore, there are $280 \times 4 = 1120$ quarts in this tank.

6. **C.** The increase is $0.15 \times 200 = 30$. Adding this to the original gives the current amount he can bench press, which is 230 pounds.

7. **A.** It is important in this problem to go piece by piece. On Tuesday, it was $35 + 5 = 40$. Then on Wednesday, it was $40 - 10 = 30$. Finally on Thursday, it was $30 - 5 = 25$.

8. **B.** If the tree is 3 times as tall as the pole, the pole is $\frac{1}{3}$ of the height of the tree. Therefore, the pole is $\frac{1}{3}$ (14 feet, 9 inches) = 4 feet 11 inches.

9. **D.** Each crate can hold 45 boxes so 810 boxes will need $810 \div 45 = 18$ crates.

10. **C.** The first raise increased Robert's salary by $520 \times 0.04 = 20.8$ to $520 + 20.8 = 540.80$. The second increase was $540.80 \times 0.02 = 10.82$ bringing the total to $540.80 + 10.82 = 551.62$.

11. **C.** Since they perform 4 checks for each plane, they will perform a total of $4 \times 107 = 428$ checks.

12. **C.** If $\frac{2}{3}$ of the attendees are women, then $\frac{1}{3}$ are men. Since this is 500, there must be $3 \times 500 = 1500$ people attending.

13. **A.** To find the number of yards, first find $\frac{1}{2} \div \frac{3}{4} = \frac{3}{2}$ to determine the number of 1000 yard lengths between the objectives. Now, multiply to find this value in yards: $\frac{3}{2} \times 1,000 = 1,500$.

14. **D.** The capacity of the container is its volume which can be found with the formula $V = \pi h r^2$ where $\pi \approx 3.14$, r is the radius 6 (which is half the diameter) and h is the height 15. $V = 3.15 \times 6^2 \times 15 = 1695.6$.

15. **C.** The difference between each number is 7.

16. **B.** The perimeter is the sum of the lengths of each side. Since this is a square, the lengths of each side are the same so the perimeter is $5 + 5 + 5 + 5 = 20$.

Word Knowledge Answers

1. **C.** Choice C is correct; fallible means imperfect or open to error. If you know the word fallacy you would have a clue to the meaning of the word. The only other clue is the word inside fallacy—fall. That could help you remember its meaning.

2. **D.** Choice D is correct; the adjective moot means arguable or subject to debate. Since there is no context, you would need to know the word. One way to build vocabulary is to study word lists with definitions.

3. **A.** Choice A is correct. Malinger means to shirk or avoid duty or responsibility. The prefix mal- meaning bad might give you a clue as to its meaning, but context clues do not help here.

4. **A.** Levity means frivolity, or lightness in tone of speech or mannerism. The other choices do not relate to the word. This is a word that needs to be memorized.

5. **B.** Choice B is correct. Quixotic means idealistic, romantic or dreamy. The word comes from Don Quixote, Miguel de Cervantes' idealistic hero of fiction who was caught up in the romance of trying to achieve unattainable goals. The unique origin of the word is one way to remember it.

6. **C.** Choice C is correct. To execrate is to denounce, loathe or abhor. Choices A, B, and D are not related to the meaning of the word. There are no clues to figure out the meaning of the word, so it would need to be memorized.

7. **A.** A is the correct choice; fortuitous means accidental or happening by chance. Standard usage implies that it is a happy accident. The root *fortune* is a good clue to the word's meaning.

8. **D.** Choice D is correct. Gamut means extent or complete range. Even if you do not recognize the word, none of the other choices are compatible with the word emotions when you place them where gamut is in the sentence. Context clues help in this instance.

9. **B.** The adjective finite means limited, or within certain bounds. The word comes from the Latin word for limit or end. The word has the same root as the word finish as well. This is a clue to its meaning since the sentence's context does not offer that much help.

10. **A.** Choice A is correct. Neophyte means a novice or beginner. The prefix neo- means new, which may provide a clue. The other choices are not related to the word in meaning.

11. **C.** The adjective nondescript means featureless, or lacking any distinction, so choice C is correct. The prefix non- means not. The root *descript* is related to description so it is possible to figure out the meaning from the word parts.

12. **D.** Choice D is correct; raiment means garment or clothing. The origin is French. You will need to memorize this word unless you have a working knowledge of French.

13. **C.** Choice C is correct. Redress means to remedy or to set right. The prefix re- means again. The word address meaning to deal with has the same root and may provide a clue to the word's meaning.

14. **A.** Choice A is correct. Sententious means pompous or high-sounding. It is from a Latin word. Since the context clues are not helpful in this case, the word would need to be memorized.

15. **B.** Demur means to object or express opposition. Choices A, C, and D are not related to the meaning of the word. Again, there is little in the word that can be analyzed. Make sure to review vocabulary lists before the exam.

16. **D.** D is the correct choice. Corpulent means stout or overweight. Context clues are helpful here, since the other choices do not make a lot of sense. Also the word's root *corp* comes from the Latin word meaning body, another hint.

17. **B.** Choice B is correct. Laconic means concise, curt, or using very few words. The other choices are not related to the meaning of the word. Context clues do not help here. You have to know the word.

18. **A.** Choice A is correct. Litigation means prosecution, legal proceedings or legal case. Context clues are a help here. A is the only option that makes sense.

19. **D.** The adjective nefarious means evil or wicked, so choice D is correct. This comes from the Latin word for crime. It is difficult to come up with the meaning of this word without extensive background in Latin, so it is a good one to memorize.

20. **C.** Choice C is correct. Pandemic means widespread, prevalent or rampant. A clue might be the similarity to the word epidemic. The prefix pan- means general or

whole, so that provides a clue as well. Reviewing the meanings of suffixes and prefixes will help you be able to analyze words more effectively.

21.   **C.** Choice C is correct; culpable means blameworthy. The word comes from a Latin word that means to blame. Context clues are a big help here since none of the other choices make sense in the sentence.

22.   **A.** A is the correct choice. Deleterious means injurious or causing harm. The origin is a Greek word meaning destroyer. Context clues are not that helpful here.

23.   **D.** The correct choice is D. Defray means to pay or bear the expense of. There are no clues to help; you have to learn the word.

24.   **B.** Choice B is correct. Baleful means ominous or foreshadowing evil. Again it is a word that is difficult to analyze. Make sure to review lists with words and their definitions before the exam.

25.   **C.** C is the correct choice. The noun amity means friendship. It comes from a Latin noun meaning friend. If you are familiar with Spanish, you might know that amigo means friend. It comes from the same Latin root. This could be a good way to remember what the word means.

26.   **B.** Choice B is correct. Palliative means relief, remedy or cure. None of the other choices make sense based on the adjective soothing. This sentence provides enough context clues to figure out the word's meaning.

27.   **C.** Choice C is correct. Beginning is the opposite of demise, which means end, termination or death.

28.   **A.** Gregarious means sociable. There are no clues here for you to figure out the meaning; the word needs to be memorized.

29.   **B.** Choice B is correct. Masticate means to chew. None of the other words would make sense in the context of the sentence. If the word is used in a sentence, always check for context clues.

30.   **D.** Choice D is correct. Hauteur means arrogance, assuming superiority. The word is French in origin. There are no clues here to help out unless you are familiar with the French word haut meaning high.

31. **A.** A is the correct choice. Garish means showy or tawdry. This word needs to be memorized since it is not easily analyzed.

32. **B.** Choice B is correct; tacit means inferred, unstated. It comes from a Latin word for silent. The other choices do not relate to the word's meaning.

33. **C.** The adjective supine means flat, lying on one's back, so choice C is correct. It has its origins in Latin.

34. **A.** Choice A is correct. Ubiquitous means omnipresent or seeming to be present everywhere. It comes from a Latin word meaning everywhere. It's a good word to learn.

35. **D.** Choice D is correct. Macabre means gruesome, or suggestive of death. Context helps here as gruesome is the best fit.

Paragraph Comprehension Answers

1. **B.** The passage states that the main topic that the two debated was extension of slavery in new U.S. territories, not states. The statements in choices A and C are both true.

2. **D.** This is the advice that doctors are giving people. There is no mention of getting vitamin D from other sources than the sun. Nothing is said about tanning machines and the doctors are not advising not being in the sun for long periods so choices A, B and C are incorrect.

3. **B.** This is not what the passage says; it says that she took the name after she was freed by the New York State Emancipation Act of 1827 making her a free person not a slave. Choices A, C and D are all supported by the passage.

4. **C.** The passage states that the Smart Truck III offers armored protection against roadside attacks, which could include explosive devices. Choices A and B are not stated in the passage and choice D is not correct either.

5. **B.** The passage states that SE tax consists of Social Security and Medicare taxes. Those taxes are included with income tax in any quarterly estimated tax payments. Choices A and C are not correct.

6. **D.** The passage states that the self-employed person must first figure net profit (or loss). Choice A is tempting, but the self-employed person pays income taxes only if there is a net profit. Estimated taxes are paid quarterly and choice C is not logical as a self-employed person would not receive a paycheck.

7. **A.** Feng Shui is a philosophy, not an energy source. Choice B can be inferred from the passage. Both choices C and D are stated in the passage.

8. **D.** It is stated in the passage that the vaqueros taught the Anglos the cattle business. The passage doesn't suggest anything about Anglos' ability to speak Spanish or use chaps.

9. **C.** The primary theme of the passage is the various appeal processes available in the court system. Choice A is too general, and choices B and D are not appropriate, as they are not discussed in the passage.

10. **D.** All of the statements are directly supported by the passage.

11. **D.** All of the statements are directly supported by the passage. OSHA provides workers with all of these services.

12. **A.** OSHA standards are enforced by OSHA itself, which is part of the Department of Labor. Congress passed the legislation which created OSHA.

13. **B.** The passage states that fossils are the remains of animals and plants that were buried, mineralized and thus preserved. Choices A and C, although true, are not the best description. Choice D is incorrect.

14. **B.** The passage infers that the fossils were fragile and easily broken, but the casts didn't break, because the scientists were able to study them. It is true that the casts were heavier, but that is not the primary reason. Neither choice C nor choice D is correct.

15. **D.** All of the statements are directly supported by the passage. Choice B is not directly stated, but can be inferred from the information in the passage.

Mathematical Knowledge Answers

1. **B.** For any right triangle, $a^2 + b^2 = c^2$ where c is the hypotenuse and a, b are legs.

$$15^2 + b^2 = 25^2$$
$$225 + b^2 = 625$$
$$b^2 = 400$$
$$b = 20$$

2. **B.** $3^2 - 4(2-3)^2 = 9 - 4(-1)^2 = 9 - 4 = 5.$

3. **A.** The product represents multiplication and "is" can be interpreted as "equals".

4. **D.** When multiplying, distribute the x^2 and remember to add exponents when two terms have the same base: $x^2(x^2 - 7) = x^{2+2} - 7x^2 = x^4 - 7x^2.$

5. **B.** The perimeter represents the sum of the length of each side. Since this is a square, the sides all have the same length. There are four sides, and if x represents the length, the perimeter is $x + x + x + x = 20$. Solving this equation, the length of each side is 5 and the area is then $5 \times 5 = 25.$

6. **C.** As an equation, this statement is $0.75x = 150$. Dividing both sides by 0.75 results in $x = 200.$

7. **A.** There is no indication that one machine's failure will affect the other. Therefore, the probability one will fail is not affected by the other. In other words, the failures are independent. To find the probability two independent events will both occur, multiply the probabilities. $0.20 \times 0.35 = 0.07.$

8. **C.** The angles of an equilateral triangle all have the same measure and in any triangle, the sum of the interior angles is $180°$. Therefore, the angles in an equilateral triangle can be found using the equation $3x = 180$ which results in $x = 60.$

9. **C.** Cross multiply and then solve as any other linear equation.

$$\frac{7}{2w} \quad \frac{1}{4}$$
$$2w \quad 28$$
$$w \quad 14$$

10. **A.** Since this is addition, the parentheses can be ignored and like terms can be collected to simplify the expression.

$$(x + 1) + (-2x - 5) = x + 1 - 2x - 5 = x - 4$$

11. **B.** With one exception, any inequality or equation will remain true if you multiply both sides by a nonzero constant. The only exception is when you multiply an inequality by a negative constant. This will result in the inequality flipping directions.

12. **C.** By the order of operations, perform the subtraction first.

$$\sqrt{25\,16}\ \sqrt{9}\ 3.$$

13. **D.** The perimeter of a circle is where r is the radius. Therefore, $2\pi r = 16\pi$ and $r = 8$. The area of the circle is then $\pi r^2 = \pi \times 8^2 = 64\pi$.

14. **D.** Sarah has saved $6 \times 50 = 300$. Robbie has saved twice this and $2 \times 300 = 600$. Finally, Terrance saved 4 times as much: $4 \times 600 = 2400$.

15. **C.** Factor out an x and then factor the resulting trinomial.

$$x^3 + 4x^2 + 4x = x(x^2 + 4x + 4) = x(x + 2)^2$$

16. **B.** Let the measure of the smallest angle be x. The largest angle is $3x$ and $x + 3x + 20 = 180$. Solving this equation, the measure of the smallest angle is $x = 40$ and the measure of the largest angle is $3 \times 40 = 120$.

Electronics Answers

1. **B.** The symbol represents a battery.

2. **B.** The symbol at B represents a normally closed switch. D is a resistor, F is a diode, and H is a motor.

3. **B.** The symbol at H is an electrical motor and the only consumer.

4. **C.** Point C would have a higher voltage, because it is before the resistor in the circuit and resistors cause a drop in voltage.

5. **D.** The circuit shown has only one pathway for current, and is therefore a series circuit. A parallel circuit will have more than one pathway, and zener and inductive are not types of circuits.

6. **A.** Component F is a diode, and it allows current to flow in only one direction, indicated by the position of the arrow in the wiring diagram.

7. **C.** A wattmeter measures current flow over time. A voltmeter measures voltage, an ampmeter measures current flow, and an Ohmmeter measures resistance.

8. **B.** A generator converts mechanical power to electrical power.

9. **A.** The black wire is hot, a neutral wire will be white, ground will be green or bare, and AC systems do not have a "negative" wire.

10. **D.** Ohm's law states R = V/I, or Resistance (ohms) = Voltage (volts) / Intensity (or current, measured in amps).

11. **C.** Random Access Memory (RAM) and Read Only Memory (ROM) are both types of computer memory. A Subscriber Identity Module card, or SIM card, is a small card that stores data in cell phones.

12. **C.** Using Ohm's law, V/R = I, therefore 120V/10 ohms = 12 amps.

13. **B.** Household current is AC, alternating current, and standardized at 120 volts.

14. **A.** Hertz. Watts is a measure of power, Ohms are amount of resistance, and Amps are the amount of current.

15. **D.** Using Watts' law, P/V = I, calculate $^{120}/_{12}$ = 10. Power is measured in watts.

16. **A.** 12 volt, direct current.

Automotive Answers

1. **D.** Under-inflated tires don't roll as well as properly inflated ones.

2. **C.** Federal emission regulations require vehicles to monitor themselves and indicate to the operator when something is out of compliance.

3. **A.** Brake pads have a wear indicator, called a "squealer," that will make noise when the pads get too thin.

4. **C.** The master cylinder is a part of the brake system, but each of the other items can affect power steering.

5. **B.** The ideal stoichiometric ratio is 14.7:1 (oxygen:fuel). A ratio of 13.7:1 needs more oxygen in the mixture, and is considered rich.

6. **A.** Diesel engines don't use spark plugs to ignite the air/fuel mixture.

7. **C.** The secondary ignition system creates a high-voltage spark to ignite gasses in the combustion chamber.

8. **B.** Once a vehicle is lifted by a jack, stationary jack stands should be used to stabilize the vehicle before working underneath it.

9. **A.** A fuse will burn out or blow when its rated current is exceeded.

10. **D.** The power stroke is the explosion part of the cycle, so the valves must be closed to contain the force.

11. **A.** An airbag refers to the secondary restraint system, which does not run off of compressed air at all.

Shop Answers

1. **A.** These tools are used to work metal, which would provide a sturdy and solid pen.

2. **C.** A drill with a keyless chuck does not require the use of a special tool, the key, to change drill bits. A keyless chuck drill may be cordless, but not necessarily.

3. **B.** You will need 12 boards, each 1.5" wide and 4 feet long. $12 \times 4' = 48$ board feet total.

4. **C.** A pipe wrench is a specialized wrench for gripping and twisting round things.

5. **B.** Finishing processes should be done from coarsest to finest, so using a rasp (coarse teeth), then sander (coarse to fine abrasion), and finally steel wool (fine abrasion) is the best sequence.

6. **D.** A welding mask is used to prevent vision damage.

7. **B**

8. **C.** For both safety and environmental reasons, spills should be cleaned up immediately.

9. **A.** A lathe is used to turn wood or metal and create round forms. All of the other options are tools used in applying or finishing concrete.

10. **D.** Welding certifications are specific to each purpose, type of welding, and type of metal.

11. **B.** Screws usually are installed in a clockwise direction, but not always, especially when assembling rotating parts. A pilot hole is not always necessary, especially in soft materials.

Mechanical Comprehension Answers

1. **B.** Only displacement has a magnitude (distance) and a direction.

2. **A.** Velocity is the displacement (+100 m) divided by the time interval (50 s), which comes out to be + 2 m/s.

3. **A.** The plane is moving at constant velocity. According to Newton's First Law, the net force acting on the plane is zero. If the engines put out +100,000 N, then the air resistance must be −100,000 N.

4. **C.** When you stop a car, the brakes apply a negative acceleration (deceleration) and the car slows down (speed decreases) to a stop.

5. **D.** Weight is the product of mass and acceleration due to gravity. So, the 80-kg soldier has a weight of approximately 800 N (W = (80kg)(10 m/s^2) = 800 N).

6. **D.** The action force is the firing of the bullet. According to Newton's Third Law, the reaction force is the recoil of the rifle.

7. **B.** The force of friction opposes the direction of motion, so arrow B represents friction.

8. **C.** While in the airplane, the package has kinetic energy by virtue of its height, but no potential energy. According to principle of conservation of energy, when dropped, the package's kinetic energy increases to maximum, while the potential energy decreases to zero.

9. **B.** The masses are balanced, so the torques must be equal. The force acting on the 4-kg mass is twice that on the 2-kg mass, so the lever arm of the 4-kg mass must be half of that upon the 2-kg mass, or 5 cm.

10. **A.** Power is work divided by time. Because each soldier does the same amount of work, the soldier with the shortest time shows the greatest power. That is soldier A.

11. **D.** He needs a short lever arm on the output end where the car is. So, he should place it as close to the car as possible.

12. **C.** The two crossed belts will cause Pulley D to turn in the same direction as Pulley A. However because Pulley D is smaller, it will turn at a faster rate.

13. **D.** A screw is merely an inclined plane wrapped around a cylinder.

14. **B.** The mechanical advantage is less than one, so the output force must be less than the input force. Since the input work equals the output work, then the output distance must be greater than the input distance.

15. **D.** A hydrofoil acts like an airplane wing in the water. The curvature of the upper surface is greater than that of the lower one. Water moves faster across the upper surface and makes a lower pressure. The difference in water pressure across the two surfaces generates lift.

16. **C.** A single fixed pulley only changes the direction of the input force opposite the output force. It confers no mechanical advantage.

Assembling Objects Answers

1. B

2. D

3. C

4. D

5. B

6. A

7. A

8. B

9. C

10. B

11. D

12. D

13. C

14. A

15. C

16. A

Part III

Review of All ASVAB Test Topics

chapter **8**

General Science

Doing well on the ASVAB's general science questions can seem to depend on knowing a lot of disconnected science facts. But a good score also rides on your ability to make reasonable assumptions and guesses. For that skill, it's important to grasp the general principles behind science itself, as well as those of its specialties.

Just becoming familiar with these subjects can lead you to the right answer, but more often you'll be much better at eliminating the wrong ones, which is nearly as important. The majority of questions are multiple-choice, with one correct answer and three incorrect answers each. So, if you can eliminate two wrong answers, you'll improve your odds of choosing the right answer to 50%.

In the paper-and-pencil test, the ASVAB general science section has 25 questions that you'll have 11 minutes to answer. The CAT-ASVAB has 16 questions and an 8-minute time limit. The questions are typically drawn from the fields of physics, chemistry, human physiology, biology, ecology, and earth and space sciences.

This chapter introduces the basics of each of these disciplines.

Physics

Basic physics deals with objects and how they move, as well as gravity, energy, heat, sound, waves, and more. The discipline has a lot of overlap with chemistry, and a good understanding of physical science will improve your understanding of it too.

Objects have *mass*, which gives them weight. Mass resists being moved, and once it's moving, it resists any change in its movement. This is Sir Isaac Newton's First Law.

An object is moving at a constant speed—or a constant *velocity*—when nothing is slowing it down. Velocity is the distance traveled by an object divided by the time it traveled. An air-hockey puck continues to move far in a straight line with only one push because it touches only the air around it. To make the puck move in a different direction, it's necessary to push it that way.

Pushing an object *accelerates* it—that is, it adds velocity. As Newton's Second Law says, it takes *force* to accelerate an object, and bigger objects take more force than smaller objects to reach the same acceleration. Put another way, force (F) equals mass (m) times acceleration (a), $F = ma$.

Friction is a force between objects—it resists them moving in different directions while touching. For example, a hockey puck sliding on concrete does not move at a constant velocity—it slows down—because friction resists that movement. It acts as force that accelerates the puck in the opposite direction of its velocity.

When you push on an object, though, you are pushed back by the same amount. This is Newton's Third Law. In other words, for every action, there is an equal and opposite reaction. For example, when you push against a wall, the wall pushes back. If it did not, you would push right through it. In another example, if a man in a small boat pushes another small boat away, both boats move in opposite directions.

Gravity is a force of attraction between two objects. The greater the mass of an object, the greater its gravitational force of attraction for other objects. However, the gravitational attraction between two objects decreases as they move away from each other.

Work is force applied over a distance. If you push a stalled car across the street, you are doing work. Work (w) equals force (F) times distance (d), $w = Fd$.

Power is the work done during a certain amount of time. In other words, power (P) equals work (w) divided by time (t), $P = w/t$.

Energy is the ability to do work. *Potential energy* is stored energy. For example, a rock at the top of a hill is said to have potential energy that is released as it rolls down the hill. As it rolls down, it is said to have *kinetic energy*. In other words, gravity does work on the rock, converting potential energy to kinetic energy. Rolling the rock back to the top of the hill uses your work to add potential energy to the rock.

Heat is energy transferred from one object or area to another without the application of work. When the rock in the example above finally comes to rest, we say that friction converted its kinetic energy into heat.

In this example, the amount of heat created equals the potential energy that the rock had before it began rolling down the hill. The total amount of energy in this system remains the same throughout, but it changed from potential energy to kinetic energy to heat. This is an illustration of the *law of conservation of energy*, which says that the total energy in a closed system always stays the same.

Heat is responsible for *temperature*, but it is not the same. It takes one *calorie* of heat to raise the temperature of water by one degree Celsius, but it takes less heat to raise the temperature of the same amount of alcohol by one degree Celsius.

In matter, heat is stored as the vibration of molecules. It can transfer from one object to another—or within a single object—by *conduction*, in which the vibrating molecules influence neighboring molecules to vibrate.

In gases and liquids, heat also transfers by *convection*. Since vibrating gas or liquid molecules take up slightly more space as they vibrate, a collection of hot molecules has less density than the same number of cold molecules. That is, they have a greater volume, but the same mass as an equal number of cold molecules. As a result, hot patches of liquid or gas rise, while the dense, cold patches fall. This is convection.

Heat also transfers by *radiation*. Vibrating molecules and the charged particles within them create *thermal radiation* when they vibrate. This radiation will cause the molecules in an object that it strikes to vibrate in return. Only objects at *absolute zero*—zero Kelvin—emit no thermal radiation.

Light is a form of electromagnetic radiation, like heat. Both travel as waves through open space, but light differs by its *wavelength*—the distance between the peaks or valleys of its waves. Visible light has a shorter (smaller) wavelength than heat, but it has a longer wavelength than ultraviolet light. Radio waves have very long wavelengths, while X-rays and gamma rays have very short wavelengths.

In some cases, light is thought of as a particle known as a *photon*.

Sound is a wave of compressions that travel through matter, such as air, water, or solid objects. High-pitched sounds have short wavelengths and low-pitched sounds have long wavelengths.

The *Doppler effect* refers to the shortening of sound waves—and rising pitch—as a sound source moves toward an observer, or the falling pitch as it moves away.

A similar phenomenon occurs with light. As a light source approaches, the light's wavelength is compressed—it becomes "blue-shifted." As the source moves away, the light's wavelength is expanded—it becomes "red-shifted."

A magnetic field forms when charged particles, such as electrons, move. When electrons move in a circular pattern, such as through a wire wrapped around a metal bar, the magnetic field develops a "north" and "south" pole at either end of the bar. This is an *electromagnet*.

Allowing iron or another magnetic metal to turn from liquid to solid metal while inside a magnetic field produces a permanent magnet, in which tiny components—called domains—arrange themselves inside the metal with their own north and south ends aligned with the field.

Earth's magnetic field results from the planet's rotation together with the movement of molten metal deep within its interior.

Chemistry

Chemistry is the study of matter and its interactions. Every object, gas, and liquid is made up of molecules, and all molecules are actually collections of atoms that are bound together.

Atoms are composed of a *nucleus* of positively charged *protons* and uncharged *neutrons*, with negatively charged *electrons* that "orbit" the nucleus in a buzzing frenzy. There is almost always the same number of protons and electrons—if one outnumbers the other, the atom is an ion, and it has positive or negative charge.

The number of protons in an atom is called its *atomic number*, and that's what determines what sort of *element* an atom is. Hydrogen atoms have one proton in their nuclei, while helium atoms have two protons, and carbon atoms have six. The periodic table presents all of the elements lined up in order by atomic number, and it groups them into families made up of similar elements.

The periodic table also lists each element's average *atomic mass*—the number of protons plus the average number of neutrons per molecule. The number of neutrons in a nucleus is often the same as the number of protons—but not always. While ordinary carbon has six protons and six neutrons, carbon-13 has six protons and seven neutrons. These two forms of carbon are called *isotopes* of carbon—they have identical properties except for the fact that an atom of carbon-13 is slightly heavier. But carbon-13 is very rare, so the periodic table lists carbon's atomic mass as slightly heavier than 12 grams per mol, where a mol is 6.022×10^{23} molecules.

In general, when a solid object gains enough heat—kinetic energy—its molecules can begin to break loose from their collective clump to form a liquid. This is called a *phase change*. Give enough energy to the molecules in the liquid, and it will change phase into a gas. Subtract energy to reverse the process.

But phase changes also depend on another factor: *pressure*. Reducing the *atmospheric pressure*—literally, the pressure that the air exerts on the liquid's surface—allows you to change a liquid's phase to gas without using as much heat. For example, it takes less heat to boil a pot of water at the top of Mount Everest, where the atmospheric pressure is low, than it does at sea level, where the pressure is high.

Phase changes are *physical changes*, and are easily reversible. *Chemical changes* are not so easily reversed. When two molecules of hydrogen gas ($2 H_2$) are burned with one molecule of oxygen (O_2), a chemical change occurs when the atoms form new *chemical bonds* to create a new *compound*—two molecules of water ($2 H_2O$).

When elements combine and form chemical bonds, they form new compounds. But when they do not, they form *mixtures*. Swirling oil into water forms a mixture, for example. A *solution* is a mixture in which a *solute*, such as salt, is dissolved in a *solvent*, often water.

The pH of a solution is a measure of how *acidic* or *basic* it is. Acidic solutions have a low pH, meaning they have a high concentration of positively charged hydrogen ions dissolved in the solution. A basic solution has a pH higher than 7, and it has a lot of negatively charged OH ions dissolved in the solution. A pH of 7 is neutral.

The chemical bonds in water are *covalent bonds*, in which each pair of hydrogen and oxygen atoms share an electron. *Ionic bonds* form between atom pairs in which one partner keeps an extra electron to itself, giving this atom—this *ion*, really—a positive charge and giving the other partner atom a negative charge. Ionic bonds are common in molecules containing atoms from opposite edges of the periodic table, such as the atoms that make up salts, including sodium chloride, NaCl.

Human Physiology

Physiology is the study of how animal bodies are organized and how they function. To minimize overlap with the section on biology, this section will concentrate mostly on body components that do not require a microscope to see them.

Like all animal bodies, the human body has four main levels of organization: *cells*, *tissues*, *organs*, and *organ systems*. At the smallest level are *cells*, which are usually specialized to fulfill specific roles, according to the type of *tissue* they are part of. For example, muscle cells make up the heart's cardiac muscle, which is a tissue.

Together, cardiac muscle, valves, connective tissues, veins, arteries, and other tissues make up the *organ* that we call the heart. The heart and the body's veins, arteries, valves, blood, and so on make up the *circulatory system*, which is an *organ system*.

The *circulatory system*'s job is to bring fresh oxygen to all of the body's tissues. Oxygen-poor blood collects oxygen and releases carbon dioxide in microscopic veins called *capillaries* in the *alveoli* of the lungs, which are tiny sacs that receive air when you breathe.

The nose, nasal cavity, trachea, and lungs make up the *respiratory system*, which delivers oxygen into the body (and removes carbon dioxide from the body) through the nose or mouth, down the trachea to the lungs. There, the trachea branches into smaller passages called *bronchioles* and eventually into the small, capillary-surrounded alveoli. Muscles of the *diaphragm* help the lungs take in and expel air.

After *red blood cells* gather oxygen from the air, the blood continues moving through the circulatory system to the heart, which pumps it through the *aorta* to the rest of the body.

This bright red, oxygen-rich blood flows throughout the body in *arteries* that get smaller as they branch out. Eventually, the blood ends up in tiny *capillaries* throughout the body, and it releases its oxygen and gathers carbon dioxide as it goes, responding to the low pH in areas that are rich in carbon dioxide.

Now oxygen-poor and carbon dioxide-rich, the blood travels through capillaries to *veins*, which combine to become larger and larger—basically a reverse of the branching arteries. This blood, now dark blue, travels to the heart again, which pumps it through the pulmonary arteries back to the lungs.

Plasma makes up most of the blood—it's the liquid in which the blood's components flow. The blood also contains *platelets*, which respond to nearby injuries by breaking open to trigger *clotting*. A scab is a blood clot on the surface of the body, but clots can also form inside.

White blood cells make up part of the body's *immune system*, which protects against invaders, such as bacteria and viruses. Specialized white blood cells make *antibodies*, which attach to foreign matter in the body, often disabling it or marking it for other cells to destroy.

Once the body makes antibodies that attack specific invaders, it can "remember" them and rapidly produce similar antibodies the next time it encounters that type of invader. This is why *vaccines* work to prevent diseases, such as mumps and rubella—injecting damaged foreign bacteria or viruses into an animal allows the animal's immune system to prepare antibodies that become useful when it encounters the real thing.

Other components of the immune system include the skin, the saliva, and the digestive system, which exclude or destroy invading organisms, as well as mucus in the nose, lungs, and elsewhere, which traps invaders.

The *musculoskeletal system* includes all of the body's bones, muscles, joints, tendons, and cartilage. In general, muscles can be divided into *voluntary muscles*, which you can consciously control, and *involuntary muscles*, which operate more-or-less automatically. Involuntary muscles include the heart and muscles in the stomach.

Skeletal muscles are voluntary muscles that attach to bones through tendons. When one skeletal muscle contracts to bend bones around a joint, an opposing skeletal muscle relaxes. The two muscles switch roles in order to bend the joint in the opposite direction.

The *digestive system* involves all the components in the winding path that food and drink take through animal bodies, including the *mouth, esophagus, stomach, small intestine, large intestine, rectum*, and *anus*. It also includes the *liver* and *pancreas*, which make fluids that help to digest nutrients.

Chewed food and saliva travel from the mouth, down the esophagus, to the stomach, where involuntary muscles mix it with *gastric juice*—containing acid and special proteins—which breaks it into smaller pieces in a process called *catabolism*. From there, involuntary muscles move the food to the small intestine. In the process, it mixes with *bile* from the liver, *pancreatic juice* from the pancreas, and *intestinal juice* from the intestinal glands.

Each of these fluids breaks the food down further, until its molecules can be absorbed by the tiny, finger-like villi lining the intestine. Here, the blood picks up absorbed nutrients and travels to the liver for filtering and processing, and then takes the nutrients to tissues throughout the body.

Involuntary muscles move any undigested food to the large intestine, where bacteria continue to break down what remains and leave some nutrients to be absorbed by the local villi. Waste products from the bloodstream collect here with remaining food to make *feces*, which is briefly stored in the rectum and eliminated through the anus.

The body disposes of wastes using the excretory system, which includes the large intestine, rectum, and anus discussed above, as well as the lungs, which expel carbon dioxide. It also includes the *kidneys, bladder,* and *urethra*—the *urinary system.* The kidneys filter waste products from the blood to produce *urine,* which is routed to the bladder, where the urine is stored until it is eliminated through the urethra.

Nutrients themselves fit into one of five categories: *carbohydrates, proteins, fats, vitamins,* and *dietary minerals.* Carbohydrates are common in grain-based foods, such as bread, rice, and pasta. Each carbohydrate molecule is composed of several sugar molecules connected end-to-end, and essentially serves as a short-term sugar storage location. Plants make carbohydrates called *starches,* while animals make similar carbohydrates called *glycogen.*

Fat molecules serve as long-term, high-density energy storage, and they include animal fat, vegetable oil, butter, and most other slippery or greasy food components. Fats are *triglycerides,* each of which are made of three *fatty acids* connected to a molecule of *glycerol.* Each fatty acid is mostly composed of a chain of carbon atoms bonded to hydrogen and hydroxyl groups (oxygen bonded to hydrogen).

Proteins are molecules that organisms use for a variety of roles including aiding chemical reactions, such as digestion; acting as signaling molecules; and reinforcing cell structure. Proteins are long chains constructed from about 20 different types of *amino acids.* While every type of food contains proteins, some foods are richer in particular amino acids. *Essential amino acids* cannot be made by the body, while *non-essential amino acids* can.

Vitamins are carbon-containing compounds that the body cannot make on its own, but still requires in small amounts. There are 13 vitamins, including the well-known vitamin A, vitamin C, biotin, and vitamin D; they can be roughly divided into fat-soluble vitamins and water-soluble vitamins. Some serve in the body as signaling molecules, while others work with enzyme proteins to perform specific chemical reactions. Particular vitamins are more abundant in certain foods.

As with vitamins, the human body needs only small amounts of *dietary minerals,* which are usually found as easily accessible chemical elements, and occasionally as part of chemical compounds. Depending upon how they are defined, there are around 16 of these minerals, many of which are metals, such as magnesium, calcium, potassium, and zinc. They generally serve structural roles, help enzymes catalyze chemical reactions, or function as electrolytes.

The *nervous system* includes the *brain,* the *spinal cord,* and the body's *nerves,* and it allows thought, emotion, involuntary responses, and conscious movement. Each part of the nervous system contains impulse-conducting cells—or *neurons*—which communicate with each other through electrical signals that they send through axons and receive through dendrites. In the case of specialized nerve cells in the body, they also send signals directly to muscle fibers to command them to contract. Connections between neurons, or between a neuron and a muscle cell, are called *synapses*.

There are around 100 billion neurons in the human brain. These make up its "gray matter," while its "white matter" is composed of two glial cells, which support neurons and provide some nutritional aid. The vast majority of the nervous system's neurons are located in the brain, particularly the *cerebrum*, where conscious thought occurs.

The brain's *cerebellum*, located on the back underside of the organ, is responsible for many aspects of muscle control and emotion. The *brain stem* is located on the middle underside of the brain. It connects the brain to the body's nerves through the *spinal cord*, and it regulates the heartbeat and breathing, among other roles.

In addition to relaying sensory and motor signals, the spinal cord is also responsible for generating some reflexes. For example, when you put your hand on a hot surface, the spinal cord controls the reflex that quickly moves your hand away.

The Senses

Of course, the brain is closely linked with the senses of sight, hearing, smell, taste, touch, and balance and position. Each of these senses involves the interpretation of environmental cues by neurons that send their information to the brain for further processing.

In the sense of sight, light passes through the eye's *pupil*, and a *lens* focuses it on the back wall of the inside of the eyeball, known as the *retina*. There, two types of light-sensitive neurons react to this light, called *cones* and *rods*. Cones provide more detail and are responsible for interpreting color, while rods are better at gathering light in dim conditions, although they cannot distinguish different colors. Each type of neuron responds to light by sending electrical signals through the *optic nerve* to the brain.

In hearing, sound waves enter the ear canal and vibrate the *eardrum*—also known as the *tympanum*. This moves three small bones—the *hammer*, the *anvil*, and the *stirrup*—which pass vibrations to the *inner ear*, where they cause tiny hairs in the *cochlea* to bend. The *auditory nerve* passes these signals to the brain.

In humans, the sense of smell—or *olfaction*—involves neurons with special sensitivity to different chemicals, called *olfactory sensory neurons*. When these neurons detect chemicals that dissolve in surrounding mucus from the air, they send electrical signals through the *olfactory nerve* to the brain's *olfactory bulb*.

The sense of balance—or equilibrioception—is provided by specialized structures in the inner ear. These include the *posterior*, *superior*, and *horizontal canals*, which are three semi-circular, fluid-filled tubes. When your head moves, liquid in one or more of these canals moves, which triggers the hairs on specialized neurons that send electrical signals to the brain. Two other structures, the utricle and the saccule use a similar method to detect movement in a straight line.

Stretch-sensing neurons throughout the body provide the sense of position, or *proprioception*. Along with vision, this sense works to fine-tune the sense of balance.

Biology

Biology is concerned with a wide variety of topics, from whole organisms to the cells they're composed of. This section will discuss cell biology, cell division, biological classification, binary fission, mitosis, meiosis, genetics, some key characteristics of the main kingdoms of organisms, and ecology.

Cell Commonalities

Whether it's a free-living bacterial cell or part of a mammal's body, each cell generally carries out the main functions that define life: they undergo metabolism, maintain a stable internal environment, react to external stimuli, and reproduce. All cells also contain *cytoplasm*, the liquid that fills them; a *membrane* that separates their interiors from the outside world; and genetic material in the form of *DNA*.

Unlike animals, plants, fungi, and protists, bacteria do not have *organelles*, which are membrane-bound structures that perform specialized roles inside of cells. Single-celled organisms that lack organelles are called *prokaryotes*, while those with organelles are *eukaryotes*. See below for specific details about eukaryotic organelles.

The cell membrane is composed of two stacks of *lipids* arranged in a *bilayer*. Within each layer, *hydrophobic*—water-avoiding—lipids lay parallel to one another, pointing their hydrophilic—water-attracting—ends toward the nearest water. For the internal layer, the nearest water is in the cell's cytosol, while for the outer layer, the nearest water is outside the cell.

Proteins and other molecules protrude through the membrane to sense the outside environment, send and receive signals, provide defense, and more.

In all cells, DNA contains the genes that provide instructions for the organism's processes and structure. These are encoded in the sequence of *nucleotide bases* that make up DNA. There are four types of these bases—guanine (G), cytosine (C), thymine (T), and adenine (A)—and in the double helix of DNA, they match up almost like the teeth of a zipper. But G only pairs with C, while T only pairs with A.

Using this choosy pairing scheme, specialized enzymes unzip DNA and copy its information into RNA—a chemical relative of DNA. This *transcription* makes "mRNA" that travels to the cytoplasm, where ribosomes *translate* its sequence of bases to assemble amino acids into a string that will become a protein. Once the ribosome is finished, the protein folds up to become active, and can serve as a structural element, a chemical catalyst, a signaling molecule, or something else.

So, the sequence of *nucleotide bases* in a gene in DNA dictates the amino acid sequence in a related protein, determining its function.

Eukaryotic Organelles

The organelles of eukaryotes include mitochondria, the nucleus, rough endoplasmic reticulum, Golgi apparatuses, smooth endoplasmic reticulum, and lysosomes. Plants feature a tough cell wall and additional organelles, including the central vacuole and chloroplasts. The central vacuole is shared by fungi and protists.

The *mitochondria* are the powerhouses of eukaryotic cells, performing the *citric acid cycle* and the *electron transport chain* to produce ATP, NADH, and NADPH, which are three important cellular "fuels." Mitochondria resemble bacteria, and even contain some of their own DNA.

The *nucleus* houses the DNA of eukaryotic cells in the form of chromosomes, which are DNA molecules wrapped around proteins that help pack them into smaller space.

Rough endoplasmic reticulum contains a large number of ribosomes, and among other roles, it serves as the site of translation for proteins that will end up in the cell membrane, or will be secreted through it.

Golgi apparatuses accept newly translated proteins—especially those meant for secretion outside the cell—and modify them to bring them closer to their final functions.

Smooth endoplasmic reticulum serves as the cell's factory for making lipids, for metabolizing carbohydrates, and other functions.

Lysosomes contain special enzymes that break down waste and unneeded components.

The *central vacuole* of plants often contains water, and helps the cell maintain internal pressure, which affects the plant's overall structure. In fungi and protists, it often serves to isolate harmful materials, such as waste products.

The *chloroplasts* of plants contain all the structures necessary for *photosynthesis*—making free oxygen and organic molecules, such as sugars, from carbon dioxide, water, and sunlight. Like mitochondria, they resemble single-celled organisms and contain some of their own DNA.

Haploid and Diploid Organisms

While most prokaryotes are *haploid*, with only one chromosome per cell, most multicelled eukaryotes are *diploid*—they carry two copies of each type of chromosome, one from each parent. Two chromosomes of the same type are called *homologous chromosomes*.

In humans, a normal body cell contains 23 types of chromosomes, and a total of 46 chromosomes. Forty-four of these are known as *autosomes*, while the remaining pair are *sex chromosomes*. Human females have two "X" sex chromosomes, while males each have one "X" and one "Y" sex chromosome.

Binary Fission and Mitosis

Prokaryotes divide in a process called binary fission. This involves specialized enzymes that duplicate their single, circular DNA chromosome and move each copy to opposite sides of the cell as the cell begins to split down the middle.

The eukaryotic process of *mitosis* is similar to binary fission, but more complicated. Enzymes duplicate the chromosomes, and two spindly structures called *centrosomes* at opposite ends of the cell pull these identical chromosomes apart. The cell then divides in half to produce two identical daughter cells.

Meiosis

In eukaryotic meiosis, a normal cell makes one copy of each of its pairs of chromosomes, and homologous chromosomes literally swap parts, trading large and small stretches of DNA with each other. The result of this swapping is two homologous chromosomes that are each mixtures of the original pair—both contain portions that originally belonged to the organism's mother and father.

When the cell divides, the result is two diploid daughter cells. This step of meiosis is similar to mitosis, so in humans, these cells have 23 pairs of chromosomes, and a total of 46 chromosomes.

But when these two diploid cells divide, their homologous chromosomes separate, creating four haploid daughter cells—four gametes, such as egg or sperm cells—each carrying only one chromosome of every type.

Genetics

Because homologous chromosomes swap parts during the first half of meiosis, then separate into different gametes, the genes in these chromosomes have been distributed at random. Even though two genes may have been on the very same chromosome, they may end up separated into different gametes.

When an egg cell and a sperm cell combine, they each contribute one gene of every type. But even though two genes are the same type, they may have slightly different DNA sequences and even different effects on the organism that inherits them. Such genes are called *alleles* of one another.

Some alleles have strong effects on the offspring's appearance or behavior—that is, they create different *phenotypes*. When a *dominant* allele (sometimes called a dominant gene in this context) and a *recessive* allele exert their effects in the same organism, only the dominant allele's phenotype is apparent. The results are the same with two dominant genes. Two recessive alleles must appear together to exert their phenotype in the organism.

For example, a male with one dominant gene for brown eyes (B) and one recessive allele for blue eyes (b) mates with a female who also has a dominant brown-eyes gene (B) and a recessive blue-eyes gene (b). A *Punnett square* will illustrate the couple's chances of having offspring with blue eyes:

FatherBb

MotherBBBBBb

bbBbb

The offspring has a 25 percent chance of having blue eyes (bb), and a 75 percent chance of having brown eyes (BB, Bb, bB), since the brown allele is dominant.

Biological Classification

Taxonomy is the science of classifying species and arranging them into a logical format, especially one that emphasizes their relatedness. There are several biological classification schemes, but the most common system used in the United States involves seven major categories. Starting with the largest category and ending with the smallest, these are: kingdom, phylum, class, order, family, genus, and species.

When naming a particular organism, it is customary to use only the genus and species names. For example, humans are *Homo sapiens*.

According to one common classification system, there are six kingdoms:

- *Animalia*, which includes all animals
- *Fungi*, for yeasts and fungi
- *Plantae*, for plants
- *Protista*, for eukaryotic single-celled protists
- *Bacteria*, which includes almost all bacteria and blue-green algae
- *Archaea*, for *archaebacteria*, which are prokaryotic, single-celled organisms that show large genetic and structural differences from ordinary bacteria

Key Characteristics of Plants

Plants are eukaryotes that get most of their energy from sunlight by using photosynthesis involving chlorophyll. The kingdom Plantae includes land plants, green algae, red algae and glucophyte algae.

The land plants are multicelled plants that we see every day, including vascular plants that have stems, leaves, and roots. Mosses and liverworts are also land plants. This group probably developed from their close relatives, the green algae.

Advanced flowering land plants called *angiosperms* developed from *gymnosperms*, an older category that includes conifers, such as pine trees. Angiosperms produce a coated seed that pollinators, such as insects and birds, reach using a special tube that penetrates the cover.

Key Characteristics of Animals

All animals eat other organisms to survive, all are eukaryotes and multicellular, and nearly all can move during at least one stage of life. Almost all animals are capable of sexual reproduction and feature a complete digestive tract, including a mouth and an anus.

The kingdom includes *vertebrates*—creatures with a backbone—as well as *invertebrates*. Fish, birds, reptiles, amphibians, and mammals are vertebrates. Invertebrates include mollusks, such as snails and squids; arthropods, such as insects and crabs; nematodes, which are roundworms; and many smaller groups.

Key Characteristics of Fungi

Fungi and yeast are eukaryotes with strong cell walls, and they do not move on their own. But unlike plants, fungi don't make any of their own food.

Instead, they consume nutrients from the surrounding environment, and many types serve an important ecological role as decomposers. Multicelled fungi often grow through their food in long, hair-like strands called hyphae, while single-celled yeast produce two unconnected daughter cells after dividing.

Many fungi produce fruiting bodies, such as mushrooms, that help to spread their spores to new locations.

Key Characteristics of Protists

Protists are microscopic and eukaryotic, but most classification systems don't describe their relationships with each other very well. In general, they tend to be single-celled, although many multicelled protists exist. Some reproduce sexually and others reproduce by binary fission. Algae and some other protists can photosynthesize, while the majority cannot. In addition to algae, the kingdom includes protozoa and slime molds.

Key Characteristics of Bacteria

As mentioned before, all bacteria are prokaryotes, microscopic, and single-celled. By total mass, they are by far the largest group of organisms on Earth. Most bacteria feature a cell wall made of peptidoglycan.

Cyanobacteria (blue-green algae) and several other groups of bacteria can photosynthesize with sunlight to make their own food, but there are also bacteria that use organic or even inorganic compounds as energy.

Bacteria are haploid, have one circular chromosome each, and reproduce asexually by binary fission. However, some species are capable of sharing genes in a sex-like process called *conjugation*.

Key Characteristics of Archaebacteria

Archaebacteria are single-celled organisms that lack membrane-bound organelles, but they are not close relatives of the bacteria. They are found in some of Earth's harshest environments, but they aren't limited to these places. They can make use of many unusual nutrition sources, including ammonia or metal ions.

Some archaebacteria are photosynthetic, although they do not use chlorophyll to synthesize food. Like true bacteria, they are asexual, possess a single circular chromosome, and typically reproduce by binary fission. Unlike bacteria, eukaryotes, and other organisms, they feature cell membranes composed of unusual ester-containing molecules.

Ecology

Ecology is the study of the relationships among organisms, their environment, and the specific places where they can live. Ecologists group the environment and its organisms into a series of smaller and smaller categories.

At the top of these categories is the *ecosphere*, which encompasses the atmosphere; the *hydrosphere*, which includes all Earth's water; the *geosphere*, which includes all Earth's minerals; and the *biosphere*, which includes all organisms and their relationships with the rest of the ecosphere and with each other.

A *community* consists of all organisms in a certain area. An *ecosystem* includes a community and all the non-living—or *abiotic*—things that interact with it. A *habitat* is the general place and conditions in which a particular organism is known to live. For example, the habitat of rainbow trout is freshwater lakes and streams.

Studying an ecosystem means understanding where important abiotic components, such as minerals, water, and energy, come from and where they go. The study of energy flow begins with *producers*, such as plants, which make their own food, usually through photosynthesis. Producers also gather many of the minerals and abiotic components they need from the environment.

Primary consumers are organisms that mostly eat producers—they're herbivores. A giraffe is a primary consumer, and so is a cow. A carnivore is a *secondary consumer*, and mostly eats other consumers. A tiger is a secondary consumer. Aside from water, consumers obtain many of the abiotic components they need, such as minerals, by eating other organisms.

Decomposers get their energy from consuming the remains of dead organisms, and play an important role in returning minerals and other important abiotic components to the environment, where they can be used by producers again. Bacteria and fungi are important decomposers, but the category also includes many animals, such as cockroaches.

The complex energy relationship among organisms is known as a *food web*. Producers, primary consumers, secondary consumers, and decomposers are all examples of *trophic levels* of organisms.

Earth and Space Science

The ASVAB's earth and space science questions tend to focus on the topics of astronomy, basic geology, atmospheric science, and oceanography.

Astronomy

The largest bodies in our solar system are the *sun* and the *planets*, of which there are eight. Beginning from the closest planet to the sun, these are Mercury, Venus, Earth, Mars, Jupiter, Saturn, Uranus, and Neptune.

The Sun, Distance Units, and Planets

The sun is essentially a giant ball of hydrogen about 330,000 times heavier than Earth and 109 times its diameter. Its intense gravity compresses its hydrogen until it undergoes nuclear fusion, which releases the energy that eventually reaches us as light and heat.

The distance between Earth and the sun is known as 1 *astronomical unit*, or 1 *AU*. The distance light travels in one year is known as a *light-year*, but the sun's light reaches our planet in about 8 minutes.

A *planet* orbits the sun, has enough mass that its own gravity makes it nearly spherical, and it has very few small objects in its orbit—often because the planet has enough gravity to pull them in. By this definition, Pluto does not have enough mass to qualify a planet. Along with two other far-away objects in the solar system, Ceres and Eris, Pluto is now known as a *dwarf planet*.

Planets are divided into two groups: *Terrestrial planets* are mostly made of rocky materials, while *gas giants* are mostly made of gas, as the name suggests. In our solar system, the gas giants are far, far larger and more massive than terrestrial planets. As a result, their intense gravity compresses their gas interiors into a solid core.

The gas giants are Jupiter, Saturn, Uranus, and Neptune. The rest of the planets are terrestrial. Jupiter is the largest of the planets, at 318 times the mass of Earth, while the terrestrial planet Mercury is the smallest, with only 0.06 times the mass of Earth.

Except for Mercury and Venus, all of our solar system's planets have moons, which are rocky objects that orbit planets. Our solar system's *asteroid belt* is a collection of small, rocky objects that orbit around the sun between the orbits of Mars and Jupiter.

Other Objects

Other common objects in the solar system include *meteoroids*, which are rocky objects smaller than asteroids, ranging from the size of a grain of sand to the size of a large boulder. A *meteor*—or "shooting star"—is the bright path that meteoroids make as they enter the atmosphere of a planet. A meteoroid that actually strikes the surface is called a *meteorite*.

Comets are icy bodies that often follow a long-distance, highly elongated orbit around the sun. As they approach the sun, the hydrogen and heat that the sun emits cause comets to shed material from their surfaces. This appears as a bright "tail" pointing away from the sun.

Orbits, Rotations, and Seasons

Planets travel an *elliptical*—oval, but often nearly circular—path as they orbit the sun. The farthest planets take the most time to complete their orbits around the sun. Of course, Earth completes its orbit once every year—365 days.

Every planet *rotates*—spins—around a central line called an *axis*. Earth's axis is tilted, so different portions of the planet experience direct sunlight as it orbits the sun. This is the reason our *seasons* change. During the Northern Hemisphere's summertime, the sun's rays strike that part of the planet most directly. And when the Northern Hemisphere is experiencing winter, the Southern Hemisphere is receiving the most direct rays from the sun. Earth completes one rotation around its axis each day—24 hours.

The rotation of Earth around the sun, and the rotation of the moon around Earth sometimes causes these three bodies to line up in an event called an *eclipse*. In a *solar eclipse*, the moon temporarily gets between Earth and the sun. In a *lunar eclipse*, Earth gets between the moon and the sun.

Galaxies and Other Stars

Our galaxy, the Milky Way, contains around 300 billion stars, and has a diameter of about 100,000 light-years. The closest star to our solar system is Proxima Centauri, which is 4.2 light-years away.

Like our sun, other stars produce light and heat through nuclear fusion. As their supply of fuel—such as hydrogen or helium—begins to run out, they expand to become *red giants*. When the supply of fuel reaches a critical point, the *envelope* of a red giant crashes back in on the star and bounces back outward in a massive explosion called a *supernova*.

The material emitted in a supernova includes all the heavier elements, and this material can condense into bodies such as planets, moons, and so on. Earth and all the other matter in our solar system, except for the hydrogen, was made in an ancient star.

Geology

Geology is the study of rocks and minerals, and how they move and change over time.

Earth's *crust* is a thin layer that makes up the entire planet's surface. A large share of the crust contains silicon and oxygen. The *mantle* is a thick layer of molten rock and metal, including iron and magnesium, with a smaller share of silicon and oxygen than the crust. The *core* contains more material than the crust, but less than the mantle. It's very hot and mostly made of iron and nickel, but it's under such high pressure that it exists as a solid sphere at the center of our planet.

There are three main types of rock: igneous rock, which is formed when molten rock—*lava* or *magma*—cools; *sedimentary rock*, which is formed when small particles are compressed into solid masses; and metamorphic rock, which form from one of the other rock types under intense heat.

Igneous Rock

Intrusive igneous rock forms underground when molten rock within the earth's crust slowly cools, forming grains. Deep underneath many mountains is a core of intrusive igneous rock. Granite is an example of this type of rock.

Extrusive igneous rock forms at the surface, when magma escapes the crust to become lava and quickly cools. Volcanoes are a typical source of this type of rock. Extrusive igneous rock can contain gas bubbles or crystals, depending on the lava's temperature and composition before it cools. Spongy-looking, light-weight pumice and dense basalt are examples of this type of rock.

Sedimentary Rock

Clastic sedimentary rock forms from fragments deposited by a moving fluid, usually water. *Sandstones* are composed of quartz and other grains stuck together with much smaller pieces that were once mud. *Mudrocks* are mostly made of extremely tiny silt particles that settle out of water or another fluid. Conglomerates are mostly made of compacted gravel.

Biochemical sedimentary rocks are made up of mineral fragments deposited by organisms. Limestone is an example of this type of rock—it's composed of the calcium-rich shells and skeletons of ancient marine animals. *Chemical sedimentary* rocks form when a mineral dissolved in water is concentrated enough to form crystals.

Metamorphic Rock

Metamorphic rock can be categorized by how it formed. *Contact metamorphism* is the process in which magma intrudes into a layer of existing rock, which changes the most at the point where it comes into direct contact with magma. Changes are less significant further away. *Regional metamorphism* occurs when a large volume of existing rock is subjected to high temperature and pressure, usually because it has been pushed deep beneath the surface. The lowest level of the crust shows a great deal of regional metamorphism.

Moving and Changing

Erosion and *weathering* slowly break rock into smaller pieces. The major causes include wind, the grinding of glaciers, chemical reactions, moving water, freezing and thawing water, and intruding plants. Another process is sheet jointing, in which lower layers of rock rise and crack as erosion and other processes reduce the pressure on them by removing upper rock layers.

Plate tectonics is the term that describes our current understanding about how and why large sheets of the planet's crust float on the mantle like ice in a glass of water. Earth's *plates* are driven to move toward or away from one another by convection currents in the mantle. These currents are the result of heating and cooling magma working together with the rotation of the earth.

Where plates converge, mountain ranges or volcanoes often form. Where plates diverge—usually on the sea floor—magma wells up to fill the gap, creating new crust. Diverging plates often create a deep trench.

The Atmosphere

The atmosphere is about 78% nitrogen and 21% oxygen gases, with carbon dioxide, argon, and other gases making up the remaining 1% or so.

Closest to the planet's surface is the *troposphere*, which is the thinnest of the atmosphere's layers, even though it comprises about 80% of its total mass. This is where weather takes place.

Higher up is the *stratosphere*, where the planet's ultraviolet light-blocking *ozone layer* is located. Because of this UV absorption, the stratosphere's higher levels are hotter. Higher still is the mesosphere, where meteoroids usually burn up when they streak through the atmosphere as meteors.

Furthest out is the *exosphere*, which is mostly very diffuse hydrogen and helium molecules—some of which escape into space.

Weather

When a large body of air—an *air mass*—cools over land, it cools more quickly than an air mass that forms over water. It's also drier. Warm air expands, so the air over oceans and other water bodies tends to rise. As a result, cooler, drier air moves as *wind* from areas above land to replace rising air over water.

The coolest air forms nearer to the North and South Poles, while the warmest air forms over water near the equator. The boundary where air masses of different temperatures meet is called a *front*.

There are three main cloud types: *stratus* clouds, *cumulus* clouds, and *cirrus* clouds. Stratus clouds are large, low, and flattened-looking. Cumulus clouds are fluffy with a flat base. Cirrus clouds are high-altitude and wispy. Each type can produce rain, but cumulus clouds are most likely to produce heavy rain.

Reading and Reviewing

This introductory chapter is only a summary intended to refresh your familiarity with the science subjects covered by the ASVAB's general science questions. Each of these sciences contain far more information than any single chapter could present. But it should help you figure out which topics you most need to study in order to maximize your test performance.

Electronic devices

5. The symbol represents a battery.

chapter **9**

Arithmetic Reasoning 1: The Basics

Most of the Arithmetic Reasoning section of the ASVAB consists of word problems such as "Movie tickets cost $9.50 each. If seven people buy tickets, how much did they pay all together?" Even a one-line problem like this can involve several steps and more than one kind of math operation. Before we learn how to break down word problems, we must review the math behind them.

Operations

In math, when we say "operation," we are referring to one of the following:

- **Addition:** also known as finding the sum as in 3 + 4 = 7
- **Subtraction:** or "finding the difference" as when you subtract 14 and 3: 14 − 3 = 11
- **Multiplication:** also called "finding the product," for example: 5 × 7 = 35
- **Division:** When we find that 15 ÷ 3 = 5 we have divided 15 by 3 and found the quotient is 5.

There are relationships among the operations listed above. Addition and subtraction are inverse or opposite operations. In other words, if I perform addition such as $10 + 3 = 13$ then I can undo this addition by subtracting 3 since $13 - 3 = 10$. This works with multiplication and division too. If we start with $12 \times 5 = 60$ then we can undo this by dividing 60 by 5: $60 \div 5 = 12$. Multiplication is also related to addition. If we had the sum $5 + 5 + 5 + 5$ where we are adding four 5s, we could instead multiply 4×5 and get the same result. Essentially, multiplication is a way of combining groups of numbers.

Exponents

Exponents are a way of simplifying how we write a special type of multiplication. Consider the product $4 \times 4 \times 4$, where 4 is multiplied by itself three times. This product could instead be written as 4^3 (read: four to the third power). In this case the base is 4 and the exponent is 3.

In general a^b means to multiply a by itself b times, as you can see in these examples.

$$3^5 = 3 \times 3 \times 3 \times 3 \times 3 = 243$$
$$5^2 = 5 \times 5 = 25$$
$$2^4 = 2 \times 2 \times 2 \times 2 = 16$$

Order of Operations

Let's look at an arithmetic problem with more than one operation such as $4 \times (5 - 1)$. Which of these answers is correct?

$$4 \times 5 - 1 = 20 - 1 = 19$$
$$4 \times (5 - 1) = 4 \times 4 = 16$$

Of course, both answers can't be right, but at the same time both seem reasonable. It turns out that the second version: $4 \times (5 - 1) = 4 \times 4 = 16$ is correct. The reason for this is something called the *order of operations*. There is a specific order that operations must be performed in and as you can see below, operations inside of parentheses are always first.

1. **Parentheses.** Start with the innermost parentheses first and work your way out. For example $2[3 + (4 - 1)] = 2[3 + 3] = 2[6] = 12$.

2. **Exponents.** Next, calculate the value of any term with an exponent.

3. **Multiplication and division.** Perform any multiplication and division left to right.

4. **Addition and subtraction.** Perform any addition and subtraction left to right.

Here are some examples:

$$3(1 + 5)^2 = 3(6)^2 = 3(36) + 108$$
$$8 + 2^2(6 - 5) = 8 + 2^2(1) = 8 + 4 = 12$$

Prime and Composite Numbers

Whole numbers can be classified as either prime or composite. Prime numbers like 7 and 2 can only be divided evenly (without decimals) by 1 and themselves. It may seem like 1 should be a prime number, but by definition it is excluded. The smallest prime number is 2.

Composite numbers are numbers that can be written as the product of two or more numbers (other than 1 and itself). For example, 12 is composite because we can write it as 3 × 4. The numbers that "make up" a composite number are called factors. In our example above, we have written down two factors of 12 but there are several more; all of the factors of 12 are: 1, 2, 3, 4, 6, 12.

Each of these numbers can be multiplied by some other number to make 12. As another example, the factors of 28 are: 1, 2, 4, 7, 14, 28.

Fractions

Of course, not all the numbers we encounter are whole numbers. Many of them are fractions and it is very important to be comfortable working with fractions when taking the ASVAB.

Fractions are a way of writing a part out of some whole. The fraction ¼ represents 1 out of 4 pieces while the fraction ³⁄₇ represents 3 out of 7 pieces. There can even be more than one fraction that represents the same part of a whole. For example, ½ is the same as ³⁄₆ since 3 pieces out of 6 is half of the pieces. Finally, the top part of the fraction is called the numerator and the bottom part of the fraction is called the denominator.

Adding and Subtracting Fractions

When we have fractions with the same denominator, we can just add or subtract the numerators while the denominator stays the same.

$$\frac{1}{8} + \frac{2}{8} = \frac{3}{8}$$

$$\frac{3}{5} - \frac{2}{5} = \frac{1}{5}$$

When the fractions have different denominators, we need to find a common denominator so that we can use the same steps we did above. This isn't that bad when one of the denominators is a factor of the other. For example, let's say we are adding $\frac{2}{5} + \frac{1}{15}$. You can see that 5 is a factor of 15. In this case, take the fraction with the smaller denominator, and rewrite it so it has the same denominator as the larger number:

$$\frac{2}{5} = \frac{?}{15}$$

To figure out what the numerator should be, use the same number you would multiply to get the new denominator. In other words you would multiply 5 by 3 to get 15, so to get the new numerator, multiply 2 by 3:

$$\frac{2}{5} = \frac{2 \times 3}{15} = \frac{6}{15}$$

Now that both fractions have the same denominator, we can add straight across the top again.

$$\frac{2}{5} + \frac{1}{15} = \frac{6}{15} + \frac{1}{15} = \frac{7}{15}$$

Unfortunately, this method will not always work. If we wanted to find $\frac{3}{4} - \frac{1}{5}$, we would need a different way to find a common denominator since neither denominator is a factor of the other. In a case like this, it is easiest to multiply the denominators to get a new denominator and then change each fraction (like we did before) to a fraction with this new denominator: $4 \times 5 = 20$ (new denominator).

Rewrite each fraction:

$$\frac{3}{4} = \frac{3 \times 5}{20} = \frac{15}{20} \text{ (since } 4 \times 5 = 20)$$

$$\frac{1}{5} = \frac{1 \times 4}{20} = \frac{4}{20} \text{ (since } 5 \times 4 = 20)$$

$$\frac{3}{4} - \frac{1}{5} = \frac{15}{20} - \frac{4}{20} = \frac{11}{20}$$

Using this method, it is important to always make sure your final answer is simplified. This means that there are no factors shared by the numerator and denominator. In this case, our answer is already simplified, but if we had an answer like 6/14, we would want to rewrite it. The numerator and denominator of this fraction share a factor of 2, so dividing both by 2 gives our simplified version 3/7.

Multiplying Fractions

When multiplying fractions, there is no need to worry about a common denominator. Instead, you just multiply straight across.

$$\frac{2}{5} \times \frac{3}{8} = \frac{6}{40}$$

As with addition and subtraction, you may need to simplify your answer. In this case, since 6 and 40 share a factor of 2, our final answer would be 3/20.

There is a shortcut that can keep the numbers a bit smaller and prevent us from needing to simplify at the end. This shortcut is commonly called "cross cancelling" and only works when multiplying fractions.

Consider $\frac{2}{7} \times \frac{3}{4}$. By using cross cancelling, we can cancel the 2 and the 4 (since they share factors) and then multiply straight across:

$$\frac{2}{7} \times \frac{3}{4} = \frac{1}{7} \times \frac{3}{2} = \frac{3}{14}$$

It is also possible to multiply fractions and whole numbers by rewriting any whole number as a fraction with a denominator of 1. For example, $\frac{2}{3} \times 7 = \frac{2}{3} \times \frac{7}{1} = \frac{14}{3}$.

Dividing Fractions

The general rule for dividing fractions is to "flip and multiply." If we have a division problem with fractions, we keep the first fraction the same and multiply it by the reciprocal (the reversed fraction) of the second fraction.

$$\frac{2}{3} \div \frac{1}{3} = \frac{2}{3} \times \frac{3}{1} = \frac{2}{1} \times \frac{1}{1} = 2$$

Mixed Numbers

You may have noticed in one of the examples we ended up with a fraction that looked a little strange: $^{14}\!/_3$. A fraction where the numerator is larger than the denominator is known as an "improper" fraction. Improper fractions can be written as mixed numbers (a number made up by a whole number and a fraction) by the process outlined below.

- Divide the numerator by the denominator

$$14 \div 3 = 4 \text{ with a remainder of 2}$$

- Write the remainder as a fraction with the original denominator

$$\frac{14}{3} = 4\frac{2}{3} \text{ (this is read as "four and two thirds")}$$

Mixed numbers can be converted back to improper fractions by multiplying the whole number by the denominator and then adding the numerator. For example, to convert $5^2\!/_9$ to an improper fraction, multiply 5 and 9 to get 45 then add the 2 to get 47. The improper fraction is now $^{47}\!/_9$.

To add, subtract, multiply, or divide mixed numbers it is often easiest to just convert them to improper fractions and then follow the steps outlined earlier in this chapter.

Converting Fractions to Decimals

Any fraction can also be written as a decimal by dividing the numerator by the denominator. Using this method, we can see that $^4\!/_5 = 4 \div 5 = 0.8$.

Rounding Decimals

Often when converting a fraction to a decimal or even when working a problem involving only decimals, we will need to round our answer to a specific place value. The first few place values after a decimal point are:

tenths   hundredths   thousandths   ten thousandths

When rounding, always look at the number to the right of the place we are rounding to. If that number is 5 or larger, we round up; otherwise we round down. In the examples below, the decimals are rounded to the hundredths place. (The wavy line above the equals sign means "approximately equal to.")

$$0.0195 \approx 0.02$$
$$0.5811 \approx 0.58$$

Scientific Notation

When decimals are especially tiny it can be cumbersome to write out all of the digits. Scientific notation is a shorthand method for expressing these decimals. Using scientific notation, the decimal is written as a shorter decimal multiplied by a power of ten. The power of ten tells us how many places to move the decimal point.

Consider the number 2.36×10^{-5}. This is actually the decimal 0.0000236 which can be found by moving the decimal place 5 (since the power on the ten is −5) to the left (since the power is negative). Similarly, 0.000000589 can be written as 5.89×10^{-7}.

Scientific notation can also be used to write very large numbers by using a positive exponent. For example, $15,000,000 = 1.5 \times 10^{7}$.

Decimals as Percents

Finally, one other way to present a decimal is as a percentage. A percent is really a way of writing a decimal as a part of 100, so to write a decimal as a percentage, we multiply the decimal by 100. Therefore, the decimal 0.567 is 56.7% and the decimal 0.434 is 43.4%

Operations on Decimals

Adding and Subtracting

Adding or subtracting decimals is done just as you would with whole numbers. The only extra thing to pay attention to is lining up the decimal points before you perform the operation and using zeros as placeholder for any "gaps" that come up.

Here's an example:

Find $0.014 + 0.9 + 0.0026$.

$$
\begin{array}{r}
0\ .\ 0\ 1\ 4\ 0 \\
0\ .\ 9\ 0\ 0\ 0 \\
+\ 0\ .\ 0\ 0\ 2\ 6 \\
\hline
0\ .\ 9\ 1\ 6\ 6
\end{array}
$$

Multiplying Decimals

As with adding and subtracting, in general, you treat the numbers just as if they were whole numbers. However, once you have multiplied the numbers, you have to figure out where to put the decimal.

To place the decimal, count the number of decimal places there were total in both of the original decimals. This will be the number of decimal places in the final answer. For example, 0.411 has three decimal places and 0.2 has one decimal place. When the numbers are multiplied, the answer will have four decimal places. Notice how an extra zero was added to the right of the decimal so there would be the correct number of decimal places.

$$0.411 \times 0.2 = 0.0822$$

Dividing Decimals

Understanding how to divide two decimals starts with understanding how to divide a decimal by a whole number. It is easiest to work with this using long division and an example like $1.8 \div 4$.

We will write it out as a typical long division problem, but we will need to make sure to keep the decimal place in our answer right above where it is in the dividend (the decimal being divided). Then, we will divide as if they were whole numbers adding zeros to the end of the decimal as we need them.

```
           .   4   5
    4 | 1  .  8   0
        1     6
              2   0
              2   0
                  0
```

In order to divide a decimal by another decimal, as with $3.23 \div 0.4$, move the decimal of the divisor (the number doing the dividing , in this case 0.4) until it is a whole number. It is important to also move the decimal of the dividend by the same number of digits. With this example, we would end up with the division problem $32.3 \div 4$ which can now be solved using the steps we just learned.

chapter 10

Arithmetic Reasoning 2: Word Problems

Now that you have seen the types of skills you will need to solve arithmetic reasoning problems, it is time to look at what types of problems you are likely to encounter. As was mentioned before, problems will not be as simple as "Add 3.14 and 9.17," but instead will be set up as applied word problems.

Many people struggle with word problems, but there are many skills you can develop and things you can watch out for that can help you successfully answer any word problem you may come across. Here are some of the big ones:

- **Read the entire problem.** Before you start writing anything, read the entire problem and make sure you know what the problem is asking for. This can help you avoid doing more work than necessary and help you avoid picking a "trick" answer (discussed below).

- **Look for keywords.** When you are trying to figure out what the problem is looking for, read for words and phrases like "total," "difference," "average," "percent of," and others. There is almost always a keyword that can guide you towards the answer.

- **Watch out for multiple steps.** Some problems will require only one operation while others will require two or possibly more. Don't assume every problem will be the same.

- **Don't fall for the "trick" answers.** In the end, this comes down to reading the problem and performing all of the steps. Many questions will have answer choices that are designed to catch people who didn't follow the directions or missed a step.

Basic Word Problems

These are examples that will involve only our elementary operations like addition, subtraction, multiplication, and division.

1. **An office manager purchases 12 boxes of pens which cost $9.55 per box and 10 boxes of paper which cost $11.50 each. What is the total amount spent on these purchases?**

   A. $104.50
   B. $114.60
   C. $204.50
   D. $229.60

   The total amount spent includes the amount spent on the pens as well as the paper. For the pens, $12 \times 9.55 = 114.60$ was spent. While this is answer choice A, it is not correct since it does not include the paper which cost $10 \times 11.5 = 115$. Thus the total spent was $114.60 + 115.00 = 229.60$. Answer choice D.

2. **A 750-foot fence divides two property lines. Only 14 feet of the fence is in good condition and the remaining portion of the fence will be replaced. How many feet of the fence will be replaced?**

   A. 14 feet
   B. 736 feet
   C. 745 feet
   D. 764 feet

   The problem states that 14 feet of the fence will not be replaced, so we subtract that from the total length of the fence to find the amount that will be replaced: $750 - 14 = 736$ feet, answer choice B.

3. **A runner just ended his first week of marathon training. The first day of training, he ran 3 miles in 25 minutes. The second day of training he ran 3 miles in 23 minutes. Finally on his third day of training he ran 3 miles in 26 minutes. What was his average time for running 3 miles?**

   A. 25.29 mins
   B. 24.67 mins
   C. 24.00 mins
   D. 22.15 mins

To find the average of any group of values, first find the sum and then divide the sum by how many values there are. Here, the sum is 74. Dividing this by 3 yields the average of 24.67. Answer choice B.

Percents

Percent problems can come in many different types: finding the percent of a number, finding the percent increase or decrease, or even finding the interest on a loan. Outlined below are strategies for solving the different types of questions.

- **Finding the percent of a number.** To find the percent of any number, write the percentage as a decimal and then multiply. Remember, to write a percent as a decimal you move the decimal two spaces to the left. The decimal for 36% is 0.36 and the decimal for 45% is 0.45. Using this you can see than 36% of 50 is $0.36 \times 50 = 18$ and 45% of 195 is $0.45 \times 95 = 42.75$.

- **Percent increase and percent decrease.** Percent increase or decrease is found by taking the amount of change and dividing that by the original value. For instance, if a salary went from $500 a week to $550 a week, you could find the percent increase by subtracting $550 - 500 = 50$ and then dividing by the original value $50 \div 500 = 0.1$. This decimal is equivalent to 10%, meaning this was a 10% increase in weekly salary.

- **Interest.** Interest problems will often ask you to find the interest earned on a starting amount of money (called the principal) or to find the total amount of money owed when you include the interest. In each case, you will make use of the interest formula: $I = Prt$, where I is the interest, P is the starting amount, r is the rate (as a decimal), and t is the time in years. You must be very careful to write your time as a fraction if it is less than a year.

1. **In a group of 50 women and 40 men, 10% of the women and 15% of the men own a truck. How many in the group own a truck?**

   A. 5
   B. 6
   C. 11
   D. 14

   First, compute the number of women and men who own a truck. Since 10% of the women own a truck, $0.1 \times 50 = 5$ women own a truck. Similarly, $0.15 \times 40 = 6$ men own a truck. Therefore a total of 11 people in this group own a truck. Answer choice C.

2. **An item originally priced at $5.95 is now on sale at $3.95. What is the percentage discount on this item?**

   A. 0.02
   B. 0.05
   C. 0.34
   D. 0.51

   This is a percent decrease problem. Remember to find the percent decrease, subtract the two values and then divide by the original. $\dfrac{5.95-3.95}{5.95} = \dfrac{2}{5.95} = 0.34$. Answer choice C.

3. **A loan is made for $500 at 7% interest over 6 months. What is the total amount paid on this loan?**

   A. $17.50
   B. $517.50
   C. $535.00
   D. $710.00

   You may be tempted to just multiply 0.07 and 500, but as an interest problem you must use the interest formula. When using the formula, notice that the amount of time is 6 months or 1/2 a year. The interest earned over those 6 months is I = Prt = $500 \times 0.07 \times 1/2 = 17.5$. This is added to the principal to find the total of $517.50. Answer choice B.

Rates and Ratios

Ratios are a way of showing how two values relate to each other. Suppose that a room had 1 dog for every 2 cats. This could be stated by saying the ratio of dogs to cats is 1 to 2. It could also be written as 1:2 or ½. Knowing this ratio allows us to know the number of dogs if we know the number of cats and vice versa. If there are 6 dogs, then there must be 12 cats.

A rate is just a special type of ratio. If a car is travelling at 65 miles per hour, the car is moving 65 miles for every hour that passes. This could also be written as 65 miles/1 hour. Knowing this information, you could determine the distance traveled in 1-½ hours is 97.5 miles by multiplying the top and bottom by 1-½:

$$\frac{65 \text{ miles} \times \left(1\frac{1}{2}\right)}{1 \text{ hour} \times \left(1\frac{1}{2}\right)} = \frac{97.5 \text{ miles}}{1\frac{1}{2} \text{ hour}}$$

1. **A vehicle travels 600 miles in 12 hours. What is the rate of the vehicle in miles per hour?**

    A. 50
    B. 60
    C. 65
    D. 72

    The rate is 600 miles/12 hours and the question is asking us to convert this to a unit rate. This means the rate should be in terms of a single hour. To get that, we need to divide both numbers by 12. $\dfrac{600 \text{ miles} \div 12}{12 \text{ hours} \div 12} = \dfrac{50 \text{ miles}}{1 \text{ hour}}$. Answer choice A.

2. **For every 8 people at an event, 1 received a discounted ticket. If there are 720 people at the event, how many paid full price?**

    A. 90
    B. 630
    C. 712
    D. 810

    If 1 out of every 8 received a discounted ticket, then $720 \div 8 = 90$ received the discount. Of the 720 people, $720 - 90 = 630$ people paid full price. Answer choice B.

1. **There are approximately 12,152 feet for every 2 nautical miles. How many feet are in one nautical mile?**

    A. 3,037
    B. 6,076
    C. 15,109
    D. 24,304

    This example is also looking for the unit rate. To find this, divide both parts of the rate by 2. $\dfrac{12,152 \text{ feet} \div 2}{2 \text{ nautical miles} \div 2} = \dfrac{6,076 \text{ feet}}{1 \text{ nautical mile}}$. Answer choice B.

Area and Perimeter

While much of the geometry material you will come across will be found in the mathematical knowledge section, you are expected to be familiar with some basic concepts like area and perimeter as part of arithmetic reasoning word problems.

The perimeter around any figure is the sum of lengths of each side. If a rectangle has sides 3,4,3,4 then the perimeter is $3 + 4 + 3 + 4 = 14$.

Area represents the amount of space a figure covers and is always measured in square units. For squares and rectangles, area is found by multiplying the length by the width. In squares, this calculation is simplified because the length and the width are the same number.

1. **What is the perimeter, in feet, of a rectangular garden which measures 3 feet by 5 feet?**
    A. 2 feet
    B. 8 feet
    C. 15 feet
    D. 16 feet
    A rectangle which measures 3 feet by 5 feet has sides 3 feet, 3 feet, 5 feet, 5 feet. The perimeter is the sum of these sides: $3 + 3 + 5 + 5 = 16$ feet. Answer choice D.

2. **A rectangular room measures 13 feet by 15 feet. How many square feet of carpet would be needed to carpet this room?**
    A. 288 sq ft
    B. 195 sq ft
    C. 56 sq ft
    D. 28 sq ft
    The area of the room will determine how many square feet of carpet is needed. Since the room is rectangular, the area is $13 \times 15 = 195$. Answer choice B.

3. **How many square feet can be tiled using fifty-six 6-inch square tiles?**
    A. 112 sq ft
    B. 168 sq ft
    C. 336 sq ft
    D. 2,016 sq ft
    This is a two-step question and the first step is to find the area in square inches of each tile. Since it is a square tile, the area is $6 \times 6 = 36$ square inches. The second step is to determine the total area of 56 such tiles. This would be $36 \times 56 = 2,016$ square inches. Since the question asks for square feet, divide this by 12 (there are 12 inches in a foot). This results in 168 sq ft. Answer choice B.

Word Knowledge

In this part of the CAT-ASVAB, you will be tested on your knowledge of the meaning of words. You will have 35 questions and 11 minutes to answer them. Stay focused, but do not spend too much time if you cannot answer a question. Move on and come back to it later.

The Word Knowledge portion of the ASVAB asks two different questions: One type asks for the meaning of a word. It will give you four choices to choose from. The other type gives you a word used in a sentence. You will have four choices to choose from as well.

Remember to choose the word that is closest in meaning to the vocabulary word. It may not mean exactly the same thing. But it will be close. One excellent exam taking technique is to eliminate alternatives that you know are not correct and then pick the most likely of the remaining choices.

While it is important to build vocabulary through reading, and looking up words you do not know, there are other skills that you can employ when taking this exam that will improve your performance.

Word Origins and Derivations

English words can be created by combining a prefix or a suffix with a root. Some words have only roots, some have roots and prefixes, some have roots and suffixes, and some have all three.

For example, let's look at the word *preconception*, which means "an idea or opinion of something formed before knowing what that thing is like." For example, a person may have a preconception of what the ASVAB exam is like before ever taking it. The word *preconception* is really made up of three parts:

Prefix	Root	Suffix
pre-	concept	-ion

pre- is the prefix. It means "before."

concept is the root. It means "an idea or opinion."

-ion is the suffix. It tells you that the word is a noun and means "an action or process."

You should be able to figure out the meaning of a word formed in this way if you know the meaning of the root and the meaning of the prefix or suffix.

Root Words

It is important to have a large grasp of root words and what they mean. They can help you figure out the meaning of a word.

Here is a list of root words that are fairly common.

Root	Meaning	Example
anthro	relating to humans	anthropology
bibli or biblio	relating to books	bibliography
brev	short	abbreviate
circum	around	circumnavigate
cogn or cogno	know	cognizant
corp	body	corporation
dict or dic	speak	dictate
flu or flux	flow	influx
graph	writing	autograph
junct	join	juncture
liber	free	liberty
lum	light	illuminate
oper	work	operate
port	carry	portable
scrib	write	describe
tract	pull	traction
trans	across	transfer
voc or vok	call	vocation

Prefixes and Suffixes

Here are some common prefixes with their meanings and an example of one or more words containing each prefix:

Prefix	Meaning	Example
anti–	against	antioxidant
bi–	two	binoculars
co–	together	cooperate
contra–	against	contradiction
de–	away, from	deduct, detour
dis–	not	disrespectful
in–	into or not	insert, inorganic
mid–	middle	midlife
multi–	many	multifaceted
non–	not	nonessential
pre–	before, ahead of time	prefix, predict
pro–	in favor of, forward	proponent, propeller
re–	back, again	reentry, rewind
semi–	half, part	semiprofessional
sub–	under, below average	subway, substandard
super–	above, above average	supervisor, superintelligent
tri–	three	triangle
un–	not, opposite of	unscientific, unscramble

Here are some common suffixes with their meanings. In the right-hand column are some examples of words that use these suffixes:

Suffix	Meaning	Example
–en	to cause to be, made of	redden, earthen
–er	person that performs an action, more	picketer, thicker
–ful	full of	spiteful
–ion	action, process	rotation
–ize	cause to become	stabilize
–less	without	clueless
–like	resembling	businesslike
–ment	state of being	adornment
–y	resembling	frosty

Context Clues

Another way of working out the meaning of a word is to use context clues. Depending on the sentence that the ASVAB uses, you may have some clues from the way the word is used in a sentence.

Read the following selections. They will have words you may not know. You should be able to work out the meaning of these terms from the words or sentences around them.

Suppose you read the following sentence:

Vanessa lived in an <u>affluent</u> neighborhood.

What does the word *affluent* mean? Unless you already know the word, you can't work out its meaning from the sentence.
Now read the following passage:

Vanessa lived in an <u>affluent</u> neighborhood of expensive homes and beautifully kept lawns.

If you read this longer sentence carefully, you can figure out that *affluent* means wealthy. You can often work out what a new vocabulary word means from the context clues provided by the words and sentences around it.

Synonyms and Antonyms

A synonym is a word that has the same meaning as or a very similar meaning to another word. Tall and large are synonyms. They do not mean the exact same thing, but their meanings are similar. An antonym is a word that has an opposite or nearly opposite meaning as another word. Tall and short are antonyms.

The ASVAB asks you to find words that are synonyms, or a word that is most like the vocabulary word. Occasionally you may be asked to find the word that most nearly means the opposite of a given word, which is its antonym. Only a few questions on the Word Knowledge subtest ask you to find antonyms.

Technical Language

Every field of work has its own terminology or set of technical terms. A lawyer might use words such as tort and indictment. A doctor would use words like pharmaceuticals and arrhythmia. A military person has his or her own language too.

A carpenter, for example, must understand terms such as orbital sander and router. Jigsaw is a kind of saw to a cabinetmaker. To a clerk in a toy store it means a jigsaw puzzle. A gardener may talk about clematis, a plant, and malathion, a pesticide or weed killer. An army officer might mention deployment, which you probably know means being sent somewhere to serve.

All of these are technical terms used in specific trades or businesses.

To understand technical terms that are new to you, you can use a dictionary or glossary. You can also use context clues to figure out the meaning of a term as you read. It is important to read as much as possible to encounter such technical words. As people who want to enter the military, it would be wise to read materials that the military issues and that are free for the asking and to look up any words you do not understand.

Reading

One of the best ways to improve vocabulary is to read; read everything and anything and make sure to highlight or underline words you do not understand. If you cannot figure out their meaning from the context of the text, then look them up in a dictionary. It does not hurt to keep lists of words.

Try to use new words in a sentence. When you do this, you will more likely remember them. Try to use new words in conversations. This will also help imprint a new word on your mind.

When you take the Word Knowledge portion of the ASVAB, remember to work carefully. Do not make silly mistakes. Answer the question that is given, and good luck!

12

Paragraph Comprehension

The Paragraph Comprehension subtest will ask you questions about paragraphs. You will need to understand the information in each paragraph. Some passages are made up of two paragraphs, but the same kinds of questions will be asked about the passage. This chapter will teach you some important skills so that you will be able to answer the questions that are asked.

There are different kinds of questions that the test will cover. Basically, the questions will:

- Ask for specific information
- Ask for the main idea
- Ask what the author's viewpoint is
- Ask about the meaning of words in context
- Ask the reader to make an inference or draw a conclusion

Finding Specific Information

On the Paragraph Comprehension subtest you will sometimes be asked if you can remember a specific fact about a paragraph or passage you have read. For example, a paragraph might contain a sentence like either of the following:

The river lay two hundred and fifty feet below, at the bottom of the ravine.

Relations between Britain and its American colonies began to deteriorate after the French-Indian War ended.

The Paragraph Comprehension subtest might ask you such questions as "How far is it from the top of the ravine to the river?" or "When did Britain and its colonies begin to quarrel?"

The test always includes questions like these where the answers can be found right there in the selection. Always check back to verify that you have chosen the correct answer. Some sample questions follow.

1. Having trouble falling asleep or frequently waking during the night can have serious consequences. People who suffer from insomnia report that in addition to feeling fatigued, they have trouble concentrating and thinking clearly, their attention span is shorter, their judgment is poorer, and their tempers are more easily provoked. In a study of 100 people with insomnia that had lasted for longer than three weeks, 39 participants reported that they were lagging behind at work, 30 that they failed to achieve some important goals, and 17 that they felt more irritable. Researchers estimate that over half of chronic sleeplessness is the result of emotional upset. Depression and anxiety are major factors. Other causes common in young people include such illnesses as migraine and asthma, medications such as cortisone and respiratory drugs, and stimulants such as caffeine and nicotine. Even substances that seem to help may cause problems. Alcohol may relax a person into sleep, but results in frequent awakenings.

   Which effect of insomnia was most widely reported by the people in the study?

   A. They were failing to achieve important goals.
   B. They felt more irritable.
   C. They were lagging behind in their work.
   D. They were suffering from depression.

   The correct choice is C. Thirty-nine participants in the study reported that they were falling behind at work. Notice that depression (Choice D) was a CAUSE, not an effect, of sleeplessness. Don't make the mistake of confusing causes and effects in this kind of question!

2. What lies under the ice covering central Antarctica, the continent at the South Pole? In 1974, an aircraft beaming radio waves onto the ice discovered that there was water beneath the two-and-a-half-mile thick sheet of ice. In 1996, scientists discovered that the water was a lake 1,600 feet deep and more than 5,000 square miles in size. How did such a lake form? The surface ice kept the ice below it insulated from the cold air. Heat rising from the rocks that lay below the ice and pressure from the surface ice combined to warm and gradually melt this bottom layer of ice. The water collected in pockets in the rock. Over thousands of years, this water wore away enough rock to form a lake.

   When did the bottom layer of ice melt?

   A. After the lake formed
   B. After the water collected in the rock
   C. Before the water collected in the rock
   D. In 1974

The correct answer is C. The bottom layer of ice melted first. Then this water collected in pockets in the rock. In order to answer this question, you must look back at the passage and find the information that you need. Careful reading is key here.

Main Ideas

The main idea of a selection is what the selection *as a whole* is all about. Read the next example and decide which is the main idea.

3. During the period of Reconstruction following the Civil War, twenty African Americans served in the House of Representatives and two served as senators. All were elected from the southern states. Thirteen of the twenty-two had been slaves before the Civil War. All the rest were born as free men. Their educational level compared well with that of other congressmen of their time. Ten of the African-American congressmen had attended college and five were graduates. Six were lawyers, three were preachers, four were farmers, and the rest were skilled in various trades. On the whole, the African-American political leaders were able and honest public officials.

   Which of the following states the main idea of this passage?

   A. African-American congressmen were from the North as well as the South.
   B. African-American congressmen were intelligent and honest, but not as well-educated as their white counterparts.
   C. Thirteen out of twenty-two African-American congressmen were ex-slaves.
   D. African-American congressmen were about as well educated as their white counterparts.

   The correct choice is D. This idea is stated in the passage in language that resembles the language used in the question. It also is given a great deal of attention. Almost half the passage is devoted to the educational level of these men.

   Usually the author doesn't state the main idea in the passage. You have to figure it out.

4. In the United States money is manufactured by the United States Mint. The government chooses the designs and the metals for each coin. Artists begin by working on a clay model, then they finish the design on a plaster model. These models are much larger than the actual coin. A final steel coin of the proper size is then made from this plaster model. When a design is chosen it is sent to the U.S. Mint for manufacture. A metal mixture is used to make the coins. This is called an alloy, which is a mixture of metals like nickel, zinc, or copper. These are melted and mixed, then rolled out into strips the exact thickness of the coin that is to be pressed from it. One machine punches out the correct size coin and another imprints the coin with the design. These coins go to banks first. From there they are dispensed for people's use.

   The main idea of this passage is:

   A. a machine punches out the correct size for a coin
   B. coins are made from a metal mixture
   C. there are many processes in making coins
   D. artists first make a clay model of a coin

Choice C is the correct answer. Although the author never states the main idea, the passage is mostly about the many processes that go into making coins. The other choices are all included in the passage. But they are not the main idea.

Often a question on the subtest will ask what a good title would be for a paragraph. This is another way of asking the main idea.

5. The earth, the other planets, the sun, the moon, and the stars we see in our sky make up only a tiny portion of the universe. They are among the billions of stars and other heavenly bodies that make up the Milky Way, the galaxy we live in. Moreover, the Milky Way is not particularly large—some galaxies are much larger—and there are more than a million galaxies in the universe. Outer space is filled with strange and exotic bodies. There are giant blue and red stars many millions of times larger than the sun, and "tiny" white dwarf stars the same size as Earth, but millions of times heavier. There are pulsars, flashing stars that appear to switch their illumination on and off thousands of times every second. And there are brilliant stars called novas, which briefly burn more brightly than anything else in our night sky, apart from the moon.

Stars are visible to us because they give off light. Some heavenly bodies give off no illumination and are invisible to us. However, we know they exist because they emit radio waves that radio telescopes can detect.

A good title for the above passage would be:

A. Galaxies
B. Inside the Milky Way
C. Our Huge and Complex Universe
D. The Night Sky

Choice C is the correct answer. This title takes in all that the passage is about. Choices A and B cover just sections of the passage. Choice D is too vague to be a good title.

Author's Viewpoint

An author's viewpoint about a subject influences what is written. If you read the sentence "James deserved to be fired," you would gather that the author has a poor opinion of James. If you read the sentence, "Football requires more strength and more smarts than all the other sports put together," you would see that the author has a high opinion of the game of football.

Read the following example and decide how the author regards a proposed new truancy law.

6. Recently legislators in this state have proposed that parents be punished for their children's truancy—excessive absence from school. The new law, if passed, would impose fines and even jail sentences on parents whose children are judged to be truants by the school administration. We think this new law would be a disaster. Although parents are responsible for their children, we must be realistic. Some parents have little control over their children's behavior, particularly in the case of delinquent teenagers. These parents need help from trained

professionals—social workers and psychologists—not fines and jail time. In many cases, fines would fall on already overburdened and low-income single parents. And what would be the benefit if inadequate parents were jailed and their children turned over to an overcrowded foster care system?

Which statement below best reflects the author's view of the proposed truancy law?

A. It is a fine idea, but it would be hard to implement.
B. Parents most in need of help would be punished instead.
C. Parents must be punished if their children cut school.
D. Delinquent students should be handled by psychologists and we need additional funds to pay for these professionals.

Choice B is correct. The author states that the parents of delinquent children need help, not punishment.

Sometimes the question is posed as a statement that an author would agree with. Read the next example and answer the question.

7. Once acupuncture was considered mysterious. But today acupuncture is an acceptable treatment in Western medicine. It is even recommended by the American Medical Association for certain symptoms. Insurance companies have begun to pay for acupuncture treatments as well. But what is acupuncture? Say the word and the most common image that appears is the picture of a person sitting in a chair with needles stuck in his or her ear. But acupuncture is a great deal more than simply sticking needles into a body.

Acupuncture was first discovered in China during the period from 2696 to 2598 B.C. by Huang Di. During this period, and later periods, books were written that became the basis of Chinese medicine.

The oldest existing book on acupuncture was written by Zhen Jiu Jia Y. Jing. It dates from 300 C.E. During the Ming Dynasty, (368–1640), a text on acupuncture written by Zhen Jiu Dei Cheng became the basis for all modern acupuncture treatment. In 1671, a Jesuit priest brought acupuncture to Europe via France. In 1683, a Dutch surgeon, Wilen pen Rhijne recommended the use of acupuncture during surgery.

In the early 1900s, in the United States, Franklin Bache, MD, the great grandson of Benjamin Franklin, wrote an article on acupuncture. In 1916, Sir William Osler, MD, writing in the *Principles and Practice of Medicine,* recommended acupuncture as a treatment for lumbago.

After the 1920s, acupuncture was rarely ever used in the United States. Then in 1971, when James Reston, a reporter for the *New York Times* on assignment in China, had an appendicitis attack. The Chinese suggested surgery using acupuncture anesthesia. His post operative was relieved by acupuncture as well. This occurrence was widely reported in the American press and acupuncture became a viable alternative in the Western mind.

The author of this passage believes:

A. Acupuncture is good for most illnesses.
B. Acupuncture has been used for many centuries.
C. Acupuncture cannot cure headaches.
D. Acupuncture is less expensive than other treatments.

Choice B is correct. There are many details that point to this being the correct answer.

Context Clues

In the sentence "His head felt *febrile*," what does the word *febrile* mean? If you don't know the word's meaning, you won't be able to figure it out from this short sentence. Now read the following passage. Again, try to figure out what the word *febrile* means.

> The doctor saw the child's flushed cheeks. His head felt *febrile*. Her diagnosis was confirmed when she took his temperature—104 degrees. He had a high fever.

If you read this passage carefully, you can probably figure out that *febrile* means feverish. The words and sentences around it helped you to work out its meaning. You were able to figure out the meaning of *febrile* from the context of the selection.

Read the example below about arteriosclerosis and use context clues to work out the meaning of the word *cumulative*.

8. **There was an *ominous* feeling to the night. It was very quiet, in contrast to the noisy confrontations that had occurred over the past few days between the government soldiers and the inhabitants of the small rural town. The streets were empty now, and the soldiers were back in their barracks. But there were rumors that rebel soldiers had heard about the troubles in the town and had promised to come to the aid of the townspeople. Miguel had heard that the rebels might emerge from the nearby mountains and attack at any moment. The boy lay awake wondering what horrors the night might bring to himself, his friends, and family.**

   Another *ominous* situation might be:

   A. the quiet just before a hurricane strikes
   B. the aftermath of a hurricane or tornado
   C. the relief when an expected storm doesn't occur
   D. being in the midst of a battle in war time

   Choice A is correct. An *ominous* situation is the period just before something bad happens. During this time, one can feel the signs of trouble about to occur.

   Read the next example and decide on the meaning of the word *centenarian*.

9. **Jeanne Louise Calment of France was the oldest woman in the world. She died in 1997 at the age of 122. There are no records of any other human living this long, although many people have survived past the age of 100. In fact there are over 15,000 *centenarians* living in America today. Scientists know very little about aging, but many attribute increased *longevity* to better diets and improvements in health care.**

   A *centenarian* is

   A. a person 100 years or older
   B. a person who is exactly 100 years old
   C. a person who was born in the 19th century
   D. a doctor who treats people over 100 years old

Choice A is the correct definition of *centenarian*. The clue is in the sentence that refers to people over 100 years old. Another clue is the root word "cent", which means 100 in Latin.

Inference

We often make inferences and draw conclusions on the basis of the information we possess. If we drive down the street we live on at 9:30 p.m. and all the houses are in darkness, we might draw the conclusion that a storm has caused a power outage. We cannot be sure we are correct. Maybe all our neighbors are out for the evening. We must make the best inference we can based on what we know and what makes the most sense.

Read the example below and make the best inference you can.

10. **Modern art has puzzled many people. One reason is that often modern art does not present a realistic picture. Instead the painting may just consist of patterns of color and shapes. Some of the greatest works of modern art were ridiculed when they were first shown to the public. Even now that modern art is widely accepted, there have been problems. Once a painting by Matisse, a great modern artist, was hung upside down in a museum. Over 116,000 people saw the painting, many of them experts in art, before someone noticed that the painting was wrong way up. At another exhibit for an unknown artist, the paintings were highly praised by experts. Imagine their embarrassment when the experts found out that the show was a trick. The paintings had been done by a chimpanzee playing around with brushes and paint.**

    What can you infer from this passage?

    A. Art experts can be relied on to understand modern art.
    B. Modern art is just a trick and not real art.
    C. Chimpanzees can be more talented artists than people.
    D. The paintings done by the chimp looked like modern art.

    Choice D is the correct inference. The chimp's paintings of shapes and colors looked like modern art, and so fooled the experts.

    Sometimes, it helps if you can draw upon your own life experiences and prior knowledge when you answer a question. It is because we know about power outages that we could guess that this might explain why all the houses were in darkness. Often your own experience combined with material in the story makes you sure of the answer.

11. **According to an ancient Greek legend, a great inventor named Daedalus was once imprisoned on an island by an angry king. His young son, Icarus, was with him. The inventor had a plan of escape. He made two pairs of wing-shaped frames and also collected seagull feathers. Then he created two pairs of wings, one for himself and one for his son, by sticking the feathers onto the wing frames with wax. He taught the boy how to use the wings, but warned him not to fly too high because the hot sun might destroy the wings. Icarus promised to be careful. However, once they were in the air, soaring over the ocean, he forgot what his father had told him. The young boy felt so powerful and free, that he never considered the danger of flying too near the sun. For a while,**

Icarus climbed higher and higher in the sky, closer and closer to the sun. Then he stopped climbing and began to fall. As he plunged downward, he remembered his father's warning, but it was too late. Icarus fell into the sea and drowned.

Why did Icarus plunge into the sea?

A. He became dizzy and passed out.
B. The force of gravity is less powerful in the upper atmosphere.
C. The wax that held the feathers onto the wings melted.
D. He was unable to hold his arms outstretched any longer.

The correct choice is C. Your own experience tells you that wax melts if it gets near anything hot; whatever it is holding together comes apart. Also, you read the warning that Daedalus gave to his son.

Reading and Comprehending

These skills will help you do better on the Paragraph Comprehension subtest. Other steps you can take to improve your performance include:

- Reading more than watching television

- Paraphrasing what you read

- Figuring out the meaning of a word from its context

- Asking yourself what the main idea of a passage that you read is

- Telling a friend about something you have read

Mathematics Knowledge 1: Algebra and Probability

Algebra

In algebra, symbols (variables) are used to represent numbers in either an equation such as $x + 5 = 6$ or in an expression such as $x - 2$. On the ASVAB, you are expected to be familiar with working with many different types of algebra problems.

Algebraic Expressions

Algebraic expressions are when you have operations between variables and numbers but no equals sign. These expressions are made up of terms which may contain one or more variables.

Expression	Terms
$x - x^2 + 1$	$x, x^2, 1$
$6xy + 5$	$6xy, 5$

Any time you have a number in a term like $5x$, it represents multiplication. In this case, it is shorthand for 5 times x. In the example above, $6xy$ is the same as 6 times x times y. The number in front is called the coefficient and if there is no coefficient shown, it is assumed to be 1. The coefficient in $5x$ is 5 and in $6xy$ is 6 while the coefficient of y is 1.

Terms are said to be "like terms" if they have the same variable and exponent such as $5x$ and $3x$ or y^2 and $4y^2$. If an expression contains like terms, it can be simplified by combining them or adding the coefficients. For example, the expression $5x + 7x + 2$ can be written as $12x + 2$ by combining the $5x$ and the $7x$.

Evaluating Algebraic Expressions

To evaluate an expression simply means to plug in the values of the variables and perform the operations to see what number you get. As you saw in the arithmetic reasoning section, the order of operations is very important and it must also be followed when evaluating an expression.

Suppose $x = 5$ and $y = 10$. Evaluating the expression $2(x + 5) - y$ would mean to substitute 5 for x and 10 for y.

$$2(x + 5) - y = 2(5 + 5) - 10 = 2(10) - 10 = 20 - 10 = 10$$

Factoring Algebraic Expressions

Factoring can be thought of as undoing a multiplication that has already occurred. There are two types of factoring problems you may come across on the ASVAB:

Common Factor. If the terms in an expression share a factor, then that factor can be taken out and used to rewrite the expression as a multiplication. The hard part is identifying what factors are shared by the terms (if any). For example, let's try to factor the expression $5x^2 - 25x$.

Both terms share a factor of 5 and a factor of x (remember $x^2 = x \times x$). Dividing each term by $5x$ gives $x - 5$. The last step is to rewrite the expression using the term we just divided by and the result: $5x^2 - 25x = 5x(x - 5)$.

Here are some more examples:

$$x^2 + 3x = x(x + 3) \text{ since both terms share a factor of x.}$$

$$30x^4 + 2x^2 = 2x^2(15x^2 + 1) \text{ since both terms share a factor of } 2x^2.$$

Trinomial of the form $x^2 + bx + c$. These special types of expressions have a step-by-step process you can use to factor them and the answer will always have the same form regardless of the numbers you start out with. This can be shown by working through factoring an example such as $x^2 + 2x - 15$. Since this expression involves x, the factored answer will be of the form $(x)(x)$. Within the parentheses, a number will be added or subtracted. The work is to figure out what these numbers will be and whether they are added or subtracted.

If the last number in your trinomial is negative, then both numbers in the parentheses will have opposite signs; otherwise they will have the same signs. In this case the last number is -15 so the factored answer will have opposite signs in the parentheses: $(x -)(x +)$.

To finish the problem, you need to find two factors of the last number that add or subtract to the middle coefficient. Here that means you need to find two factors of 15 that add or subtract to 2. If you think about it, 5 and 3 are factors of 15 and $5 - 3 = 2$. These are the numbers!

Since you have to subtract the 3, it will be with the minus sign and the 5 will go on the other side. The final answer will be $x^2 + 2x - 15 = (x - 3)(x + 5)$. Here are some more examples:

$$x^2 - 6x - 7 = (x + 1)(x - 7)$$
$$x^2 + 6x + 8 = (x + 2)(x + 4)$$

Solving Linear Equations

To solve an equation means to find the value for the variable that makes the equation true. You can probably look at $x - 3 = 4$ and see that $x = 7$ would make the statement true. Most of the time, equations are more complicated so it is worth learning the steps you would use to solve them when the value isn't easily seen.

Linear equations are equations with a variable that doesn't have an exponent. The example in the previous paragraph is a linear equation as is $3x + 1 = 4$. All linear equations can be solved by keeping one goal in mind: get the variable on one side and the number on the other. As long as you do this within the "rules" (anything you do to one side of the equation, you must do to the other side), you will always end up with your answer.

Consider the equation $x + 6 = 11$. To get the x by itself, the 6 needs to be moved to the other side. However, you can't just move a number to the other side of an equation. To correctly move a number or a variable from one side of the equation to the other, you perform the opposite operation to both sides of the equation. In other words, since the 6 is being added to the x, you will subtract it from both sides of the equation to move it.

$$x + 6 - 6 = 11 - 6$$
$$x = 5$$

What if there is a number multiplying the x? In this case, you will divide both sides of the equation by that number. To solve $5x = 30$, divide both sides by 5 to get $x = 6$. As before, perform the opposite operation to both sides.

It is possible to have to do both of these steps or to even move variables in this way as you can see in the examples below.

Solve: $5x - 3 = 2$

$5x - 3 + 3 = 2 + 3$ (add 3 to both sides)

$5x = 5$ (divide both sides by 5)

$x = 1$

Solve: $2x - 4 = x - 1$

$2x - 4 + 4 = x - 1 + 4$ (add 4 to both sides)

$2x = x + 3$

$2x - x = x + 3 - x$ (subtract x from both sides)

$x = 3$

Solving Quadratic Equations

Quadratic equations are equations that contain the square of a variable such as $x^2 - 1 = 25$ or $5x = x^2 + 1$. Many quadratics can be written as $x^2 + bx + c = 0$, where b and c are numbers. In this case, they can be solved just by factoring and then setting each term to zero. When you do this, you end up with two linear equations that can be solved in the way we just discussed. Here are some examples:

Solve $x^2 - 2x - 8 = 0$

$(x+2)(x-4) = 0$ (factor the trinomial)

$x + 2 = 0 \quad x - 4 = 0$ (set each term to zero)

$x = -2 \quad x = 4$ (The result of solving these is your final answer.)

$$\text{Solve: } x^2 - 4x + 3 = 0$$
$$(x-3)(x-1) = 0$$
$$x-3=0 \quad x-1=0$$
$$x=3 \quad x=1$$

Inequalities

Not everything in algebra can be classified as an expression or an equation. Sometimes you will work with inequalities. In an inequality, one side is possibly larger or smaller than the other side. The symbols used are:

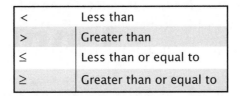

<	Less than
>	Greater than
≤	Less than or equal to
≥	Greater than or equal to

Luckily, inequalities can be solved the same way you solve linear equations. There is one very important thing to remember: *any time you divide or multiply by a negative number you must switch the inequality.* Here are some examples:

Solve: $\quad x+5 < 3$
$$x+5-5 < 3-5$$
$$x < -2$$

Solve: $\quad -2x+4 \geq 8$
$$-2x+4-4 \geq 8-4$$
$$-2x \geq 4 \quad \text{(Here the direction is flipped since you divide by –2.)}$$
$$x \leq -2$$

Probability

The probability of an event is the likelihood of that event occurring and can be expressed as a percentage, a fraction, or a decimal. The probability of any event will never be larger than 1 or smaller than 0. Mathematically, the probability of an event is found by the following equation:

$$\frac{\text{number of ways the event can occur}}{\text{total number of possible outcomes or results}}$$

Here are some examples:

A bag contains 3 red, 5 blue, and 6 green marbles. A marble is randomly selected. What is the probability the marble is red?

There are a total of $3 + 5 + 6 = 14$ marbles in the bag. When one is randomly selected, any one of these could be selected so this represents the total number of possibilities. The number of red marbles is 3. So the number of ways the event can occur is 3. Finally, the probability is $3/14 = 0.214$ or 21.4%.

A fair six-sided die is rolled. What is the probability an even number comes up?

On a six-sided die, there are the numbers 1, 2, 3, 4, 5, 6. Since only 3 of these are even, the probability is $3/6 = 0.5$.

Complementary Events

Suppose you knew the probability of an event occurring was 30%, but you were instead interested in the probability the event doesn't occur. The event you are interested in is called the "complement" of the original event. It turns out that the probability of the complement can be found by subtracting the probability of the original event from 1.

Here are some examples:

The probability of flipping a weighted coin and getting tails is 0.40. What is the probability of flipping this coin and getting heads?

Since the only possibilities are heads and tails, the probability of heads is $1 - 0.40 = 0.60$.

A bag contains 3 red, 5 blue, and 6 green marbles. A marble is randomly selected. What is the probability the marble is not blue?

To find this probability, first find the probability of a blue marble and then subtract that value from 1. The probability of a blue marble is $5/14$. This means that the probability of not picking a blue marble is $1 - 5/14 = 9/14 = 0.643$.

Finding "and" Probabilities

In probability, when you want to find the probability of one or more events occurring at the same time or one after the other, you are finding an "and" probability. Many times, this probability can be found simply by thinking it through. For example, what is the probability a number which is even and larger than 3 is rolled when a six-sided die is rolled? You already know the number of possibilities is 6, so how many ways can a number be rolled that is even and larger than 3? Only 4 and 6 satisfy both properties so the probability is $\frac{2}{6} = 0.33$.

In cases where the events can be thought of as not influencing each other, the events are said to be independent. The probability of an "and" event with independent events can be found by multiplying the probabilities.

Here are some examples:

> The probability that any machine produced in a factory will malfunction in a day is 0.18. What is the probability that 3 machines produced in this factory will malfunction in a day?

It is reasonable to assume that one machine malfunctioning will have no effect on the probability another machine malfunctions. Therefore, these events are independent and the probability can be found by multiplying $0.18 \times 0.18 \times 0.18 = 0.006$.

> Two die are rolled. What is the probability both land on an even number?

Since the probability one lands on an even number is $\frac{3}{6}$ and the events are independent, the probability is $\frac{3}{6} \times \frac{3}{6} = 0.25$.

Finding "or" Probabilities

If you are interested in whether or not one or both of the events A or B occur, you are interested in the "or" probability. This can be found by adding the probabilities of each event and then subtracting the probability that both events occur. This value is subtracted because it is double counted when we add the probability of A and the probability of B. By far, the most common mistake is to forget to subtract this value.

Here are some examples:

> A single fair die is rolled. What is the probability the resulting number is odd or larger than 3?

The probability the number is odd is $\frac{3}{6}$ and the probability the number is larger than 3 is $\frac{3}{6}$. Finally, the probability the number is odd and larger than

3 is $\frac{2}{6}$. Using the idea above, the probability the number is odd or greater than 3 is $\frac{3}{6} + \frac{3}{6} - \frac{2}{6} = \frac{4}{6} = 0.67$.

A class of 30 students has 15 people who are in the band, 20 people who are in the chorus, and 10 people who are in both. If a student in this class is randomly selected, what is the probability the person is in the band or in the chorus?

The probability the person is in the band is $\frac{15}{30}$ while the probability the person is in the chorus is $\frac{20}{30}$. Finally, the probability the person is in both is $\frac{10}{30}$. The "or" probability is then: $\frac{15}{30} + \frac{20}{30} - \frac{10}{30} = \frac{25}{30}$ or 0.83.

chapter 14

Math Knowledge 2: Geometry

In addition to understanding basic geometry principles, geometry problems on the ASVAB may require arithmetic skills, algebra skills, or both. In this chapter, we will review the geometry definitions and concepts you will need on test day.

Angles

When two lines meet at a point, they form an angle. Angles are commonly measured in degrees where an angle of 360 degrees is one full revolution around. There is a lot of terminology surrounding angles, which we will review below.

- **Acute angles** have a measure between 0 and 90 degrees.

- **Right angles** have a measure of 90 degrees.

- **Obtuse angles** have measures between 90 and 180 degrees.

- **Straight angles** have a measure of 180 degrees.

When dealing with pairs of angles, they may be either complementary or supplementary. Complementary angles have a sum of 90 degrees whereas supplementary angles have a sum of 180 degrees:

Finally, when lines intersect (or cross) the angles on opposite sides of the lines are equal. These are called vertical angles.

Triangles

A triangle is a closed geometric figure with three sides. The interior angles of any triangle add to 180 degrees and as with angles, there are several special types of triangles.

- **Isosceles triangles** have two sides which are the same length. The angles that are opposite these sides are also equal.

- **Equilateral triangles** have three sides of all the same length. In these triangles, each angle is 60 degrees.

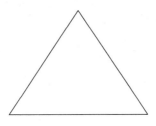

- **Right triangles** have one angle which is a right angle (90 degree). The side opposite this angle is the longest side and it is called the hypotenuse.

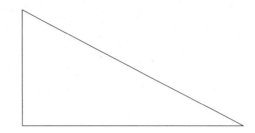

Area

The area of any triangle can be found using the formula $A = \frac{1}{2}bh$, where b represents the length of the base and h represents the height of the triangle. For example, the triangle below has an area of $\frac{1}{2} \times 5 \times 3 = 7.5$.

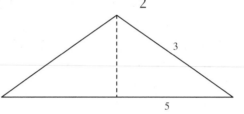

The Pythagorean Theorem

Right triangles have a special property that makes it possible to find the lengths of any side if you know the lengths of the other two sides. Consider the right triangle below.

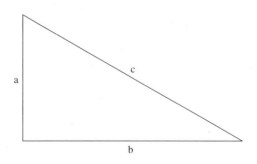

The Pythagorean theorem states that $a^2 + b^2 = c^2$ where a and b are the lengths of the legs (as in the figure) and c is the length of the hypotenuse.

Circles

You are probably already familiar with the idea of a circle. Mathematically, a circle is a closed figure where all of the points on the line are the same distance from some center. This distance from the center is called the radius and the distance from one point on the circle to a point opposite it is called the diameter. The diameter is always twice the radius. In the image below, the solid line represents the diameter while the dashed line represents the radius.

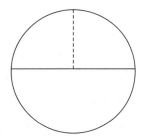

As with other shapes, it is possible to define area and perimeter for a circle. The area of any circle is found by using the formula $A = \pi r^2$ where r is the radius and π is the Greek letter pi. This letter represents a constant that is approximately 3.14.

The perimeter of a circle is called its circumference and represents the distance around the outside of the circle. The circumference of a circle is found using the formula $C = 2\pi r$.

Volume

The volume of a three-dimensional object is the amount of space (in cubic units) the object takes up. You should be comfortable finding the volume of rectangular solids and of cylinders.

For a rectangular solid, the volume is the product of the length, width, and the height. For example, the volume of the solid below is $3 \times 4 \times 7 = 84$ cubic units.

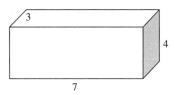

The volume of a cylinder is found by taking the area of the circle it is based on and then multiplying that by the height of the cylinder. The formula is $V = \pi r^2 h$ where r is the radius and h is the height. The cylinder below has a volume of $\pi \times 2^2 \times 5 \cong 3.14 \times 4 \times 5 = 62.8$ cubic units.

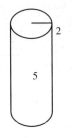

chapter **15**

Electronics

Describing Electricity

Electricity is generated for human consumption by transforming other forms of energy. The main system of generating electricity is by mechanically rotating a magnetic field near a wire resulting in electromagnetic induction and the flow of current. Chemical generation is the transformation of chemical, reactive energy into electricity. Solar generation uses specialized photosensitive cells to transform the sun's energy into electrical current.

Electromagnetic energy travels in waves that are measured in terms of their amplitude and frequency. If you imagine the perfect wave for surfing, you can remember which is which. Frequency is the rate at which the waves travel to shore. High frequency means they are coming in rapid succession, and a low frequency describes a greater spacing between them. Height of the wave is amplitude. A professional surfer can ride a wave of high amplitude, and a beginner would start out at low amplitude. This is where we get the terms AM (amplitude modulation) and FM (frequency modulation) to describe our radio bands.

Substances that electricity flows through easily are called conductors. Many metals such as silver, copper, and gold, as well as water, are good conductors. Insulators inhibit the flow of electricity. Rubber, wood, and many ceramics are good insulators. Materials such as silicon that partially conduct electricity are considered semi-conductors.

Current

Simply put, current is the flow of electricity. Direct current (DC) flows in one direction only. Alternating current (AC) reverses direction at regular intervals. These intervals are measured in complete cycles per second, or Hertz (Hz). When AC current is converted to DC, the process is known as rectification.

Describing Circuits

Because electricity needs a pathway, circuits are necessary to direct and control electrical power to final consumers. A circuit is simply a system through which electric current flows. A closed circuit is a completed circuit allowing for the transfer of power. An open circuit has a disruption and electricity is unable to flow. For example, turning a light on with a switch will close the circuit, allowing electricity to flow through the light bulb. Flipping the switch off will open the circuit, stopping the flow of electricity through the bulb.

The simplest circuit is a series circuit, which has only one pathway. Current flows in one path through every single part of the system. Interruption in any portion will cause the circuit to open. A classic example is a strand of lights in which one bulb fails and the entire strand goes dark.

A parallel circuit is more complex, with multiple pathways for current flow, allowing the circuit to continue to operate despite the failure of a single component. If a strand of lights is a parallel circuit, one bulb can burn out and the rest stay lit because there is another pathway for the current.

In common practice, most circuits are a combination of the two, known as a series parallel. Most modern strand lights are wired this way. If one bulb burns out, all the lights that are wired in series with it will also go dark. However, because of the parallel circuits, other segments of the strand can still receive power.

Parts of a Circuit

Now that you know what circuits are, you're ready to learn about some of the parts that enable us to control them. Switches open or close the circuit, turning it off or on. Complex components allow us to regulate or increase the flow of electricity. The direction and pattern of flow can also be controlled. In wiring diagrams, line drawings that describe circuits, symbols are used for each of these components. You can view the symbols in many places online, including www.kpsec.freeuk.com/symbol.htm.

Amplifier: device that increases the strength of a current or signal

Circuit breaker: a circuit-protection device that goes open when the circuit is overloaded and can be reset

Diode: a device allowing electrical current to pass only in one direction

LED (light emitting diode): creates light when current passes through it

On-off switch: switch that opens or closes a circuit, and remains in position as set

Momentary or push switch: switch that passes current only while engaged

Resistor: resists current in a circuit; resistors are marked with a coded series of three to five colored bands; match exactly when replacing one

Rectifier: device for converting AC to DC power

Cathode: place where current flows out of a polarized electrical device

Anode: place where current flows into a polarized electrical device

Ground: a large conducting body (such as the earth) used as a common return for an electric circuit and as an arbitrary zero of potential

Rheostat: a variable resistor that regulates current

Potentiometer: device that provides for adjustable voltage or signal

Transformer: an electromagnet that can increase or decrease voltage

Generator: a mechanical device capable of creating electrical current

Capacitor: a device that stores electricity in the form of a charge

Relay: a switching device for allowing control of a circuit by a control switch without all the current flowing through the switch

Transistor: an electronic relay capable of switching or amplifying current or power

Inductor: an electromagnet that stores electricity as magnetism

Regulator: controls voltage output

Oscillator: creates a repeating pattern

Fuse: circuit protection device that goes open when the circuit is overloaded, and then must be replaced

Fuse rating: the predetermined point of failure of a fuse

Breaker: circuit-protection device that switches open when the circuit is overloaded, and can be reset

Ohm's Law

This set of formulas allows us to describe how electricity behaves in a circuit. First, let's define the terms in the equation.

Current (I): rate of electron flow; "I" refers to "intensity"

Ampere/Amps: measurement unit of electric current

Voltage (V): potential energy difference in a circuit

Volt: amount of force, or "push" of electrons in a circuit.

Resistance (R): the opposition to flow of electricity

Ohm: unit of electrical resistance

Here's the equation:

$$V = I \times R \text{ (Voltage = Current multiplied by Resistance)}$$
$$R = V/I \text{ (Resistance = Voltage divided by Current)}$$
$$I = V/R \text{ (Current = Voltage divided by Resistance)}$$

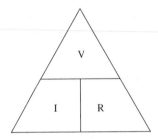

The simplest way to remember the three Ohm's law equations is to use the triangle above. Simply cover the letter representing the value you want to calculate. For example, if you want to know how much voltage is in a system, cover the V. The I and R are still visible and should be multiplied to find the voltage.

Let's try a real example now by finding the amount of amps in a 12 volt circuit with a resistance of 3 ohms. Cover the letter of the value you do *not* know, in this case, the "I." You'll be left with V/R. Plug in your numbers, $12/3$, and you get a value, I, of 4 amps.

Watt's Law

Derived from Ohm's law, this formula enables you to calculate power.

Power (P): amount of work done in a unit of time

Watt (W): the measurement unit of electric power

Wattage: the amount of electric power required by a device

Kilowatt: one thousand watts

Megawatt: one million watts

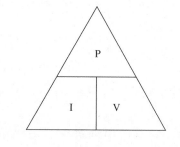

$P = I \times V$ (Power = Current multiplied by Voltage)

$I = P/V$ (Current = Power divided by Voltage)

$V = P/I$ (Voltage = Power divided by Current)

Watt's law can be remembered and used in the same way as Ohm's law. For example, if a 45 watt light bulb is plugged into a 120 volt system, how much current does it draw? Cover the "I" leaving you with P over V. Plug in your numbers, $^{45}/_{120}$, and you will get 0.375 amp.

Working with Electricity

Before you work with electricity, please refer to the guidelines at the end of this chapter.

Wire

Wire, often copper, is the basic "roadway" of transmitting current. Insulation keeps the electricity contained and prevents the circuit from grounding out and malfunctioning.

Wire thickness, or gauge, is measured with a number designation. A larger number denotes a smaller wire diameter, and a smaller gauge number denotes a larger wire diameter. For example, a Number 6 wire is thicker than a Number 10. In the United States, AC household power is color coded. Neutral is always indicated by white, while both black and red can indicate positive, or "hot." Green or bare wires are used for ground.

Wire is rated as to the current it can carry. Overloading this amount can result in heat creation generated by the resistance of the wire itself.

Tools

Ammeter/ampmeter: a meter used to measure current in amps

DVOM: digital volt ohm meter

Multimeter: A multimeter can measure circuit attributes such as voltage, resistance, and current flow (volts, ohms, and amps).

Voltage indicator: a simple tool for testing if voltage is present on a circuit

Voltmeter: an instrument that measures difference in voltage

Electric meter: an instrument that measures and records power usage

Safety equipment: includes specialized clothing, gloves and footwear

Consuming Electricity

In the United States, most electricity is supplied by a vast network of power plants, transformers, and power lines known as "The Grid." Sometimes this is also referred to as "shore power," meaning you are tapping into a publicly accessible power supply. Independent generators, both diesel and gasoline, supply power in situations where shore power isn't available or sufficiently powerful. Large Naval ships, such as aircraft carriers, generate their own power through the use of nuclear turbines and other advanced technologies.

In the United States, residential power is supplied in both 120V and 240V systems. High-usage electric appliances such as stoves and heaters requiring large amounts of power are typically on a 240V system, while the majority of devices require only 120V.

High voltage describes any voltage deemed to be potentially dangerous, generally greater than 40 volts. Low voltage typically describes components that are operated by DC voltage, generally at a power of 12V in a vehicle. In a residential system, a transformer converts the voltage for end uses such as low-voltage lighting.

BTU: British Thermal Unit, a measurement of heat energy

Kilowatt (kW): one thousand watts

Kilowatt-hour (kWh): one thousand watts acting over a period of 1 hour, the standard measurement unit for household electrical power consumption

Power Storage

Batteries use chemical reactions to store electricity to be discharged when needed. An alkaline battery uses a high pH, or basic, chemical solution to accomplish this. Often found in cell phones and laptops, rechargeable batteries like Li-Ion (Lithium Ion) and Ni-MH (Nickel Metal Hydride) are more powerful and able to store larger amounts of power.

Safety

Electricity is incredibly dangerous to work with, in part because of the speed with which it moves. Follow all precautions, and educate yourself about hazards and best practices. Never perform electrical repair you are not qualified to do. Some basic tips include, but are NOT limited to:

- Turn off the power and confirm with a voltage tester that there is no voltage present before performing any repairs.
- Inspect all cords and equipment regularly to be sure they are in good condition.
- Thoroughly inspect all safety equipment to insure it is in proper working order before use.
- Be particularly careful when working in damp or wet areas, since water is a conductor of electricity. Never operate electrical equipment while standing in water.
- Outlets installed near water should be GFCI protected. A GFCI, or Ground Fault Circuit Interrupt, contains a circuit breaker and is designed to reduce the risk of electrocution.
- Use polarized and 3-prong plugs as designed.
- Comply with building codes.

Conclusion

With a basic understanding of electronic principles, you should be able to score well on this subtest of the ASVAB. Memorize the symbols and learn the vocabulary. Use the triangle system to remember your formulas, and be sure to use the correct law for the situation at hand. Classes, books, and online resources offer many opportunities for in-depth study of the vast and rapidly changing field of electronics.

If you are interested in electronics, a magazine subscription might keep you informed of the latest developments and newest technologies.

chapter **16**

Auto Information

Vehicles are designed all over the world with constant updates and improvements, and every manufacturer has a different idea of the perfect vehicle. This has resulted in so many variations that it would be impossible to cover them all, so we'll focus more on the larger principles at work, rather than specific proprietary systems. Terminology changes as well as technology and one component can have several names.

Cars are complex machines with multiple systems working together. Whether you have prior automotive experience or not, it is essential to understand each system. As you read through the sections, consider the following: Is the system sealed or open? What are its components? How does it interact with other parts of the car? How do other forces work within the system (friction, hydraulics, air flow, or electricity)? How can you tell when it's operating properly and when it's not? We'll start with how a combustion engine creates power, and then move onto the rest of the individual systems necessary to use that power in a drivable vehicle.

Engine Mechanical

The internal combustion engine is the central power plant in an automobile. The components that make up an engine are all important to meet the requirements of internal combustion.

Compression

First an engine must be able to build compression; this is achieved by the piston moving up and down inside the cylinder. In order to allow enough space for movement of the piston in the cylinder, pistons are slightly smaller in diameter than their cylinder, necessitating the use of piston rings to form a tight seal. To change the up-and-down movement of the pistons to rotational movement, a crankshaft is employed with connecting rods joining them together. The pistons, rings, connecting rods, crankshaft, and cylinders are all housed together in the engine block. When the block is capped off with a cylinder head, everything is in place to create compression.

Air/Fuel Mixture

Next there needs to be a method of getting air and fuel into the cylinders, and exhaust gases out. For this purpose, intake and exhaust valves are fitted in the cylinder head at the top of each cylinder; the valves can be opened and closed as needed.

Timing

For everything to work, the timing of valve operation must be in unison with the crankshaft, and therefore the attached pistons. To accomplish this, there is a camshaft which is rotated in time with the crankshaft by either a timing chain or belt. Most modern camshafts are located in the cylinder head and are referred to as overhead cams (OHC), while engines with the camshaft in the engine block are referred to as overhead valve engines (OHV).

Ignition

All that is needed now is to be able to ignite the compressed air/fuel mixture. Gasoline engines use a spark plug installed in the cylinder head for this, while diesel engines simply depend on the pressure and heat created by compression to achieve ignition.

Lubrication and Cooling

Finally, to keep all this in working order, the engine contains a pressurized oil lubrication system to reduce wear and prevent damage to the moving parts. The cooling system deals with the extreme temperatures created during combustion.

Four Steps of Internal Combustion

Now that we have an engine that can meet all the requirements for internal combustion, we can perform all the steps a four-stroke motor needs to create power.

1. Intake stroke (suck)
   - Intake valves open
   - Pistons move down
   - Sucks in the air/fuel mixture
2. Compression stroke (squish)
   - Intake and exhaust valves close
   - Pistons move up
   - Compresses air/fuel mixture
3. Power stroke (bang)
   - Intake and exhaust valves remain closed
   - Ignition of compressed air/fuel mixture causes it to burn
   - Pushes pistons down causing rotation of crankshaft
4. Exhaust stroke (blow)
   - Exhaust valves open
   - Pistons move up
   - Pushes out spent air/fuel mixture (exhaust)

So as you can see, it took two complete rotations of the crankshaft (four strokes) for each cylinder to produce power. You can remember this with "suck, squish, bang, and blow" and of course the whole thing is repeated hundreds of times a minute when the engine is running!

Engine Management

The engine management system is responsible for achieving and maintaining the ideal air/fuel ratio for complete burning of the fuel during the combustion process. This ideal ratio is known as the stoichiometric mixture. For gasoline engines, the stoichiometric mixture is 14.7 molecules of O_2 to 1 molecule of fuel (usually expressed 14.7:1). Any ratio below this, for example 12:1, indicates too much fuel or a "rich" mixture. Conversely, any ratio above the ideal, such as 16:1, would point toward too much oxygen, or a "lean" mixture. In a carbureted engine, the attempt to achieve this mixture is controlled by fixed passages of a certain size that are calibrated to the engine. In modern fuel injection systems, the mixture can be constantly adjusted by the powertrain control module (PCM) based on inputs from various sensors.

Ignition System

The ignition system provides a high-voltage spark to ignite the compressed air and fuel mixture at the correct time in a gasoline internal combustion engine.

Essentially, starting at the battery, primary voltage travels to an ignition coil. When this voltage is temporarily removed by electronic control or mechanical breaker points, the ignition coil produces a pulse of secondary high voltage, which must then be conducted to the spark plug. In a distributor ignition system, this connection is through the coil wire, rotor, distributor cap and spark plug wires. An alternate method of transferring this voltage is the distributorless, or coil over plug system. As you might expect, this system has no distributor, and each cylinder has a separate ignition coil managed by an electronic control module. In both systems, once the high voltage reaches the spark plug in the engine, electricity arcs across a gap and ignites the air/fuel mixture in the cylinder. The spark must arrive at the correct time, which is generally before the piston reaches the top of its compression stroke. This is referred to as an "advanced" ignition timing and is required because of the slight delay between the moment of spark and the burning of the air/fuel mixture.

Partial failure of the ignition system will cause a loss of engine performance, while complete failure will cause the vehicle to stop running altogether.

Fuel-Delivery System

The components of the fuel system include:

Fuel gauge: indicates tank fill level

Fuel filter: removes debris and impurities from fuel

Fuel lines and hoses: allow for transfer of fuel from tank to engine

Fuel pump: moves the fuel through the system

Fuel tank: stores fuel for use by the combustion engine

The fuel system is a one-way system, allowing for the storage and transfer of fuel needed for the combustion process of the engine in a vehicle. The fuel pump moves fuel from the tank through the filter, lines, and hoses, making it available to the engine management system, which in turn supplies the appropriate amount of fuel to the combustion chambers of the engine.

Fuel systems can fail either by not delivering the correct amount of fuel to the engine, causing the engine to stop or run intermittently, and by leaking fuel externally through a damaged tank, hoses, clamps, or connections.

Air Intake System

The air intake system provides a supply of filtered air needed for the combustion process to the engine. Its components include:

Air filter: cleans incoming air to keep engine free of debris

Intake manifold: distributes air to all cylinders from a central point

Supercharger: belt-driven pump used to force air into intake manifold

Turbocharger: exhaust-driven pump used to force air into intake manifold

Intake pipes and hoses: connect intake components to provide the sealed delivery of clean air

On a normally aspirated engine, outside air is sucked in through the air filter to the intake manifold, which distributes the air to the individual engine cylinders. With turbo- or supercharged engines, a pump is added to the air intake system to force extra air to the intake manifold for use by the engine. Pipes and hoses route the air between different components.

Failure of the air intake system can cause a poorly running engine, possible mechanical damage and poor fuel economy. Restrictions in the air intake (most commonly a clogged air filter) will cause the engine to work harder and use more fuel than normal. Leaks in the system (split hoses, loose connections, etc.) affect both the air/fuel mixture formed by the engine management system and allow dirt and debris into the engine.

Exhaust System

The exhaust system transfers harmful gases created by the engine during the combustion process safely away from the passenger compartment while reducing noise levels and environmental emissions in the process. Here are its components:

Catalytic converter: emissions-control device that converts exhaust gases like carbon monoxide and hydrocarbons to less harmful substances such as carbon dioxide, nitrogen, and water

Exhaust manifold: collects exhaust gases at the cylinder head from individual cylinders to a single exhaust pipe

Exhaust pipes: allow for needed connections between other exhaust components

Exhaust hangers: secure exhaust components to vehicle frame or chassis

Muffler: reduces noise emissions caused by the expelling of exhaust gases from a combustion engine

Generally the exhaust gases will flow from the engine, be collected by the exhaust manifold, then pass through the catalytic converter and finally the muffler(s) with exhaust pipes as needed between components.

The most common failure of exhaust systems is leakage, causing an unsafe condition for occupants of the vehicle. Excessive noise caused by a loose and/or worn component is also a failure, but not as critical. Exhaust pipes and mufflers tend to corrode from the condensation of water vapor. Catalytic converters can fail by becoming inefficient or by the catalytic material becoming loose.

Engine Cooling Systems

Purpose of the cooling system: Absorb and dissipate the extreme heat created by the engine combustion process in order to maintain a constant engine temperature, both for the protection of the engine's mechanical components and to maintain efficient running. It is a closed system that circulates coolant through all parts of the system. Here are the system components:

Coolant: Also called antifreeze, coolant is a chemical mixture that raises the boiling point and lowers the freezing point of water, generally a 50/50 mixture of Glycol and water.

Hoses: allow for flexible connections between cooling system components

Overflow tank or reservoir: collects coolant expelled by radiator cap caused by normal expansion during operation

Water pump: circulates coolant through the system; can be belt-driven, electric, or have an auxiliary water pump in addition to the main water pump

Radiator: reduces coolant temperature by transferring heat to the air; usually located at the front of the vehicle

Radiator cap: maintains constant pressure in the cooling system

Radiator fan: pushes or pulls air past the radiator to aid in heat dissipation especially when the car is at a standstill

Thermostat: opens and closes at a predetermined temperature to control flow of coolant in order to maintain a constant temperature

Water jacket: area of engine block around cylinders containing antifreeze

The water pump circulates coolant through the engine passages and water jacket where the heat is absorbed from the engine. Then, at a predetermined temperature, the thermostat opens, allowing coolant to flow through the radiator where heat is transferred to the passing air. Finally, the cooled antifreeze is returned to the engine where it can absorb more heat, maintaining a constant engine temperature. All this must occur in the sealed recirculating system at a constant pressure.

System failure would be indicated by the engine overheating, usually indicated by a temperature gauge or warning lamp. Typical causes of system failure are leaks from one of the components (water pump, radiator, hoses, etc.), lack of coolant circulation (thermostat stuck closed, blockage in passages, pump not operating correctly, etc.), and lack of airflow past the radiator (failed or broken fan, debris covering radiator, etc.). Continued overheating will damage the engine to the point it will not run so should be addressed promptly.

Lubrication System

Just as it sounds, this system lubricates the engine to help slow wear and prevent damage. It's a closed system containing either synthetic or petroleum based oil, according to the car manufacturer's recommendations and engine specifications. Synthetic oils were developed in part to allow for longer time spans and mileage between oil changes, as well as some increase in fuel economy.

Oil circulates within the engine block and drains down to the oil pan below it. The oil pump pushes the oil through the oil filter back into the engine block where the cycle continues. A cap on the engine allows oil to be added when necessary, and the dipstick allows you to measure how much oil remains in the system.

Lubrication system failures range from annoying (an occasional drip on the driveway) to catastrophic (complete loss of oil pressure). Catastrophic failure results in major engine damage and could be due to oil pump failure, blockage in the system, or a broken component that causes the pressure to drop.

Electrical System

The electrical system stores and maintains direct current (DC) electrical power needed by various consumers on a vehicle. This system can be split into two parts: engine electrical (starting/charging) and body electrical. At the center of both parts is the battery. Here are the system components:

Battery: electrical power storage device, typically a lead-acid type containing an electrolyte solution of sulfuric acid and water

Alternator: mechanical generator run by the engine that generates electrical current

Voltage regulator: controls the amount of voltage produced by the alternator, based on the battery's state of charge; usually built into the alternator

Starter: electric motor responsible for cranking the engine, causing it to "turn over"

Consumer: any component that requires electrical power to operate (e.g., lights, power windows, control modules, ignition system, sound system)

Fuses: circuit-protection device designed to blow if too much power flows through a circuit. Rated in amps based on circuit requirements.

Relays: switching devices used to control an electrical circuit

Switches: provide operator input for control of electrical circuits

Direct Current (DC): one-way electrical system used in automobiles, typically 12 volt

The engine electrical consists of a starter motor responsible for starting the engine and an alternator that generates DC voltage once the engine is running. The alternator contains a voltage regulator to monitor and maintain the level of charging based on the vehicle's current electrical needs. The body electrical encompasses all the consumers requiring electric power to operate and the circuits required to control them (switches, fuses, wiring, relays, etc.). For a consumer to operate (e.g., a light to shine), the vehicle must provide both positive (battery) and negative (ground) pathway for the flow of voltage and proper operation.

When the key is turned to start position, the starter motor engages and rotates the engine consuming a large amount of the battery's stored power. Once the engine is running, the starter is disengaged and the alternator, which is turned by a belt on the running engine, will start to recharge the battery. Once the voltage regulator determines that the battery has been fully recharged, it decreases the voltage output of the alternator to prevent overcharging of the battery while still providing enough power for the vehicle's electrical consumers.

Failure of the vehicle's electrical system is easily noted by things not operating, such as the starter motor not turning or a light not lighting up. This can be caused by lack of available voltage (dead battery), the inability to provide power to the consumer (blown fuse, broken wire, faulty switch, etc.), or a faulty consumer (burned out bulb, bad starter, etc.).

Driveline

The driveline consists of the components that allow the transfer of the power created by the engine to the driving wheels.

Basically, the constant power created by the engine is transferred to a transmission containing different gear ratios that allow for variable output speeds. This power is then transferred to a differential gear and finally connected to the drive wheels by axles.

Manual transmissions operate with a fixed coupling to the engine called a clutch, which must be disengaged by the driver when changing gears or coming to a stop. The gear selection must also be controlled directly by the driver by means of the shifter.

Automatic transmissions contain a fluid coupling to the engine called a torque converter, which allows for the vehicle to remain in gear while stopped. Gear selection while driving is controlled hydraulically based on several inputs such as engine speed, vehicle speed, and load.

Front-wheel-drive vehicles utilize a combination transmission and differential called a transaxle not requiring the use of a driveshaft.

Rear-wheel-drive vehicles contain a driveshaft that connects the output of the transmission to the input of the differential.

Four-wheel-drive vehicles require a transfer case attached to the output of the transmission to allow power transfer to both the front and the rear wheels. As such, a four-wheel-drive vehicle also requires the addition of a front driveshaft, front differential, and front axles.

Differential gears are necessary to allow the drive wheels to turn at different speeds with a constant input while cornering. Limited slip differentials provide the added benefit of transferring power to the wheel with the most traction.

Suspension

The purpose of the suspension system is to provide a buffer between the passenger compartment of a vehicle and the wheels by compensating for uneven driving surfaces. Without a proper suspension system, vehicles would have a very rough ride and it would be very difficult to maintain control. Manufacturers use many types of suspension and configurations. Independent, semi-independent, multi-link and torsion bar suspension are some examples. Here are the components of the suspension system:

Wheels: many configurations; encompass tire, hub, wheel bearing, valve stems, etc.

Springs: provide cushion and insulation from bumps and irregularities in the driving surface; common types include coil, leaf, and air springs

Shocks absorbers and struts: hydraulically dampen the recoil of springs, providing for better handling

Sway bars: reduce body roll when cornering, allowing for better control

Swing arms or control arms: allow for independent vertical movement of individual wheels

Ball joints: a ball-and-socket type of joint that allows for numerous angles of free movement

Bushing: typically rubber components that provide a stiff yet somewhat flexible connection point for suspension components

Torsion bar: a substitute for springs, based on the twist and return of the bar

Failure of the suspension system can be noted by a change in handling characteristics, harsh or excessively bouncy ride, vibrations, and unusual noises.

Spring failure or fatigue is generally indicated by a low or uneven ride height and a rougher ride. An excessively bouncy ride would indicate that the hydraulic shocks or struts have lost their ability to dampen the action of the springs. Noises and vibrations typically point to worn or loose components such as ball joints and bushings. Faulty suspension, while not always immediately critical, should be inspected because it can be unsafe. Under- or over-inflated tires will affect handling as well as fuel economy. It is important to maintain inflation at the PSI (pounds per square inch, a measurement of air pressure) recommended by the vehicle manufacturer. Tire tread should be monitored for wear and condition.

Steering System

The steering system allows for the directional control of a vehicle by the driver. Components are listed below.

Steering wheel: driver's means of directional control

Steering column: connects the steering wheel to the steering gear or rack

Steering rack: steering gear in a rack-and-pinion system

Steering gear box: transfers steering column input to the pitman arm

Pitman arm: connects steering gear box to the center link

Center link: transfers steering motion to the tie rods

Idler arm: stabilizes the other end of the center link

Tie rods: final connection point between wheels and steering mechanism

Power steering pump: provides hydraulic pressure on power assist steering system to ease movement of steering components

Power steering fluid: hydraulic fluid used in power steering systems

The two most common steering systems are rack and pinion and steering gear box, either of which can be power assist or manual. With a rack and pinion, the steering request from the steering wheel is transferred directly through the steering column to the rack that is attached to both wheels by tie rods. On a steering gear, the request is transferred out of the steering gear box via a pitman arm attached to the "drag" or center link, which is attached at the other end to an idler arm. Movement of the center link is then transferred to the wheels by tie rods.

Failure of the steering system can be indicated by excessive free play in the steering wheel, vibrations while driving, unusual steering characteristics and, in the case of a power steering system, loss of power assist indicated by increased difficulty turning the wheel. Lack of power assist is caused by a loss of hydraulic pressure commonly caused by leakage of power steering fluid, a failed pump, or a malfunctioning power steering belt. Free play, vibrations, and a change in steering characteristics indicate worn or bent steering components.

Brake System

The brake system provides controlled stopping of a vehicle through the use of hydraulic pressure and friction material. The two common designs of friction material are disc and drum; they both fundamentally work the same way. Anti-lock brakes (ABS) use additional electronic parts to help avoid "locking up" the brakes while still working under the same principles.

Components common to disc and drum systems:

Brake fluid: hydraulic fluid used to build and transfer pressure

Master cylinder: creates hydraulic pressure when brake pedal is depressed

Brake booster: provides power assist to master cylinder reducing the amount of force needed at the brake pedal; can be operated either by engine vacuum or hydraulic pressure

Brake lines and hoses: allow for the transfer of pressure in brake hydraulic system

Disc brake system components:

Brake caliper: on a disc brake system, the hydraulic component at each wheel that squeezes the brake pads against the brake rotor

Brake pad: a flat piece of friction material on a disc brake system

Brake rotor: round disc that receives the pressure from the brake pad

Drum brake system components:

Brake shoe: crescent shaped piece of friction material

Wheel cylinder: the hydraulic component that pushes the shoes into the drums

When a driver presses the brake pedal, hydraulic pressure is built up by the master cylinder and transferred via the brake lines and hoses to each wheel. In a disc brake system, the caliper squeezes the brake pad to the rotor, creating friction and causing the wheel to stop turning. Drum brakes work when the brake shoe presses against the inside of the brake drum causing friction and stopping the vehicle.

When you take your foot off of the brake pedal in either system, the hydraulic pressure drops, allowing for the release of friction and the wheel to turn again.

Brake failure would be indicated by loss or reduction in stopping ability, commonly caused by allowing air into the system, a brake fluid leak or a failed hydraulic component (master cylinder, caliper or wheel cylinder). Excessive noise is usually an indication of worn friction material and requires replacement of pads or shoes.

Conclusion

Numerous resources exist to help you learn more about automobiles. A great place to start is the owner's manual of your own car. Observing and maintaining a vehicle directly will give you the practical experience to support the theories and knowledge you've just acquired. Public libraries contain manuals and guides, and sometimes even online access to professional databases. Trade, technical, and community colleges offer courses that usually allow you to "get your hands dirty" and gain more direct knowledge.

17

Shop Information

Safety First

Any discussion of shop information must begin with a discussion about safety precautions. We'll start with eye protection. Many workshop tools used can send splinters, metal pieces, or even sparks flying. Safety glasses are fine for many operations, but welding requires specialized visors. Ear protection is evaluated with a Noise Reduction Rating (NRR). A higher NRR means the earplug or ear muff offers more protection against louder noises. Both fumes and dust can damage your lungs, and require different types of respirators. The best source of information regarding which respirator you need is the National Institute for Occupational Safety and Health (NIOSH). For many jobs, gloves are a small but critical piece of safety equipment because glues, solvents, and oils can leach through your skin and affect your health. Welding gloves insulate your hands and arms from heat and protect your skin from sparks. Clothing should always be appropriate to your task. In general, overly loose or flowing clothing is dangerous. Specialized textiles like leather and Nomex are essential in some situations. Extreme care and best practices should be followed when electricity is used around water; other facets of electric safety are covered in Chapter 14 on Electronics. Maintaining a well-lit, clean, and orderly work area will greatly reduce your risk of accidents and improve your efficiency. When working with any material, it is best to consult the Material Safety Data Sheet (MSDS) to learn what hazards it poses, and what level of safety equipment is required.

Materials

Probably the first consideration in any project is materials. Modern suppliers offer a broad range of both types and qualities of material. Appropriateness to end use, size, density, thickness, quality, and ratings should all be considered in your choice. All materials have a "grain," or orientation of internal structure, which must be considered when cutting, bending, or joining.

Wood is classified by "grade," and often labeled as suited to exterior or interior application. Plywood is board-formed wood made from several layers glued together and is available in many formulations, such as hardwood, softwood, or marine. OSB, or oriented strand board, is particleboard made of wood chips bonded together with resin and glue under high pressure. MDF, medium-density fiberboard, is a popular resin-bonded light-duty material made of bonded wood fibers. Dimensional lumber, or "board," is milled from solid hard or soft wood. The measurement system refers to the size of the wood <u>before</u> it is planed into standard sizes and dried. Therefore, the common "2 by 4" actually has the dimension of approximately 1.5" × 3.5".

Metal can be purchased in sheet, stock (similar to "boards"), and wire. Thickness of both flat stock and wire is denoted by gauge, and the larger the number, the <u>smaller</u> the dimension. Aluminum, steel, and copper are a few of the readily available metals. Galvanized metal has been treated, usually with a coating of zinc, to reduce the possibility of corrosion.

Masonry materials range from natural rock to high-tech engineered products. Stone, brick and block have been used since ancient times because of their strength and durability. Masonry can be dry-laid, or without glue, or wet-laid by bonding with an adhesive such as mortar or grout. Concrete is a mixture of aggregate (particles such as sand or gravel), cement, and water. Rebar, steel rods, and expanded wire mesh are often used to add strength to concrete structures. The most recent development is the bonding of cement, fibers, and additives to create durable and fire-resistant boards for use in siding and other applications.

Ways of Powering Tools

Hand-Powered Efficiency

We tend to think of tools in terms of power tools, but hand tools are still essential for many tasks. Gears reduce the force needed to crank an eggbeater-style hand drill, and a speed handle is a crank that increases rotational speed even more.

Common on automotive tools, a ratchet is a one-way gear that allows for tightening or loosening a fastener without lifting the tool off of the fastener.

Battery Portability

Many modern tools come with rechargeable battery packs, so the tool is truly mobile. The development of higher voltage batteries has made many cordless tools as powerful as their corded cousins.

Electric Power

Electric tools plug in. Larger electric tools require a good power supply, sometimes requiring their own dedicated circuit and heavy gauge extension cords. Saws and air compressors are two examples.

Pneumatic Productivity

Pneumatic tools use compressed air to operate. In general, pneumatic tools are used in professional auto and wood shops because it is efficient to operate one compressor and power all of the tools with it. Numerous tools can operate at the same time without a loss of power, as opposed to an electrical system which can easily be overloaded.

Measuring

Accurate measuring is critical for success with shop projects. Here are some of the tools you might use to achieve that accuracy:

Ruler: a graduated tool for measuring length

Squares, t-square: for checking a 90-degree angle

Protractor: for measuring any angle in degrees

Level: for checking horizontal or vertical trueness

Plumb bob: a weight hanging from a string used to measure vertical trueness

Gauges: Feeler gauges are thin strips of metal that measure gaps. Run-out gauges measure wobble, usually of rotating parts. Pressure gauges measure pressure in a system.

Calipers: measure thickness of materials

Micrometer: measures with extreme accuracy

Dial indicator: accurately measures small movements and displays them on a dial

Drilling and Boring

Drilling can be done with a handheld power drill. Battery powered cordless versions, electric, and compressed air powered are all available. A drill mounted on a table is called a drill press, and has great precision. The specific spinning part that is in direct contact with the material is called a bit, and a chuck is the part of the drill that holds the bit.

Center punch: creates a dent to help start drilling a hole

Metal punch: a hollow tool used to create a hole in metal

Twist bit: classic spiral-shaped drill bit

Wood boring bit: a bit with a sharp point attached to a flat chisel, used to make holes quickly in wood

Masonry bit: a drill bit with an attached chisel at the point for drilling block and stone

Stepped bit: a single bit capable of boring different sized holes in metal with the same tool

Cutting

Some cutting tools are designed for specific materials and uses, but most power saws can cut a variety of materials when fitted with the appropriate blade.

Chisels: hand tools used to gouge material

Shear: used to cut sheet metal, has one stationary blade

Snips: handheld tool used to cut metal with a scissor motion

Bolt cutters: used to cut bolts and heavy gauge wire

"Stanley" blade: a light duty handheld utility knife for softer materials; usually retractable

Cross-cut saw: classic handsaw for cutting boards to the correct length

Miter saw: used in conjunction with a miter box to cut precise angles

Chop saw: a powered form of a miter saw

Japanese saw: a flexible saw for fine, angled, or complex cuts

Bow saw: often used to rough cut wood, such as firewood

Hack saw: used to cut metal and pipe

Jeweler's saw: a high-tension blade used for fine cuts in metal

Coping saw: used for fine cuts in wood

Bandsaw: a power saw with a flexible blade in a continuous loop

Jig saw: a power tool able to cut curves and scrolls

Hole saw: a cylindrical saw installed on a drill, used for making holes

Circular saw: a handheld tool with a disc-shaped blade and many applications

Table saw: a table version of a circular saw

Tile saw: a specialized type of saw for masonry applications with a water-cooled blade

Rip saw: a saw used to cut with the grain in order to reduce wood in thickness

Fastening

Driving

All threaded fasteners such as screws and bolts should be installed with a twisting motion. Many screw driver variations exist beyond the popular phillips and flat-head, and it is important to match the screwdriver bit to the screw head accurately to avoid damaging the fastener or component. The fairly common Hex or Allen wrenches have a hexagonal head, and are often used in bicycle repair and furniture construction.

Wrenches grip a fastener from the outside for twisting on and off.

Box wrench: a fixed, closed tool used for grabbing all sides of a fastener at the same time

Open-ended wrench: has one side open, generally a c-shape

Combination wrench: has one open-ended side and one boxed

Adjustable wrench (Crescent): an adjustable open-ended wrench

Pipe wrench: an adjustable wrench designed to grab and turn round objects

Socket: the isolated head of a wrench used with standardized and interchangeable drivers such as a ratchet or impact wrench

Impact wrench: a power tool that uses a rotating hammering action to loosen and tighten

Torque wrench: a specialized driver that indicates when the specified amount of force is applied when tightening

Striking

Hammers and mallets are for driving smooth, unthreaded fasteners such as nails and brads.

Claw hammer: use the head for striking nails, and the claw for pulling them back out

Ball peen: a hammer with one spherical side and one cylindrical side. Used to form metal, insert tacks, and strike punches

Mason's hammer: has a chisel-shaped end for scoring and chipping masonry and a striking head

Sledge hammer: used for driving chisels, demolition, etc.

Dead-blow hammer: a specialized hammer filled with weights that shift to create solid and accurate impact without recoil

Nail gun: a power tool, often pneumatic, used to "shoot" nails into the base material

Mallets: made of rubber, plastic, wood, leather, etc. For striking chisels and applying force without damage

Additional Tools and Shop Helpers

Here are some additional tools/gadgets to help you around the shop:

Pliers: two-handled grasping tool with a central pivot point

Needle-nose pliers: the grasping end is tapered to a point for versatility

Slip joint: the central pivot point can be changed, increasing or decreasing the size of what can be gripped

Locking (vice grip): Pliers that can be locked in a grasping position as a clamp

Clamps: hold your work securely in place; examples include C-clamps, spring clamps, and vice

Lathe: used to create cylindrical and round objects of assorted materials

Router: a high-speed tool used to create grooves, gouges and curves, and to cut and round edges

Planer: power tool that shaves boards to an even thickness

Hand plane: a hand tool that evenly removes thin shavings of wood with a sharp blade

File: a toothed tool that removes surface material incrementally; examples include bastard, crosscut, and rat-tail

Rasp: similar to a file, it removes surface material more quickly than a file because of its coarser teeth

Anvil: a solid iron surface used as a support for forming and bending metal

Flexible shaft tool (Dremel): a versatile tool used with varied attachments to carve, buff, polish, grind, etc., with great precision, control, and detail

Fasteners

Purpose, exposure, load, and material type all affect fastener selection. Outdoor and marine projects need very different fastener materials than light-duty indoor projects. Stainless steel, copper, bronze, and galvanized steel are able to withstand elements.

Nails

Nails are driven into materials with a striking motion, and often have smooth sides and a flat head. Countersinking a nail refers to hammering it using a punch so that the head lies below the surface of the material. Nail length is designated by the a number followed by a *d*, and larger numbers are longer nails. For example, a 2d nail is 1" long, and an 8d nail is 2.5" long.

Common nails: sturdy nails with a flat head used in a broad range of applications

Finishing nails: smaller gauge wire nails with a smaller head that can be countersunk for interior and fine applications

Double-headed nails: temporary nails with two stacked heads for easy removal

Screws and Bolts

Because of the corkscrew-shaped threads wrapped around their shafts, screws "grab" materials as they are joined and offer more security than a smooth nail. Bolts work on the same principle, but are designed to match an internally threaded part. Screws and bolts are both measured by diameter, spacing of threads (pitch) and length from tip to under the head.

Wood screws: have a pointed tip and tapered shaft

Sheet metal screw: have a pointed tip and constant size shaft

Machine bolts: have a blunt, flat end

Machine screws: small bolts

Lag: describes a large-scale, heavy-duty screw or bolt

Nuts: internally threaded piece of metal

Wing nut: a nut with attached flanges ("wings") to make grasping easier

Other Fastening Components

Washers: used with screws, bolts and nuts; have a flat surface with a hole in the center and are used to protect a base material, secure a fastening, or distribute force more evenly; types include shakeproof/lock, jaw, flat, spit-lock, and plain

Cotter pin: a locking device used to secure a nut onto a bolt

Rivet: a permanent fastener that is not easily removed. Rivets have a head on the front side of the joint and are physically expanded on the back side joining and securing flat materials together. Pop rivets are commonly used, but many specialty types and applications exist. A rivet gun, bucking bar, and manual riveter are three possible tools used for riveting.

Staples: U-shaped fasteners used to attach flat materials or fencing to a support.

Joining Materials

Ways of attaching materials together without individual fasteners are specific to each type. Metals are often joined by welding. MIG, TIG and Arc (shielded metal arc welding, SMAW) welding all use electricity in a high-voltage arc to weld. Oxy-acetylene welding uses the combination of two gases to fuel the welding flame without electricity. Soldering joins metal or wire by liquefying a material of a lower melting point to act as glue. Glues can be water- or solvent-based, and the manufacturer's recommendations will help you choose the right one for your material. Epoxy and other two-part glues bond when the catalyst and the resin are mixed, forming a material that hardens to form a very strong bond.

Finishing

Sanders are power tools that remove surface material through friction and abrasion. Sandpaper is made by attaching abrasive material to a backing. The size of the particles, or grit, is rated on a numerical scale, with larger numbers being the finest grits and lower numbers being the coarsest. Finer grits create and are used on smoother surfaces.

Sanding block: a flat piece of wood or other stock with sandpaper wrapped around it, used to remove material evenly

Steel wool: fibrous steel fibers wrapped together and used as a fine abrasive

Drum sander: sander with a cylindrical abrasive surface

Belt sander: a handheld sander with sandpaper mounted on a belt

Orbital sander: a handheld sander for detail and small-scale work

Conclusion

Visiting your local hardware store or home improvement center can boost your shop knowledge, and many offer free workshops. Spending some time in a workshop of any type will boost your knowledge and skill level. Several knowledgeable and skilled woodworkers host television programs designed to clearly demonstrate techniques and correct tool usage.

chapter **18**

Mechanical Comprehension

Describing Motion

Motion is a change in position. There are three aspects to describing motion: displacement, velocity, and acceleration. *Displacement* (Δd) is a change in an object's position from some reference point. For example, if you walk 10 m forward, then you have changed your position by a *distance* (10 m) in a *direction* (forward) from some reference point. Note that displacement has both a magnitude (i.e., how far you've gone—distance) and a direction (e.g., forward—often, positive is used to denote going away from the reference point, while negative is used to denote coming towards the reference point). People often use displacement and distance interchangeably, but remember that displacement has a direction, whereas, distance does not.

Velocity (v) is the rate of change of displacement over some time interval (Δt). You can calculate it by dividing displacement by a time interval (v = Δd/Δt). For example, if you travel 10 m forward in 2 s, then your velocity is 5 m/s forward. Like displacement, velocity has a magnitude (i.e., how fast or slow—speed = 10 m/s) and a direction (e.g., forward—again, positive usually denotes going away from the reference point, while negative usually denotes coming towards the reference point). Like displacement and distance, people often use velocity and speed interchangeably, but remember that velocity has a direction, whereas, speed does not.

Acceleration (a) is the rate of change of velocity over some time interval. You can calculate it by dividing the change in velocity (Δv) by the time interval ($a = \Delta v / \Delta t$). So, if you travel from rest (0 m/s) forward to 5 m/s in 2 s, then your acceleration is 2.5 m/s/s or 2.5 m/s^2 forward. Like displacement and velocity, acceleration has a magnitude (2.5 m/s^2) and a direction (e.g., forward—again, positive usually denotes going away from the reference point, while negative usually denotes coming towards the reference point). Note that a negative acceleration is called a *deceleration* and means that the object is slowing down. So, now that we have described motion, let's look at the cause of motion—forces.

Force and Newton's Laws of Motion

A *force* is simply a push or a pull on an object. It's what causes motion. Sir Isaac Newton summed up forces in his three laws of motion:

1. **Law of Inertia:** An object at rest will remain at rest ($v = 0$ m/s) or an object in motion will remain in motion at constant velocity in a straight line unless acted upon by an outside force. In other words, if an object is at rest or moving at constant velocity in a straight line, then there is no net force acting upon it ($F_{net} = 0$). For example, if you roll a ball on a frictionless surface, the ball will keep moving in a straight line at constant velocity— you don't need to keep pushing it for it to remain in motion.

2. **F = ma:** Any object that is accelerating or decelerating must have a net force acting upon it. The net force is the product of the object's mass and acceleration ($F_{net} = ma$). The unit of force is called the newton (N), which equals 1 kg·m/s^2. For example, a rolling ball on a real surface will slow down and eventually stop because a net force of friction is acting opposite the ball's direction of motion.

3. **Law of Action and Reaction:** For every action, there is an equal, but opposite, reaction ($F_{action} = -F_{reaction}$). If the air gets let out of a balloon in one direction (F_{action}), the balloon will move away in the opposite direction ($F_{reaction}$).

Let's look at some common forces that we deal with in mechanics.

Gravity

Gravity is an attractive force between two masses. Your most common experience of gravity is weight (w). The weight of an object is caused by the attractive force between Earth's mass and an object's mass. You can calculate any object's weight by multiplying its mass (in kg) by Earth's acceleration due to gravity (g, 9.8 m/s^2 [w = mg]). For example, a 5 kg bowling ball has a weight of approximately 50 N (for a quick calculation, it often helps to round g to 10 m/s^2).

Friction

Friction is a force that acts between any two materials that are moving past each other. It is caused by tiny bumps in the surfaces of the objects and it opposes motion. Friction is caused by two surfaces rubbing together. If you rub your hands together, the heat that you feel is due to friction. The force of friction depends upon the types of material and how much they are pressed together. For example, concrete block sliding on a paved road has more friction than when it slides on an icy paved road. Mathematically, the force of friction can be calculated by multiplying the coefficient of friction (μ) by the object's weight ($F_f = \mu W$ or $F_f = \mu mg$). The coefficient of friction is related to the nature of the surfaces. For example, the coefficient of friction between a block of wood and concrete is 0.62, while between a block of wood and a wooden board, it is 0.2. So for the same block of moving wood, the force of friction would be greater on a concrete surface than on a wooden surface.

Friction also occurs when objects move through a fluid like air or water. When a paratrooper falls through the sky, the air molecules rub against him and cause friction. We call this friction **air resistance**. Similarly, when a submarine moves through the water, the water molecules rub against it, thereby causing friction, which we call **drag**.

Normal Force

When a box sits motionless on the floor, gravity pulls it downward. Yet that box does not fall through the floor. That's because the floor pushes up on the box with a support force called a **normal force** (F_N). The normal force is equal, but opposite to the weight of the box ($F_N = -w$ or $F_N = -mg$).

Tension

Tension is a force that stretches an object like a string, rope, or spring. The tension is transmitted equally through all parts of the rope or string. For example, if a person stands on a scaffold suspended on either end from two ropes, then total tension in the two ropes must balance the weight of the person and the scaffold.

Pressure

Pressure is actually the application over an area of surface. Pressure is calculated by dividing the force by the area of application ($p = F/A$). So, if a box on the floor weighs 100 N and the area of the box's bottom surface is 0.01 m², then the pressure exerted by the box on the floor is 10,000 N/m². The unit of pressure is the pascal (Pa), which is equal to 1 N/m². So, the box exerts a pressure of 10,000 Pa.

Torque

Torque (τ) is a turning force that causes an object to rotate. When you turn on a faucet, you apply a torque to the handle. A torque is produced when you apply a force with some "leverage" at a distance from the center of rotation. This distance is called a **lever arm** (d). A torque is the product of an applied force (F) and the lever arm ($\tau = Fd$). For example, if you apply a 10 N force with a 0.5 m wrench to a bolt, then you are applying a 5 N·m torque. Note that if you apply the same force with a 1.0 m wrench, then the torque is 10 N·m. Torques cause an object to rotate either clockwise (positive) or counterclockwise (negative).

Newton's laws of motion apply to rotational motion as well. Here are two examples:

- **Newtons's First Law:** If an object is balanced about its center of rotation, then the sum of the torques acting upon it are equal ($\tau_{net} = 0$). Two children balanced on a see-saw have no net torque acting on them. Likewise, an object spinning about its center of rotation at constant rotational velocity has no net torque acting upon it.

- **Newton's Second Law:** If the rotational velocity of an object is accelerating or decelerating, then a net torque must be acting upon it. If you get on one side of a see-saw and no one else is on the other side, you exert a net torque on the see-saw and you fall downward. In other words, your weight applies a net torque causing it to spin about its center of rotation.

Torques play important roles in machines like levers, gears, and things that spin.

Buoyant Force

If you drop a tennis ball in air, it falls. But if you drop a tennis ball in water, it floats. The water or fluid exerts an upward force on the tennis ball. This force is called the **buoyant force** (F_B). Buoyant force opposes gravity. The buoyant force on an object is equal to the weight of the fluid displaced by the object. Let's look at an example of a diver underwater. If the diver is suspended so that she is neither rising nor falling, then the buoyant force equals the force of gravity—we call this neutral buoyancy. If the diver is sinking, then the force of gravity must be greater than the buoyant force. If the diver is rising, then the buoyant force must be greater than the force of gravity. Buoyant force is also related to the density of the fluid. Your buoyancy in the Great Salt Lake would be more than in a freshwater lake because saltwater is denser than fresh water.

Work, Energy, and Power

Work

When you apply a force to an object over some distance in the direction of motion, you do **work** on that object. For example, when you pick up a box, you apply a force that lifts the box upward. The box moves upward, so you have done work on the box. Now, suppose you walk forward after you lifted the box. In this case, you have done no further work on the box, even though your muscles are exerting a force to keep the box up. Why haven't you done work? The force you apply to the box was upward, but your motion was forward. So, *work can only be done on an object if the direction of the applied force is in the same direction as the object's motion.*

Work can be calculated by multiplying the applied force times the distance moved ($W = Fd$). If you apply a net force of 10 N that slides a box along the floor forward 10 m, then you have done 100 N·m of work. The unit of work is joules (J). One joule is equal to 1 N·m, so you did 100 J of work on the box. When you do work on an object, you change its energy. So, before we talk about how work and energy are related, let's look at energy.

Energy

Simply stated, energy is defined as the ability to do work. There are two major types of energy, kinetic energy and potential energy. *Kinetic energy* (KE) is the energy of motion and is related to the velocity of the object ($KE = \frac{1}{2}mv^2$). An object at rest has no kinetic energy. *Potential energy* (PE) is stored energy.

There are many types of potential energy. *Gravitational potential energy* is energy by virtue of the height of an object. If you pick up a box, you change its height and increase its gravitational potential energy. You can calculate its potential energy by multiplying the weight of the box times the height (PE = wh or PE = mgh). Substances contain **chemical potential energy** by virtue of the energy stored in their chemical bonds. Gasoline has lots of chemical potential energy.

There is a principle called the *conservation of energy*, which states that energy cannot be created nor destroyed, but merely converted from one form to another. Suppose you hold a ball in the air above the ground. That ball is not moving so it has no kinetic energy. However, that ball is at some height above the ground, so it has gravitational potential energy. When you let go of the ball, it falls. As it falls, its potential energy gets converted to kinetic energy. During the fall, as the height decreases, so does the potential energy. But at the same time, the ball's velocity increases, so does its kinetic energy. When the ball hits the ground all of the potential energy has been converted to kinetic energy, so the kinetic energy is at its maximum.

So, how are work and energy related? There is a principle called the **work-energy theorem**. Basically, when you do work on an object, you change its kinetic energy ($W = \Delta KE$). For example, when you do work on a ball to lift it to some height, you increase its energy, in this case, its gravitational potential energy. If you push a box to slide it across the floor, you are doing work on the box and increasing its kinetic energy. Because work and energy are related, they are measured in the same units, joules.

Power

Power (P) is the rate by which work is done. Consider moving the 100 N box 10 m across the floor. If you move that box in 10 s or in 20 s, you do the same amount of work. However, if you do it in 10 s, then you have more power. Power is calculated by dividing work by the time interval over which the work was done ($P = W/\Delta t$). The unit of power is called the **watt** (W) and is equal to one joule per second.

Machines

Basic Principles of Machines

Work and energy are related to machines. A **machine** is a device that multiplies applied forces or changes the direction of applied forces, but does not change the amount of work. Basically, you do work on a machine (input work, W_{in}) and the machine does work on an object or load (output work, W_{out}), but the total amount

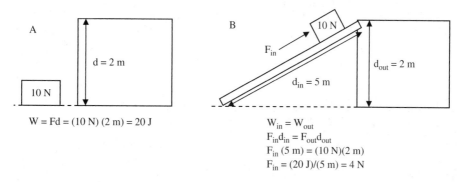

FIGURE 18-1 • (A) To lift a 10 n box to the top of a 2 m loading dock requires a force of 10 N and 20 J of work. (B) Pushing the box up a 5 m long ramp requires only 4 N of force. The machine (ramp) reduces the input force by increasing the input distance, yet the work done remains the same.

of work remains the same ($W_{in} = W_{out}$). So, machines operate on the principle of conservation of energy. When you apply an *input force* (F_{in}, which is sometimes called an **effort force**, F_e), the machine applies an *output force* (F_{out}, which is sometimes called a **resistive force**, F_r). The output force can be greater or less than the input force. The ratio of the output force to the input force is called the machine's **mechanical advantage** ($MA = F_{out}/F_{in}$ or $MA = F_r/F_e$). Because the work remains the same, the machine changes the ratio of the output to input forces by changing the output and input distances. You can see this with an example of a simple machine, the inclined plane or ramp as shown in Figure 18-1.

Machines may simply change the direction of motion without providing a mechanical advantage. One example is a pulley, which we will discuss later in this chapter.

In an ideal machine, the input work equals the output work. However, real machines do not have all of the input work available for output work. Some of the energy is lost to friction. So, a real machine has an **efficiency** (eff), which is the ratio of output work to input work (eff $= W_{out}/W_{in} \times 100\%$). Real machines have an efficiency of less than 100%.

Machines can be classified as simple machines or complex machines. The six types of *simple machines* are inclined plane, screw, wedge, lever, pulley, and wheel and axle. In contrast, *complex machines* are combinations of simple machines. So let's look at various types of simple machines.

Inclined Plane

As shown in Figure 18-1, an *inclined plane* reduces the input force by increasing the input distance. A ramp is an inclined plane. Even a hill is an inclined plane.

Screw

A *screw* is merely an inclined plane that is wrapped around a cylinder. The input force is the torque that you apply in turning the screw and the input distance is the length of the ramp made by the threads. The closer the threads are together, the longer the input distance. The output distance is the amount of force the screw provides to hold the materials together. A bolt is a type of screw. A nut is also a type of screw with the inclined plane on the inside.

Wedge

A *wedge* is merely two inclined planes attached together at the base. The input force is the force that you use to hammer the wedge in place. The edges are the ramps that supply the increased input distance. The output force is the force the wedge uses to split the wood (each side does half). The output distance is the width of the split. An axe is an example of a wedge.

Lever

A *lever* is a device that uses torques to magnify forces. It consists of a lever arm and a center of rotation called a **fulcrum**. Levers come in three classes as shown in Figure 18-2. What distinguishes one class from another are the placement of the input and output force relative to the fulcrum, the direction of the input and output forces, and the lengths of the input and output lever arms. Levers can be used to magnify forces, to propel objects faster, or to move objects further than the distance which you must apply.

Pulley

A simple pulley consists of a wheel and rope. A single fixed pulley changes the direction of the applied force, but does not have a mechanical advantage. However, when you string a fixed pulley together with one or more movable pulleys (block and tackle), you gain mechanical advantage as well. You can decrease the input force by increasing the input distance (i.e., the length of rope that you must pull to raise the load). The number of pulleys is proportional to the mechanical advantage (see Figure 18-3). The arrangements of block and tackles varies. For example in Figure 18-3, with the rope attached to the movable pulley, the direction of the input and output forces is the same. If the rope was attached to a hook on the fixed pulley, then the direction of the input and output forces would be opposite.

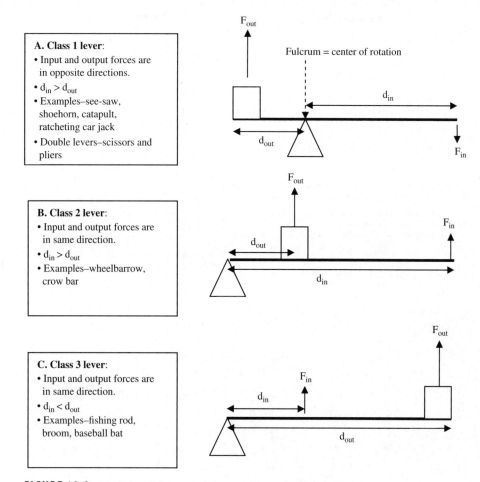

A. Class 1 lever:
- Input and output forces are in opposite directions.
- $d_{in} > d_{out}$
- Examples–see-saw, shoehorn, catapult, ratcheting car jack
- Double levers–scissors and pliers

B. Class 2 lever:
- Input and output forces are in same direction.
- $d_{in} > d_{out}$
- Examples–wheelbarrow, crow bar

C. Class 3 lever:
- Input and output forces are in same direction.
- $d_{in} < d_{out}$
- Examples–fishing rod, broom, baseball bat

FIGURE 18-2 · Principles of the various classes of levers (A) Class 1, (B) Class 2, (C) Class 3.

Wheel and Axle

A wheel and axle is basically two wheels of different sizes attached to one another (Figure 18-4). A rope or belt can be placed around the wheel to apply the input force. A rope or belt can be placed around the axle to apply the output force. Because the circumference of the wheel is larger than the circumference of the axle, the input distance is larger than the output distance. This gives a mechanical advantage and reduces the input force needed.

In some cases, it may be desirable to reverse the arrangement of the wheel and axle from that shown in Figure 18-4 (i.e., apply the input to the axle and the output to the wheel). This means that the machine will require a greater

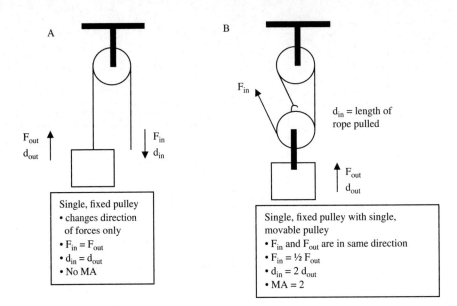

FIGURE 18-3 · Principles of pulleys (A) single fixed pulley, (B) single, fixed pulley in combination with one movable pulley (single block and tackle).

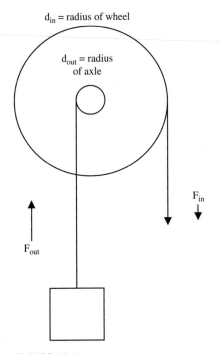

FIGURE 18-4 · Principle of wheel and axle. The larger radius of the wheel compared to the axle gives a longer input distance and, therefore, gives a mechanical advantage.

input force than output force, but the output distance is greater than the input distance. This is exactly what happens in the wheels of a bicycle and car.

There are some special cases of wheels and axles, such as gears and belts and pulleys. **Gears** are toothed wheels that can transfer motion from one to another (see Figure 18-5). The teeth of one gear interlock with the teeth of another. Depending upon the size and number of teeth on each gear, the configuration can provide mechanical advantage.

Belts and pulleys are another special case of wheels and axles. Like gears, belts and pulleys can also transfer motion. The configuration of the belts will determine the direction that the pulleys turn (Figure 18-6). If the belt is looped around two pulleys, then they will turn in the same direction. If the belt is crossed as it is looped around the pulleys, then they will turn in opposite directions. The sizes of the pulleys involved and which one has the driving force will determine mechanical advantages. A drive attached to the lager pulley will have a mechanical advantage.

As mentioned before, complex machines are combinations of simple ones. For example, bicycles use wheels and axles (the wheels and pedals), belts (chains), and gears to change the input force.

FIGURE 18-5 · The large gear has more teeth and turns more slowly than the small gear. The two gears move in opposite directions. If the drive is on the large gear, then the torque on the large gear is less than the torque on the small gear, so there is a mechanical advantage. The configuration can be reversed if the drive is on the small gear.

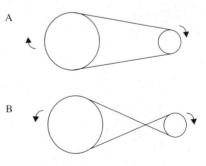

FIGURE 18-6 · The arrangements of belts on pulleys determine their direction of motion. (A) A simple loop moves the pulleys in the same direction. (B) A crossed loop moves the pulleys in opposite directions. The relative sizes of the pulleys and which one is driven will determine whether there is a mechanical advantage.

Fluid Dynamics

Fluids can be used to do work and transfer forces. Earlier, we talked about pressure as a force applied to an area. Fluids, such as water, will transmit pressure. So, the pressure applied to one side of a hose containing water will be transmitted to the other side. This equal transmission of pressure can be used to multiply forces in connected containers.

Blaise Pascal, a French physician, discovered that the shape of the container or hose has no effect on the pressure. So, connect a small piston (A_1) filled with fluid to a wider one (A_2) filled with fluid. When you apply pressure by pressing down on the small piston (F_1), the fluid transmits the same pressure to the larger piston $(P_1 = P_2$ or $F_1/A_1 = F_2/A_2)$. The pressure pushes up on the wider piston. Because the area of the wider piston is larger, the force applied to the wider piston (F_2) is also larger $(F_2 = F_1A_2/A_1)$. This is the principle of the hydraulic press and hydraulic jack.

Moving fluids can also create forces. Consider an airplane wing as it moves through a fluid such as air. The upper surface is curved more than the bottom one. As the plane moves through the air, air travelling at a constant speed, the air passing across the upper surface has to go farther and faster. According to Bernoulli's principle, as the velocity of a fluid increases, the pressure decreases. So, the air pressure on the upper surface of the wing is less than that on the lower surface. This difference in air pressure between the wing surfaces makes an upward force called **lift**. Air foils or spoilers on race cars are reverse wings. They cause a downward force of air pressure that keeps the cars on the road.

chapter 19

Assembling Objects (CAT-ASVAB Only)

Simply stated, the Assembling Objects subtest is an assortment of visual puzzles designed to test mechanical aptitude and spatial reasoning. For some people, these skills are innate and come naturally. Preparation for this part of the ASVAB is slightly different from that of the other subtests, and is accomplished by learning and practicing problem-solving strategies rather than memorizing words or formulas.

This chapter explains specific strategies you can use to improve your ability to solve these problems quickly and accurately. First, realize that these puzzles can be solved in both a "positive" and "negative" way. If you are using a positive method, you're searching for the *correct* answer. A negative method is searching for *wrong* answers that can be eliminated from the options. Using a combination of both methods is an efficient way to accurately solve the puzzles.

Each question shows an unlabeled set of shapes on the left, which will combine exactly to match one of the four possible answers. The shapes and symbols are diverse and often complex, but break down into two main categories.

Puzzles

The first category of questions is essentially jigsaw puzzles in which you are supplied a set of pieces and are asked to envision how they'll fit together correctly. Pieces can fit together, or occasionally, stack. Be aware that the pieces may not be at the same scale in the answer (a circle might become larger or smaller, for example).

Attachments

The second main type of questions are attachments that ask you to link the shapes together properly. These puzzles mimic assembly of an object, and test your ability to attach slot A to slot B. Keep in mind that the shapes must also match.

General Strategies

- Process of elimination: Rule out the solutions that obviously don't match the goal set, and evaluate the remaining possibilities.
- Match the shapes.
- Count the sides, especially of more complex or abstract shapes.
- Confirm that *all* parts agree.
- Methodically work left to right, eliminating options as you go.
- Pay attention to small details.

Specific Strategies

Matching Shapes

Look for shapes to correspond exactly to the base set on the left. In the example below, answer A is correct, because all of the base set shapes are present and match. Answer B is almost a match, but a circle has been substituted for the oval.

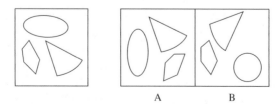

A   B

Scan for unique shapes that can help you narrow down your solution options. An unusual shape such as a horseshoe or pie may help you quickly pinpoint a possible match. In our next example, the star is included in correct answer B, but left out of A.

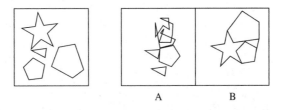

A   B

Matching Angles

Compare angles carefully. In the example below, notice that both the base set and correct answer A contain a square, but answer B contains a parallelogram (vertices are not right angles) so it is not a match.

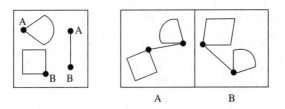

A   B

Counting

Because all of the set pieces will be present in the solution, simply counting shapes can sometimes guide you towards the correct answer. There are seven shapes in the set below and correct answer A, but only 5 in answer B. In some instances, the placement of pieces will create additional shapes or spaces, so this method isn't foolproof and your answer should be verified by careful observation.

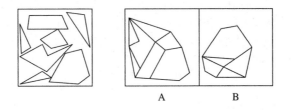

A   B

In the set below, we are shown a plus-shaped form and 4 quadrangles. Both A and B match the goal set in that regard, and it's hard to tell at first glance which is correct because of the rotation of the shapes. However, if you look closely at the goal set, you will count 1 smaller quadrangle and 3 medium-sized ones. In the incorrect solution A, you can count 3 smaller quadrangles and only 1 medium sized one. Answer B has the correct shapes, and you can spot the 1 small quadrangle in the lower left corner of the completed puzzle.

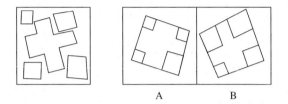

A   B

Count the number of sides, especially with more complex shapes. The shape that is shaded below in the base set is complex and hard to describe, but you can easily count that it has 8 sides, and match it to the 8-sided shape in correct answer A. The similar shape in set B has only 6 sides, so it is not an exact match.

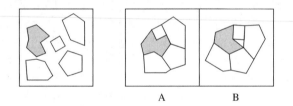

A   B

Flipping

As you may have already noticed, shapes can be rotated in any direction. However, be on the lookout for mirror image flipping, which is not considered a match. If you take a close look at the shaded shapes below, you can see that in answer A, the shape has been flipped as well as rotated. The shaded shape in answer B has simply been rotated, and the rest of the shapes correspond to the base set, so it's the correct answer.

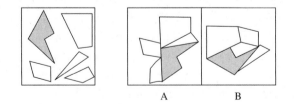

A   B

Layering

Some of the puzzles require that the pieces be stacked, or layered. Let's take a look at one of these and see how to solve it. At first glance, answer A seems to match the goal set best, but it is lacking the small triangles of the goal set, and the rectangle is a slightly different dimension. Correct answer B has all the proper parts stacked. Each "pie" has a small triangle stacked on it, and the long rectangle is placed beneath them and only partially visible.

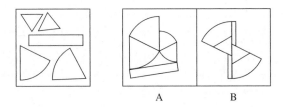

A   B

Attachment Points

When solving the attachment point questions, look very closely at *where* the point is placed on the shape. Is it placed in a corner, or in the middle of a straight side? In this example, answer A is wrong on two counts. The attachment point is in the center of the triangle instead of at the vertex and the attachment on the 7-sided figure is in the middle of a side instead of the vertex. Answer B is correct because the attachment points match, as well as the shapes.

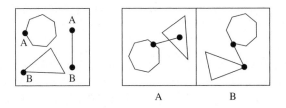

A   B

When faced with asymmetrical shapes, be sure to confirm that the attachment points are on the correct side of the shape. In this example, the oval has a small line detail near one end, making it asymmetrical. Answer A has both attachment points at the correct placements, while incorrect answer B has the placement of the attachment point at the wrong end of the oval. If you look closely, the squiggle shape in answer B also has its point at the wrong place, on the inside of the curve rather than the outside.

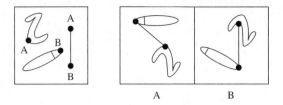

If there is a line through the attachment point, make sure your answer follows that line. In the goal set below, the line from point A in the wedge follows through the intersection of the two straight sides. In correct answer B, this attachment line position is maintained, and the rounded shape is correct as well. Answer A is wrong because the attachment line has been rotated out of position and intersects the arc of the pie instead. In addition, the abstract shape has been flipped and no longer matches the goal set.

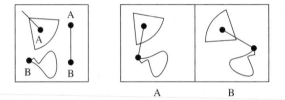

With strategies and practice, doing well on the Assembling Objects test is possible for even the least visual among us. Playing video or board games that involve fitting shapes together will sharpen your skills. Putting together a jigsaw puzzle, especially one with few color changes, will help as well. Assembling a 3-D puzzle or model, without following the instructions, is a third way of training your brain.

Part IV

ASVAB Practice Tests

chapter 20

ASVAB Practice Test 1

General Science Questions

1. Viruses do NOT do which of the following things?
   A. Carry genetic material.
   B. Reproduce.
   C. Excrete wastes.
   D. Adapt to the environment through natural selection.

2. Fungi get all their nutrients from
   A. photosynthesis
   B. consuming the material surrounding their cells
   C. consuming live plant cells
   D. consuming inorganic chemicals

3. Of the following, which type of animal is an invertebrate?
   A. Octopus
   B. Amphibian
   C. Reptile
   D. Bird

4. Mitochondria provide eukaryotic cells with
   A. energy in the form of carbohydrates
   B. lipids
   C. proteins
   D. energy in the form of ATP

5. Water can erode rock by all of the following EXCEPT
   A. freezing and thawing in cracks
   B. crashing rocks against each other
   C. saturating and drying clay-containing rocks
   D. conducting heat to rocks

6. Which of the following is NOT a sedimentary rock?
   A. Sandstone
   B. Limestone
   C. Marble
   D. Shale

7. Which of the following does NOT affect how water currents circulate in the ocean?
   A. Differences in water salinity.
   B. Differences in water temperature.
   C. Heavy cargo ship traffic.
   D. Wind on the water's surface.

8. Which of the following sequences is arranged from highest altitude to lowest?
   A. Troposphere, stratosphere, exosphere
   B. Exosphere, troposphere, stratosphere
   C. Exosphere, stratosphere, troposphere
   D. Troposphere, exosphere, stratosphere

9. The two most abundant elements in the earth's atmosphere are
   A. hydrogen and helium
   B. carbon dioxide and oxygen
   C. nitrogen and oxygen
   D. hydrogen and carbon dioxide

10. Transpiration and evaporation can lead directly to
    A. cloud formation
    B. sublimation
    C. runoff
    D. accumulation

11. Which two elements are most common in the earth's crust?
    A. Iron and calcium
    B. Potassium and oxygen
    C. Silicon and oxygen
    D. Calcium and sodium

12. The asteroid belt is located between the orbits of
    A. Mars and Jupiter
    B. Mercury and Venus
    C. Uranus and Neptune
    D. Earth and Mars

13. The continental crust and oceanic crust are part of the
    A. stratosphere
    B. magnetosphere
    C. atmosphere
    D. lithosphere

14. During intense exercise, muscles begin to produce
    A. oxygen
    B. phosphorous
    C. lactic acid
    D. amino acids

15. Red blood cells are produced in
    A. muscles
    B. kidneys
    C. the central nervous system
    D. bone marrow

16. Plants make carbohydrates in a form called
    A. lipoproteins
    B. acetyl-CoA
    C. triglycerides
    D. starch

17. The process of cell division that results in sperm or egg cells is called
    A. mitosis
    B. transcription
    C. meiosis
    D. base substitution

18. Which of the following shows parts of the electromagnetic spectrum in order of increasing wavelength?
    A. X-rays, visible light, radio waves
    B. X-rays, radio waves, visible light
    C. Radio waves, visible light, x-rays
    D. Visible light, radio waves, x-rays

19. The frequency of a wave directly refers to
    A. speed
    B. height
    C. rate
    D. size

20. Every object with mass is attracted to every other object with mass due
    to the effect of
    A. thermodynamics
    B. relativity
    C. momentum
    D. gravity

21. An ion carries a positive or negative charge because it does not have the
    same number of
    A. neutrons and positrons
    B. protons and electrons
    C. neutrons and protons
    D. quarks and electrons

22. The atomic number of an element is a measure of
    A. radioactivity
    B. weight
    C. number of protons in the nucleus
    D. electrical charge

23. A nanometer is a unit of measurement equal to
    A. one-tenth of a meter
    B. one-millionth of a meter
    C. one-billionth of a meter
    D. one billion meters

24. When the body changes food into a form that it can use for nutrition, it
    is called
    A. digestion
    B. circulation
    C. respiration
    D. defecation

25. If two species of organisms in the same community share the same niche, they may
    A. cooperate to obtain resources
    B. produce resources for each other
    C. compete for resources
    D. consume equal amounts of resources

Arithmetic Reasoning Problems

1. Three brothers agree to share the cost of a gift for their parents. The gift costs $600 and one of the brothers can contribute only $125. The remaining will be shared equally between the other two brothers. How much will each of the two brothers contribute?
    A. $219.10
    B. $237.50
    C. $300.00
    D. $475.00

2. Michelle purchased a sweater at $14.35, a hat at $12.50, and a pair of pants at $49.99. Ignoring sales tax, how much did Michelle spend?
    A. $64.74
    B. $65.74
    C. $75.84
    D. $76.84

3. In the past three weeks, a couple has paid $45, $30, and $42 for babysitting respectively. What is the average amount the couple has spent on babysitting in the past three weeks?
    A. $39.00
    B. $43.50
    C. $58.50
    D. $117.00

4. A map is drawn such that 1½ inches represents a mile. On this map, two cities are 17¼ inches apart. How many miles apart are the two cities?

    A. $11\frac{1}{2}$ miles

    B. $15\frac{3}{4}$ miles

    C. $18\frac{3}{4}$ miles

    D. $25\frac{7}{8}$ miles

5. The distance between two bases is 1,960 miles. A cargo plane flew from one base to the other in 3½ hours. Assuming constant speed, what was the speed in miles per hour of the cargo plane?
    A. 480 mph
    B. 560 mph
    C. 653 mph
    D. 980 mph

6. Andy began his first assignment of the day at 7:53 a.m. and completed it at 11:02 a.m. How long did Andy work on this assignment?
    A. 3 hours 2 minutes
    B. 3 hours 9 minutes
    C. 4 hours 7 minutes
    D. 4 hours 47 minutes

7. What is the next number in the sequence: 5, 15, 35, 75
    A. 90
    B. 95
    C. 125
    D. 155

8. 30% of 250 is
    A. 30
    B. 60
    C. 75
    D. 83

9. Jackson went out to lunch and dinner in one day. For lunch, he left a 10% tip of $1.75 while for dinner he left a 20% tip of $6. Including tips, how much did Jackson spend on lunch and dinner?
    A. $19.50
    B. $36.00
    C. $41.75
    D. $49.50

10. Including a 3 foot 7 inch attachment, a pipe section is 17 feet 2 inches long. How long is the pipe section without the attachment?
    A. 12 feet 2 inches
    B. 13 feet 7 inches
    C. 14 feet 5 inches
    D. 20 feet 9 inches

11. A large crate can hold 15 lbs 3 ounces of potatoes. If a shipment has 23 such crates, how many pounds of potatoes is contained in the shipment?
    A. 243 lbs 6 ounces
    B. 345 lbs 1 ounce
    C. 349 lbs 5 ounces
    D. 351 lbs 9 ounces

12. Casey walked 112 miles over 2 weeks. If Casey walked the same number of miles every day, how many miles did he walk each day?
    A. 8 miles
    B. 16 miles
    C. 56 miles
    D. 224 miles

13. A cylindrical tank can hold 410 gallons of water when full. This morning the tank was ⅛th full. Since then, 21 gallons of water has been used. How much water is currently in the tank?
    A. 30.25 gallons
    B. 32.50 gallons
    C. 51.25 gallons
    D. 60.50 gallons

14. In an organization with 3,500 members, only half attended the most recent meeting. Of those who attended, 20% voted against a rule change. Assuming all attending members voted, how many voted in favor of the rule change?
    A. 350
    B. 700
    C. 1,400
    D. 2,800

15. A recipe requires 2¼ cups of sugar to make 1 pound of dough. How much sugar should be used to make 3½ pounds of the dough?

   A. $4\dfrac{1}{2}$ cups

   B. $5\dfrac{3}{4}$ cups

   C. $6\dfrac{1}{8}$ cups

   D. $7\dfrac{7}{8}$ cups

16. A board measuring 14 feet is cut into three pieces. The longest piece is 6 feet while the remaining two pieces are of the same length. How long is each remaining piece?

   A. 2 ft

   B. 4 ft

   C. 8 ft

   D. 20 ft

Word Knowledge Questions

This test is about the meanings of words. Each question has an underlined word. You may be asked to decide which one of the four words in the choices is a synonym or most nearly means the same thing as the underlined word. It may ask which one of the four words means the opposite. Some of the underlined words are used in sentences. In this case decide which of the four choices most nearly means the same thing as the underlined word as used in the context of the sentence.

1. Avocation most nearly means
    A. profession
    B. hobby
    C. advertisement
    D. education

2. His cumulative score of 15 put him in the lead.
    A. last
    B. best
    C. total
    D. amazing

3. Some people say she has a strong personality, but I find her domineering.
    A. attractive
    B. silly
    C. quiet
    D. overpowering

4. Tenacious most nearly means
    A. stubborn
    B. flexible
    C. strengthening
    D. capable

5. Shelly refused to buy the new television because she felt the price was <u>exorbitant</u>.
   A. out of bounds
   B. fair
   C. unusual
   D. foreign

6. The audience was shocked that his speech was so <u>incoherent</u>.
   A. eloquent
   B. long
   C. terse
   D. unintelligible

7. The thief <u>fabricated</u> the reasons that he had taken the painting from the museum, but no one believed his story.
   A. made up
   B. memorized
   C. recited
   D. recalled

8. Although Jonathan kept looking for a way to get around the problem, a solution was <u>elusive</u>.
   A. hidden
   B. useful
   C. deceptive
   D. unimportant

9. <u>Choreography</u> most nearly means
   A. importance
   B. pause
   C. dancing
   D. religion

10. <u>Dogmatic</u> most nearly means
    A. obstinate
    B. passive
    C. dull
    D. personable

11. <u>Mitigate</u> most nearly means
    A. assure
    B. surprise
    C. alleviate
    D. concede

12. <u>Amnesty</u> most nearly means
    A forgetfulness
    B. pardon
    C. allergy
    D. understanding

13. His older brother was always his favorite <u>cohort</u>.
    A. kinsman
    B. person
    C. teacher
    D. companion

14. She had always felt that her grandfather was <u>magnanimous</u>.
    A. rich
    B. ineffective
    C. generous
    D. overbearing

15. Jamie often liked to <u>fondle</u> her new kitten.
    A. feed
    B. stroke
    C. train
    D. discipline

16. <u>Soliloquy</u> most nearly means
    A. understanding
    B. applause
    C. censorship
    D. monologue

17. <u>Probity</u> most nearly means
   A. education
   B. integrity
   C. productivity
   D. discipline

18. <u>Trenchant</u> most nearly means
   A. deep
   B. angry
   C. forceful
   D. quiet

19. <u>Jocund</u> most nearly means
   A. severe
   B. excited
   C. overweight
   D. lighthearted

20. <u>Iconoclast</u> most nearly means
   A. destroyer
   B. seriousness
   C. immigrant
   D. drama

21. <u>Homogeneous</u> most nearly means
   A. desirous
   B. poor
   C. similar
   D. illegal

22. <u>Indigent</u> most nearly means
   A. immigrant
   B. careful
   C. needy
   D. mediocre

23. Exemplary most nearly means
    A. commendable
    B. insignificant
    C. attentive
    D. uniqueness

24. We all agreed that Randy was often overly garrulous.
    A. playful
    B. entertaining
    C. talkative
    D. critical

25. The author has long had a reputation for being a polyglot.
    A. generous person
    B. person who is scholarly
    C. informative person
    D. person who speaks many languages

26. Vincent has been acting puerile for most of the day.
    A. childish
    B. unstable
    C. unhappy
    D. deceptive

27. Laura had been feeling vertiginous since she got up that day.
    A. aggressive
    B. disliked
    C. dizzy
    D. embarrassed

28. The doctor was unable to corroborate any symptoms of heart palpitations.
    A. cull
    B. confirm
    C. stimulate
    D. explain

29. <u>Carnage</u> most nearly means
    A. banishment
    B. strength
    C. foreclosure
    D. slaughter

30. <u>Ameliorate</u> most nearly means
    A. injure
    B. contend
    C. improve
    D. agree

31. <u>Diminutive</u> most nearly means
    A. hidden
    B. tiny
    C. mediocre
    D. pleased

32. <u>Acclimate</u> most nearly means
    A. harass
    B. compare
    C. censor
    D. adjust

33. The word most opposite in meaning to <u>querulous</u> is:
    A. complaining
    B. aggressive
    C. amiable
    D. critical

34. The weather report warned the storm could <u>wreak</u> havoc along the coast.
    A. show
    B. conceal
    C. tarry
    D. cause

35. Paul considered his sister's behavior to be <u>maudlin</u>.
    A. dishonest
    B. overemotional
    C. exceptional
    D. humorous

Paragraph Comprehension Questions

1. The Underground Railroad offered some slaves in the South a way to escape to the North and to freedom before the Civil War. It had no tracks or engines. It was a system of ordinary people helping slaves, hiding them in barns and attics, feeding them and giving them directions to the next family, until they reached the North.

    Which of the following statements isn't true?

    A. The Underground Railroad was available to all slaves.
    B. The Underground Railroad wasn't a real railroad.
    C. Ordinary people hid the slaves from the law.
    D. All of the above statements are true.

2. Scientists are undertaking a complicated experiment. They are trying to find what they believe are the building blocks of the universe. Hundreds of feet underneath the surface of the earth, near Geneva, Switzerland, physicists are looking for sub-atomic particles that are not possible to find in a normal laboratory environment. They are using a device called an atom smasher to create the conditions that existed when the Big Bang took place, which resulted in the creation of the universe. The Big Bang theory hypothesizes that around 15 billion years ago, the universe all of a sudden just expanded, like a balloon that has popped. The proponents of the theory say that the universe started from nothing. They do not know what existed before the Big Bang, but they say that as the universe expanded, it cooled. It continues to expand and cool to this day.

    Physicists near Geneva, Switzerland, are looking for

    A. an atom smasher
    B. conditions that existed when the universe started
    C. sub-atomic particles
    D. what happened before the Big Bang

3. Fannie Mae is the nickname for the Federal National Mortgage Association (FNMA). It is what is known as a Government Sponsored Entity (GSE). Fannie Mae is authorized by the U.S. Congress to enhance the availability of mortgage money for the residential housing market. It securitizes mortgages in the form of mortgage-backed securities, which are then sold to investors, creating a secondary mortgage market to

increase the supply of money available for mortgage lending. Fannie Mae was founded in 1938 by Congress, as part of President Roosevelt's New Deal.

Which of the following statements isn't supported by the above passage?

A. Fannie Mae securitizes mortgages as mortgage backed securities.
B. President Roosevelt founded Fannie Mae.
C. A secondary mortgage market increases the supply of money available for lending.
D. FNMA is considered a GSE.

4. Tornadoes are funnel-shaped, rotating columns of air usually surrounded by debris and dust that make the funnel shape clearly visible. However, not all such funnels are tornadoes. In order for meteorologists, or weather scientists, to consider a funnel of air a tornado it must be in contact with both the ground and the cloud base. Tornadoes can be relatively mild weather events, but they can also produce massive destruction, stirring winds up to 300 miles per hour. These destructive tornadoes are usually caused by a type of thunderstorm called the supercell. A supercell thunderstorm is characterized by a rotating updraft of air.

The primary purpose of this passage is to

A. Urge readers to prepare for tornadoes.
B. Give a history of tornadoes.
C. Suggest ways to prevent tornadoes.
D. Describe and define tornadoes.

Questions 5 and 6 are based on the following passage.

Prior to the Army setting a standard of support for all garrisons, no matter their location, there were garrisons where soldiers spent a one-year hardship tour without their families, such as South Korea's "Area 1." Now called Red Cloud, that same once gritty garrison has been transformed under the program that the Army calls normalization. At the direction of the Pentagon soldiers, civilians and retirees bring their families with them during their more lengthy tours there. The families are fully supported, as they would be in any Army garrison in the world. There is a kindergarten through eighth grade school and a day care center. And it is not an uncommon sight to see women strolling in the garrison with baby carriages.

5. Before the normalization of "Area 1," soldiers there
    A. set a standard for all garrisons
    B. were stationed for one year
    C. would bring their families with them
    D. none of the above

6. In what is known as Red Cloud there
    A. is now a gritty garrison
    B. was once a garrison in South Korea
    C. was a program called normalization
    D. is a policy to support families

7. The Louvre is one of the most famous art museums in the world. Located in Paris, France, the Louvre has several buildings. The oldest building was built in the Middle Ages. Known as "the gallery of masters," the Louvre houses paintings and sculpture from every civilization around the world. The French leader, Napoleon, stole works of art from the Netherlands, Germany, and Italy while at war with those countries and placed the stolen art in the Louvre. Most of those works of art were returned, but many remain in the Louvre. Originally the Louvre accepted works of living artists, but today only art from artists who have died is admitted in the Louvre's collection.

    Many of the masterpieces installed in the Louvre during the time of Napoleon were:

    A. the reason for its reputation as "the gallery of masters"
    B. works of art from the Middle Ages
    C. taken from other countries during wartime
    D. none of the above

8. The New York City subway system is among the oldest and most extensive public transportation systems in the world, with 468 stations and 842 miles of track. The first underground line was opened in New York City in 1904. Right now, a bit more than half of the tracks run through the underground. The rest are either elevated or run on the ground. The New York City subway transports over 1 billion passengers annually, and

averages over 4.3 million riders on weekdays. The New York City subway is an extremely busy rapid transit rail system. It is the fourth busiest in the world, after Tokyo, Moscow, and Seoul. People are able to ride the system 24 hours a day, 365 days a year. The Metropolitan Transit Authority (MTA) operates the system.

The number of miles of underground track in the New York City Subway system is

A. 187
B. 619
C. 443
D. The question can't be answered based on the information contained in the passage.

Questions 9 and 10 are based on the following passage:

To qualify for the Earned Income Tax Credit or EITC, you and your spouse, if married and filing a joint return, must have a valid Social Security Number, must have earned income, and cannot use a married filing separate filing status. In addition, you must be a U.S. citizen or resident alien all year. You cannot be the qualifying child of another person, and cannot have any foreign earned income. Your Adjusted Gross Income (AGI) and earned income must meet the limits. Earned income includes all the taxable income and wages you get from working. There are two ways to get earned income: you work for someone who pays you or you work in a business you own or run. Pay received for work while an inmate in a penal institution, interest and dividends, retirement income, social security, unemployment benefits, alimony and child support are not considered earned income.

9. Which of the following statements isn't supported by the above passage?
   A. Dividend income is not considered earned income to qualify for the EITC.
   B. An individual who is married and filing separately qualifies for the EITC.
   C. The qualifying child of another person does not qualify for the EITC.
   D. There are limits to the amount of income earned to qualify for the EITC.

10. An individual in prison would not be able to apply for the EITC because
    A. He failed to make child support payments.
    B. Her Adjusted Gross Income was too high.
    C. He was a resident alien for the entire year.
    D. Her income doesn't qualify as earned income.

Questions 11 and 12 are based on the following passage:

> Zumba is an exercise that is set to Latin music and includes salsa, meringue, and mambo, as well as dance and aerobics. There's even a little bit of belly dancing thrown in too. Zumba developed by accident when Alberto "Beto" Perez, a gym instructor in Cali, Columbia, was on his way to a class and realized he had forgotten his workout tape. He went back to his car and took a tape with his favorite Latin hits to pinch hit. He decided to exchange his usual routine for a workout that he improvised while he went along.
>
> To his surprise his students were impressed and wanted more of this new way to exercise. People liked Zumba because it was not the usual exercise-by-numbers that can become boring. It substitutes a few steps and great music for the ordinary gym class. The steps are repeated to create a dance routine. Even if a person thinks he or she has two left feet, it is easy adjusting to the routine. Should you make a mistake, no one will ever know since everyone in the class is so very busy trying their best to be a "dancer of the stars."

11. The author of this passage believes that Zumba is different because
    A. The teacher can improvise during class.
    B. It combines Latin dancing and aerobics.
    C. Alberto Perez once forgot his music tape.
    D. The dance steps are repeated.

12. If a person thinks she has two left feet, she would be considered
    A. a boring dancer
    B. a belly dancer
    C. a Latin dancer
    D. a clumsy dancer

Questions 13 through 15 are based on the following passage:

> Family caregivers are the more than 65 million people in the United States who take care of other adults, often parents or spouses, or

children with special medical needs. Being a caregiver has a high cost, but there are support services available. One of the first tasks that people who may become primary caregivers must face is determining what stage of caregiving their family currently needs. Then, they need to carefully assess the loved one's condition so they can prepare for the challenges they will soon face. AARP (American Association of Retired Persons) provides a helpful checklist to ensure that people do a thorough assessment.

The Family Care Navigator from the National Center on Caregiving can also help people navigate the often confusing myriad options of long-term care programs in each state. Among the many questions caregivers need to ask themselves is: Will their state provide care in their home? Will they decide to hire a professional? Will the situation be temporary or permanent? The scenarios are endless. As a primary care provider, they will help a loved one decide where to live. They will help the loved one decide if they will they stay at home, home share with a relative, or live with someone else. Another duty that must be done is a home safety check. Also, caretakers should develop emergency plans and give all family members a copy, and make sure everyone knows how to execute the plan should the need arise.

13. The author of the above passage believes that
    A. Being a family caregiver requires a lot.
    B. There are many questions that must be answered by a caregiver.
    C. A home safety check can identify problem areas for those in need of care.
    D. All of the above statements are true.

14. The primary theme of the above passage can best be described as
    A. protector
    B. programs
    C. scenarios
    D. safety

15. The function of the Family Care Navigator is to
    A. create a checklist for caregivers to use to assess their family's needs
    B. analyze the level of care needed for a person
    C. prepare an emergency plan for caring for a loved one
    D. figure out the various options of care that states offer

Mathematical Knowledge Questions

1. Solve for x: $3(x + 2) = 6$
   A. 0
   B. $\dfrac{5}{6}$
   C. 1
   D. $\dfrac{4}{3}$

2. Evaluate the following expression if $x = -1$, $y = 2$, and $z = -2$: $x(y - 1) + z$
   A. 0
   B. -1
   C. -3
   D. -5

3. One of the angles in a right triangle is 30°. What are the measures of the remaining angles?
   A. 30°, 30°
   B. 60°, 90°
   C. 30°, 60°
   D. 90°, 90°

4. A circle has a diameter of 6 mm. Find the area of this circle in terms of π.
   A. 6π
   B. 9π
   C. 12π
   D. 36π

5. Which of the following is equivalent to $x(x^2 - 2x + 1) \div (x^2 - x)$?
   A. $x - 1$
   B. $x + 1$
   C. $x^2 - 2$
   D. $x^2 - 2x + 1$

6. If $-2x \geq 6$, then which of the following must be true?
   A. $x \geq 3$
   B. $x \geq -3$
   C. $x \leq 3$
   D. $x \leq -3$

7. $\sqrt{3^2 + 4^2} =$
   A. 5
   B. 7
   C. 12
   D. 49

8. Angle A and another angle measuring 20° are complementary. What is the measure of angle A?
   A. 70°
   B. 80°
   C. 160°
   D. 340°

9. Three consecutive integers have a sum of 24. What is the value of the first integer?
   A. 7
   B. 9
   C. 15
   D. 22

10. $(x^2 + 4x - 1) - (x - 5) =$
    A. $x^2 + 3x - 6$
    B. $x^2 + 5x - 6$
    C. $x^2 + 3x + 4$
    D. $x^2 + 5x + 4$

11. The length of a rectangle is 3 times the width. The area of this rectangle is 48 square inches. What is the measure of the length in inches?
    A. 4
    B. 6
    C. 12
    D. 15

12. A 10-foot ladder is leaning against a wall such that the top of the ladder is 6 feet above the ground. What is the distance from the wall to the foot of the ladder in feet?
    A. 4 feet
    B. 8 feet
    C. 12 feet
    D. 16 feet

13. Solve for x: $\dfrac{x}{5} + \dfrac{x}{4} = 9$

    A. 4

    B. 5

    C. 20

    D. 180

14. Three coins are flipped. What is the probability all three coins land on tails?

    A. $\dfrac{1}{8}$

    B. $\dfrac{1}{6}$

    C. $\dfrac{1}{2}$

    D. $\dfrac{3}{2}$

15. The sum of a number and 4 is 3 times the number. If x represents this number, which of the following is equivalent to the statement?

    A. $x + 4 = 3 + x$

    B. $x - 4 = 3 + x$

    C. $x + 4 = 3x$

    D. $x - 4 = 3x$

16. $(3x + 4)(2x - 5) =$

    A. $-x - 20$

    B. $6x - 20$

    C. $6x^2 - 7x - 20$

    D. $6x^2 - x - 20$

Electronics Questions

1. What is the resistance of a 12v circuit whose current is 2 amps?
   A. 24 ohms
   B. 6 ohms
   C. 0.5 ohms
   D. 10 ohms.

2. In a DC system, the electrical charge flows
   A. directly in both directions
   B. several directions, depending on resistance
   C. in either direction, depending on voltage
   D. only in one direction

3. This symbol represents which of the following?

   A. A resistor
   B. A fuse
   C. A parallel circuit
   D. AC voltage

4. A diode allows
   A. electrical current to pass only in one direction
   B. for the storage of electrical current
   C. voltage to be increased before use
   D. electronic switching to occur

5. The ohmic value of a resistor can be identified by
   A. the size of the resistor
   B. its location in a circuit
   C. its color bands
   D. a stoichiometric rating

6. What is the minimum current rating of a 110V circuit with a resistance of 10 ohms?
   A. 11 amps
   B. 1 amp
   C. 120 amps
   D. 60 amps

7. With AC wiring, the neutral is indicated by the color
    A. green
    B. white
    C. black
    D. red

8. To measure the current flow through a circuit, you would use
    A. an ampmeter
    B. a voltmeter
    C. a capacitor
    D. a potentiometer

9. Plug-in LED landscape lighting could operate using which voltage?
    A. 120V but not 12V
    B. 12V but not 120V
    C. Neither 120V or 12 V
    D. Both 120V and 12V

10. A DVOM can
    A. manually switch digital voltage
    B. control the voltage output of a transformer
    C. measure the current and resistance of a circuit
    D. divert voltage on a manual

11. Lineman's gloves can be made of
    A. wool
    B. rubber
    C. leather
    D. B and C

12. AM and FM stand for
    A. Anode Module and Ferrous Module
    B. Amplitude Modulation and Frequency Modulation
    C. Antique Music and Foreign Music
    D. All Music and Free Music

13. A battery is represented by the symbol
     A.
     B.
     C.
     D.

14. A closed circuit must
     A. provide a complete pathway
     B. contain switching relays
     C. be contained in an electrical box
     D. provide several pathways

15. When working on a household electrical system, you
     A. are generally dealing with low-voltage DC
     B. can make repairs as long as you have on rubber shoes
     C. should turn off the power and confirm with a voltage tester.
     D. must always connect the white wire to ground

16. A 20 amp circuit on a 120 V system is able to handle how much power?
     A. 60 watts
     B. 140 watts
     C. 2400 watts
     D. 7200 watts

Automotive Information Questions

1. If your car radio isn't working, which of these would not be a possible cause?
   A. Relay
   B. Switch
   C. Fuse
   D. Bushing

2. In a car, an automatic transmission
   A. converts engine power to electric DC current
   B. uses hydraulic fluid to regulate gear selection.
   C. regulates climate control systems automatically
   D. allows the wheels to turn at different speeds

3. How many drive shafts are in a 4-wheel-drive vehicle?
   A. 1
   B. 2
   C. 3
   D. 4

4. Which of the following is NOT a type of automotive suspension?
   A. Co-dependent
   B. Independent
   C. Multi-link
   D. Torsion bar

5. The primary purpose of the exhaust manifold is to
   A. ensure complete combustion
   B. secure exhaust components
   C. reduce emissions
   D. collect exhaust gases

6. In an internal combustion engine, a camshaft is used to
   A. operate the valves
   B. control the cooling system
   C. move the pistons
   D. start the engine

7. Secondary ignition is
   A. an auxiliary starter switch
   B. an engine module backup
   C. high voltage
   D. another term for breaker points

8. A super-charger is a type of
   A. high-voltage ignition
   B. belt-driven pump
   C. automatic transmission
   D. performance muffler

9. A 50/50 mixture of automotive coolant and water would
   A. raise the freezing point of water
   B. lower the boiling point of water
   C. Both A and B are correct
   D. Neither A nor B is correct

10. A rack and pinion steering system contains
    A. tie rods
    B. idler arm
    C. center link
    D. all of the above

11. A possible source of brake fluid loss would be any of the following EXCEPT
    A. wheel cylinder
    B. brake drum
    C. master cylinder
    D. brake caliper

12. Which part of the ignition system is located in the engine?
    A. Primary
    B. Spark plug
    C. Rotor
    D. Coil

13. A stoichiometric ratio of 16:1 would indicate
    A. an ideal air/fuel mixture
    B. a rich air/fuel mixture
    C. a lean air/fuel mixture (key)
    D. none of the above

Shop Information Questions

1. When choosing a respirator, you should consider
   A. what materials you are working with
   B. the MSDS recommendations
   C. the NIOSH ratings
   D. all of the above

2. If you want to make a hole in wood, it's best to use a
   A. center punch
   B. twist bit
   C. stepped bit
   D. chuck

3. In situations with no access to electricity, the best method of welding is
   A. metal inert gas/MIG
   B. tungsten inert gas/TIG
   C. shielded metal arc welding/SMAW
   D. oxy-acetylene/OA

4. A friend asks you to help with a home improvement project, and to bring a few of your tools. He asks you to bring a hack saw, stepped bit, and a crosscut file. You suspect you'll be
   A. building new steps to the deck
   B. constructing a brick wall
   C. turning a steel drum into a BBQ smoker
   D. replacing his air conditioner

5. Which of the following would you likely use to install a sheet metal screw?
   A. Dead-blow hammer
   B. Phillips head
   C. Metal punch
   D. Screw gauge

6. Tools powered by an air compressor are
   A. air-o-matic
   B. always heavy duty
   C. pneumatic
   D. safer than other tools

7. The reason a tile saw requires water is
    A. tiles are commonly used in wet places
    B. to allow for cutting curved shapes
    C. to cool the blade while working
    D. to help mix the mortar to set the tile

8. You want to refinish the top of your wooden coffee table. The best sander for the job is:
    A. drum
    B. orbital
    C. floor
    D. bench

9. To shake loose an extremely tight bolt you would use a
    A. ratchet and socket
    B. hammer and chisel
    C. orbital box wrench
    D. impact wrench

10. The correct fastener for installing a temporary plywood floor is
    A. screws
    B. epoxy
    C. finishing nails
    D. rivets

11. The best tool for cutting sheet metal is a
    A. shear
    B. rip saw
    C. utility knife
    D. vise

12. The following could all be used in a metal shop EXCEPT
    A. lathe
    B. Japanese saw
    C. brake
    D. grinder

Mechanical Comprehension Questions

1. Which is the magnitude portion of displacement?
   A. Speed
   B. Velocity
   C. Distance
   D. Acceleration

2. Your car accelerates from rest to +30 m/s in 2 s. Which is its acceleration?
   A. -2 m/s^2
   B. -15 m/s^2
   C. $+2$ m/s^2
   D. $+15$ m/s^2

3. Which has a net force acting upon it?
   A. Two children balanced on a see-saw
   B. A scuba diver at neutral buoyancy
   C. A bungee jumper falling from a bridge
   D. A car moving on a straight highway at a constant 30 m/s

4. Which is a force of friction?
   A. Drag
   B. Gravity
   C. Normal force
   D. Tension

5. Which is the approximate weight of a 30-kg child?
   A. 150 N
   B. 300 N
   C. 450 N
   D. 600 N

6. A cannon fires a shell at a distant target. Which is the reaction force?
   A. The firing of the shell
   B. The shell traveling through the air
   C. The impact of the shell on the target
   D. The recoil of the cannon

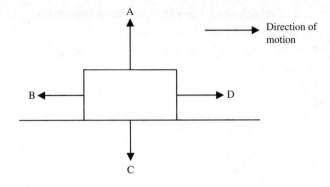

7. A box is moving along the floor as shown in the diagram. Which is represented by arrow A?
   A. Applied force
   B. Weight
   C. Normal force
   D. Friction

8. A ball rolls from the top of the hill down to the bottom. Which is true?
   A. The kinetic energy of the ball decreases to zero while its potential energy increases to maximum.
   B. Both the potential energy and kinetic energy of the ball decrease to zero.
   C. The kinetic energy of the ball increases to maximum while its potential energy decreases to zero.
   D. Both the potential and kinetic energy of the ball increase to maximum.

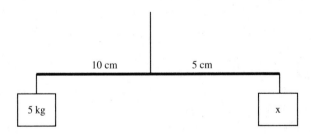

9. Two masses are balanced from a rod attached to a wire as shown in the diagram. The distances from the center of rotation are shown. What is the value of x?
   A. 1 kg
   B. 5 kg
   C. 10 kg
   D. 20 kg

10. A man pushes a crate 10 m across a wooden floor by using 50 N of force. How much work does he do on the crate?
   A. 5 J
   B. 60 J
   C. 150 J
   D. 500 J

11. Which is a class 2 lever?
   A. see-saw
   B. wheelbarrow
   C. fishing rod
   D. pliers

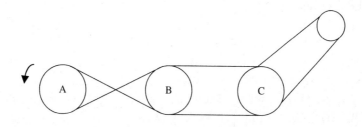

12. A belt-and-pulley system is shown in the diagram. Pulley A is the driving pulley and is spinning in the direction indicated by the arrow. Relative to Pulley A, which is true?
   A. Pulley B will turn in the same direction, but at a slower rate.
   B. Pulley C will turn in the opposite direction, but at a faster rate.
   C. Pulley D will turn in the opposite direction, but at a faster rate.
   D. All the pulleys will turn in the same direction at the same rate.

13. Which is a compound machine?
   A. Wheel and axle
   B. Bicycle
   C. Inclined plane
   D. Screw

14. A machine has a mechanical advantage that is greater than one. Which is true?
    A. The output force is greater than the input force.
    B. The output work is greater than the input work.
    C. The input distance is greater than the output distance.
    D. The efficiency is 100%.

15. If you exert 10 N of force on the piston of an air pump with an area of 0.1 m², then which pressure are you exerting on the piston?
    A. 1 Pa
    B. 10 Pa
    C. 50 Pa
    D. 100 Pa

16. The pistons of a hydraulic press have areas of 1 m² and 100 m². If you press down on the smaller piston with a given force, then how much force will the second piston raise up?
    A. The same amount of force
    B. Twice the amount of force
    C. Ten times the amount of force
    D. One hundred times the amount of force

Assembling Objects Questions

In each of the following questions, the picture at the left shows a group of parts. Answer Choices A–D show objects made from assembled parts. Choose the one that is made from the parts shown at the left.

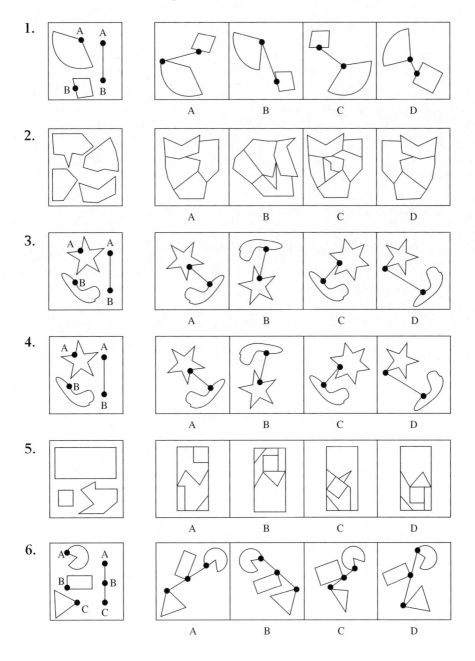

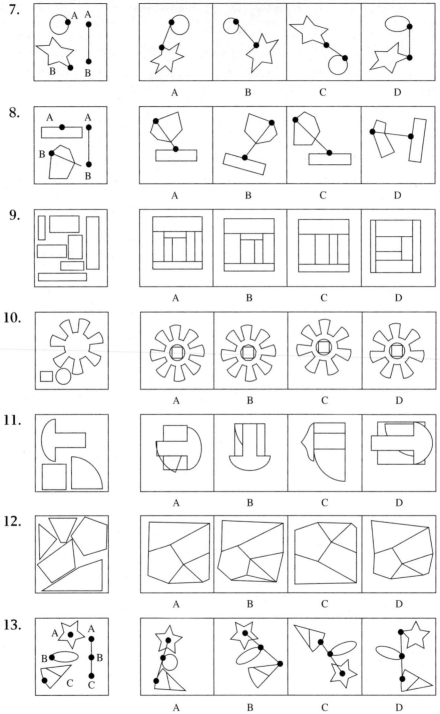

14.

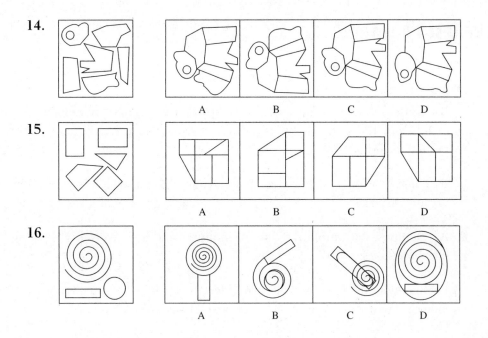

15.

16.

Practice Test 1 Answers

General Science Answers

1. **B.** Viruses do not excrete wastes, but they do carry genetic material in the form of DNA or RNA, and they reproduce and adapt to the environment through natural selection.

2. **B.** Fungi consume the material that surrounds them, which is very often dead organic material.

3. **A.** Octopuses are mollusks, and all mollusks and are invertebrates—they lack backbones.

4. **D.** Energy in the form of ATP, a common "fuel" for cells. Mitochondria also provide cells with energy in the form of NADH and NADPH.

5. **D.** Water erodes rock by all of the methods listed except for conducting heat to rocks.

6. **C.** Marble is a metamorphic rock.

7. **C.** Cargo ship traffic has no measurable effect on how water currents circulate in the ocean.

8. **C.** The exosphere is the outermost layer of the atmosphere, while the stratosphere lies just above the troposphere. The troposphere is the lowest level.

9. **C.** Nitrogen and oxygen comprise about 99% of the earth's atmosphere.

10. **A.** Cloud formation. Water turns into a gas when it evaporates, and it can condense in the atmosphere as clouds. Transpiration is evaporation from the leaves of plants.

11. **C.** Silicon and oxygen are the two most common elements in the earth's crust, making up about 74% of it.

12. **A.** The asteroid belt consists of a large number of small rocky objects that orbit the sun between the orbits of Mars and Jupiter.

13. **D.** The lithosphere is the outermost shell of a rocky planet. On Earth, the lithosphere includes the crust and part of the mantle.

14. **C.** When oxygen is in short supply, muscles use anaerobic respiration, which produces lactic acid.

15. **D.** The red bone marrow of large bones, such as the femur, produces red blood cells.

16. **D.** Plant carbohydrates are in a form called starch, while animals make a carbohydrate called glycogen.

17. **C.** Meiosis. During this process, the cell duplicates its two sets of chromosomes, then divides twice. The resulting four sperm or egg cells then contain one set of chromosomes each, which is one-half the number of chromosomes in ordinary body cells.

18. **A.** X-rays have the shortest wavelength of the set (0.01 to 10 nanometers) and radio waves have the longest (1 millimeter to 100 kilometers).

19. **C.** Rate. Frequency is the number of occurrences of a wave over a certain period of time.

20. **D.** Gravity. The attraction between two objects is proportional to their masses, and inversely proportional to the square of the distance between them.

21. **B.** Protons and electrons. In an atom with no electrical charge, positively charged protons balance the same number of negatively charged electrons.

22. **C.** The atomic number is the number of protons in the nucleus of an atom. The periodic table lists elements in order by atomic number.

23. **C.** One-billionth of a meter. The nanometer is often used for measuring objects at the atomic scale.

24. **A.** Digestion describes how the body breaks down food. The term includes both mechanical means, such as chewing, and chemical means, such enzyme-driven chemical reactions.

25. **C.** If two species in the same community share the same niche, then they prefer the same set of resources, such as food, temperature, water source, and so on. As a result, they are likely to compete for some limited resources, including space.

Arithmetic Reasoning Answers

1. **B.** First, subtract the 125 from the 600 to account for the brother who can't contribute much. This results in 475 and since it will be split equally among the remaining two brothers, they each will contribute 475 ÷ 2 = 237.50.

2. **D.** Since sales tax is ignored, this is the total: 14.5 + 12.50 + 49.99 = 76.84.

3. **A.** To find the average, add the values and divide by the total number of values. In this case, add 45, 30, and 42 to get 117 then divide by 3 to get 39.

4. **A.** Each mile is represented by 1½ inches. To find the total number of miles, figure out how many times 1½ goes into 17¼. In other words, divide:
$$17\frac{1}{4} \div 1\frac{1}{2} = 11\frac{1}{2}.$$

5. **B.** The given speed of the plane is $\dfrac{1960\,\text{miles}}{3\frac{1}{2}\,\text{hours}}$. To find the speed in miles per hour, the denominator must be 1 (for 1 hour); therefore, divide the numerator and the denominator by 3½ miles: $\dfrac{1960\,\text{miles} \div 3\frac{1}{2}}{3\frac{1}{2}\,\text{hours} \div 3\frac{1}{2}} = \dfrac{560\,\text{miles}}{1\,\text{hour}}$.

6. **B.** The easiest way to approach this is to calculate it in pieces. The time until 8 a.m. is 7 minutes. There are then 3 hours until 11 a.m. and 2 minutes until 11:02 a.m. This gives a total of 3 hours 9 minutes.

7. **D.** The difference between 5 and 15 is 10 while the difference between 15 and 35 is 20. Finally, the difference between 35 and 75 is 40. Each time, the difference is doubling which implies the difference between 75 and the next number will be 80.

8. **C.** To find the percentage of a number, convert the percent to a decimal and then multiply. 250 × 0.3 = 75.

9. **D.** 10% of the cost of lunch was $1.75. This means that lunch cost Jackson 175 ÷ 0.10 = 11.75 before the tip. Including the tip, lunch was $13.50. Similarly, dinner was 6 ÷ 0.2 = 30 before the tip and $36 after bringing the total to 13.5 + 36 = 49.5.

10. **B.** This is another example where performing the subtraction is steps is helpful. Subtracting the 7 inches from the 17 feet 2 inches would leave 16 feet 7 inches. Now, subtracting the 3 feet yields the final result of 13 feet 7 inches.

11. **C.** To find the total number of pounds, multiply 23 × (15 lbs 3 ounces). Multiplying the 15 pounds by 23 gives 345 pounds while multiplying the 3 ounces by 23 gives 69 ounces. Since there are 16 ounces in a pound, convert the 69 ounces by dividing to get 4 pounds 5 ounces. Together there are (345 pounds) + (4 pounds 5 ounces) = 349 pounds 5 ounces.

12. **A.** There are 14 days in two weeks. Therefore, Casey walked 112 ÷ 14 = 8 miles each day.

13. **A.** In the morning, there was $\frac{1}{8} \times 410 = 51.25$ gallons in the tank. After the 21 gallons were used, there were 51.25 – 21 = 30.25 gallons remaining.

14. **C.** The number attending the meeting was 3500 ÷ 2 = 1750 and 0.2 × 1750 = 350 voted against the rule change. Therefore, 1750 – 350 = 1400 voted for it.

15. **D.** To find the total amount of sugar needed, multiply the amount used by the number of pounds of dough: $2\frac{1}{4} \times 3\frac{1}{2} = 7\frac{7}{8}$.

16. **B.** Not counting the longest piece, the two smaller pieces are 14 – 6 = 8 feet in length total. Since they are of the same length and there are two of them, they must each be 8 ÷ 2 = 4 feet long.

Word Knowledge Answers

1. **B.** An avocation is something that a person is interested in or does in addition to his job or profession; it is a hobby. If you study the parts of the word it can help you figure out its meaning. The prefix a- means away from while vocation means profession. So the word means away from a profession, another way to say hobby. None of the other choices are correct.

2. **C.** Cumulative means a total; it does not mean last, best or amazing. If you think about the word accumulate, which means amass, you get a clue to the meaning of the word.

3. **D.** The word domineering means overpowering. The word dominate gives you a hint to the meaning of the word. When considering which answer is correct, always look for other words that you know the meaning of that are related to the word in the question.

4. **A.** Stubborn is the correct answer. Words such as tenacity or tentacle might give you a clue to the meaning of the word. It does not mean flexible. That is the opposite of tenacious. Choices C and D are also incorrect.

5. **A.** Choice A is correct. Context clues should help you figure out that Choice B, C, and D are incorrect. Another clue is found in the prefix ex-, which means out of or from and often imports a negative connotation.

6. **D.** Choice D is correct. The prefix in- means not; so does the prefix un-. This is a clue that the words may be related. Context clues do not help a great deal here.

7. **A.** Context clues will help you figure out the meaning of this word if you do not know it. Place the other words where fabricated is in the sentence and see if they make sense. Only made up makes sense there.

8. **A.** Hidden is the correct choice. If you think of the verb elude, which means to get away from, it will help. None of the other words are related to the meaning of elusive.

9. **C.** Dancing is correct. If you think of the word chorus, which has to do with singing, it will point you in the right direction. The other choices are incorrect.

10. **A.** Obstinate is the correct choice. The root dogma, which means strong belief, gives you a clue to the right choice. The other choices are not related to the word.

11. **C.** Mitigate means to make milder or alleviate. There are words which you will need to memorize to know their meaning. This is one of them. So it is important to review lists with words and their definitions. That is one way to build vocabulary.

12. **B.** Amnesty is a pardon, typically granted by a government. Don't be confused by choice C just because it also begins with the letter a. This is another example of a word that needs to be memorized.

13. **D.** Choice D is correct. A cohort is a companion or partner. The prefix co- means together and helps you to find the correct meaning. The other choices do not make any sense if used in the sentence.

14. **C.** Magnanimous means generous. Context clues do not help with this word, which comes from the combination of two Latin words: magna meaning great and animus meaning soul or mind. Reviewing word lists will help build your vocabulary.

15. **B.** Choice B is correct. Fondle means to stroke or handle with kindness. The adjective fond meaning liking helps in determining the correct definition.

16. **D.** A soliloquy is a monologue in which a person talks to himself or herself, often used in drama and literature. The prefix soli- should provide a clue since it is similar to solo, or alone. The other choices are not related to the meaning of soliloquy.

17. **B.** Probity means complete integrity. It is another word that needs to be memorized.

18. **C.** Choice C is correct. Trenchant is an adjective meaning forceful or cutting, as a trenchant argument. Nothing can help you figure out its meaning, so be sure to review word lists before you take your exam.

19. **D.** Jocund means lighthearted. The words jolly or jocular might give you a clue to its meaning.

20. **A.** An iconoclast is a person who destroys things, often religious images or ideas. The word icon, or image, provides a small clue.

21. **C.** Choice C is correct. Something similar is said to be homogeneous. The prefix homo-, which means same or like, is your clue here.

22. **C.** Indigent means needy or poor and comes from a Latin word meaning needy person. This is another word that just has to be learned.

23. **A.** 23. The adjective exemplary means commendable, worthy of noticing. The prefix ex- meaning out of doesn't offer much help here.

24. **C.** Garrulous describes a person who is talkative. Since any of the other choices could fit in the sentence, the meaning has to be learned.

25. **D.** A polyglot is a person who can speak and write multiple languages. The prefix poly- means one of many and provides you with a clue to the correct choice. It is important to review prefixes and suffixes to learn their meanings so you can analyze words.

26. **A.** Choice A is correct; puerile means childish or immature. It comes from a Latin word for child. Context clues do not help in this instance. However, a knowledge of roots would help.

27. **C.** Vertiginous means dizzy or affected by vertigo. Some of you might be familiar with the word vertigo. That would give you a good clue about the word's meaning. The context of the sentence does not help with this one.

28. **B.** Corroborate is a verb synonymous with confirm and means to support with other evidence. The other choices are incorrect. The co- prefix could help you figure this one out.

29. **D.** Choice D is correct. Carnage means slaughter, usually in a large scale and in a war. The word has a Latin root that means flesh.

30. **C.** C is the correct choice. Ameliorate means improve or make better. It is another word that needs to be memorized so make sure to review word lists with definitions. Reading also helps you develop a good vocabulary.

31. **B.** Diminutive means tiny or very small. You might see part of the root minute in the word. Minute means almost the same thing as diminutive.

32. **D.** Choice D is correct. Acclimate means to get used to or adjust to a new environment. The presence of the word climate could offer a clue along with the prefix a-, meaning to or towards.

33. **C.** C is the correct choice. Amiable is the word most opposite in meaning to querulous, which means argumentative. The word quarrel might help you understand the meaning of querulous. Then you would be able to choose the word that means the opposite. Amiable which means friendly comes from a Latin root meaning friend.

34. **D.** Choice D is correct. Wreak means to cause or bring about. It comes from an Old English word. You need to know this one.

35. **B.** Choice B is correct. Maudlin is to be overemotional or weepy. Yet another word that needs to be learned.

Paragraph Comprehension Answers

1. **A.** The Underground Railroad could only be accessed by some slaves, not all, so choice A is an incorrect statement. Choice B is a correct statement, as is choice C. Choice D is not correct.

2. **C.** According to the passage, scientists are looking for the building blocks of the universe, sub-atomic particles. They are not looking for an atom smasher since they have one. The atom smasher can create the conditions that existed when the universe started, so this is incorrect. Scientists are not looking to find out what happened before the Big Bang either.

3. **B.** The last sentence states that Congress founded Fannie Mae, making choice B an incorrect statement. The others are all accurate.

4. **C.** The primary purpose of this passage is to describe and define tornadoes; several characteristics of tornadoes are given. Choices A, B, and C are relate to tornadoes, but are not the purpose of the passage.

5. **B.** The first sentence states that soldiers would spend a one-year hardship tour without their families. Later in the paragraph, it states that the tours were longer. Neither choice A nor C is correct.

6. **D.** The fourth sentence states that soldiers and their families are fully supported at Red Cloud, as they would be at any garrison in the world. Choice A is clearly incorrect as is choice B. The normalization program was not in Red Cloud; Red Cloud came about because of the normalization program.

7. **C.** The third sentence states that Napoleon stole works of art from other European countries during wars with those countries, so choice C is correct. There is no suggestion that choice A is correct. While the Louvre was built in the Middle Ages, there is no reason to believe that choice B is correct.

8. **C.** The second sentence states that a bit more than half of the tracks are underground. If you do the math you will find that 443 is 53% of the tracks.

9. **B.** The passage states in the first sentence that one cannot use a married filing separately status and qualify for the Earned Income Tax Credit (EITC). The other statements are correct.

10. **D.** The last sentence states that income earned in a penal institution does not qualify as earned income and that person would not be able to apply for the EITC.

11. **B.** The passage clearly communicates the idea that Zumba is different because of the combination of Latin dance steps and aerobics. Teachers do not improvise in a Zumba class since the steps are set up. Choices C and D are not correct either.

12. **D.** The expression "two left feet" refers to someone who is clumsy and not a good dancer. All of the other choices are incorrect.

13. **D.** All of the statements are directly supported by the passage.

14. **A.** The primary theme is stated in the first sentence. Protector is closest in meaning to caregiver, a person who gives care, or protects, another.

15. **D.** This is stated in the passage. The other options are done by the caregiver or other agencies. Choice A is performed by the AARP. Choices B and C are performed by the caregiver.

Mathematics Knowledge Answers

1. **A.** Apply the distributive property and then solve as a typical linear equation.

    $$3(x+2) = 6$$
    $$3x + 6 = 6$$
    $$3x = 0$$
    $$x = 0$$

2. **B.** Plug in the values to the corresponding variables and be sure to follow the order of operations.

    $$-1(2-1)-2$$
    $$= -1(-1)-2$$
    $$= 1-2$$
    $$= -1$$

3. **B.** All right triangles have an angle of 90° and the sum of the angles in any triangle is 180°. Since one angle is 30° and the other angle is 90°, the last angle must be $180° - 30° - 90° = 60°$

4. **B.** The area of a triangle is πr^2 where r is the radius. If the diameter is 6, the radius is 3 and the area is $\pi \times 3^2 = 9\pi$.

5. **A.** Factoring both terms results in the expression $x(x-1)^2 \div x(x-1) = x - 1$.

6. **D.** Divide both sides by –2 to solve and be careful to flip the inequality since you are dividing by a negative number.

    $$-2x \geq 6$$
    $$x \leq -3$$

7. **A.** In general, it is not true that $\sqrt{x^2 + y^2} = x + y$. By the order of operations, perform the operations within the square root first.

    $$\sqrt{3^2 + 4^2} = \sqrt{9+16} = \sqrt{25} = 5$$

8. **A.** Complementary angles have a sum of 90°. Therefore the measure of angle A is $90° - 20° = 70°$.

9. **A.** Let the first integer be represented by x. The next two will then be $x + 1$ and $x + 2$. The fact that the sum is 24 results in the equation $x + (x + 1) + (x + 2) = 24$ which has a solution of $x = 7$.

10. **C.** Distribute the negative and then add:

$$(x^2 + 4x - 1) - (x - 5) =$$
$$x^2 + 4x - 1 - x + 5 =$$
$$x^2 + 3x + 4$$

11. **C.** Let the width be represented by x. Then, the length will be $3x$ and the area will be $3x^2 = 48$. Solving this equation results in $x = 4$ which is the measure of the width. Therefore, the length is $3 \times 4 = 12$.

12. **B.** The ladder and the wall make a right triangle with a hypotenuse of 10 feet and a leg of 6 feet. For any right triangle, $a^2 + b^2 = c^2$ where c is the length of the hypotenuse. In this case:

$$6^2 + b^2 = 10^2$$
$$36 + b^2 = 100$$
$$b^2 = 64$$
$$b = 8$$

13. **C.** Multiplying both sides of the equation by 20 will clear the fractions:

$$20\left(\frac{x}{5} + \frac{x}{4}\right) = 20 \times 9$$
$$4x + 5x = 180$$
$$9x = 180$$
$$x = 20$$

14. **A.** Coin flips are independent, which means you can multiply the probability of tails on a single flip by itself 3 times: $\frac{1}{2} \times \frac{1}{2} \times \frac{1}{2} = \frac{1}{8}$.

15. **C.** The sum of a number and 4 can be represented by $x + 4$ while 3 times a number can be represented as $3x$. Finally, the "is" can be represented by an equals sign.

16. **C.** Use F.O.I.L. (first, outer, inner, last):

$$(3x + 4)(2x - 5) =$$
$$6x^2 - 15x + 8x - 20 =$$
$$6x^2 - 7x - 20$$

Electronics Answers

1. **B.** Using Ohm's law, $R = V/I$, so $12V/2 = 6$ ohms resistance.

2. **D.** DC (direct current) voltage only flows in one direction regardless of voltage or resistance.

3. **B.** Fuse

4. **A.** A diode allows electrical current to pass only in one direction.

5. **C.** Resistance is color coded on resistors with a series of standardized colored bands describing their ohmic rating. Refer to a table or chart for their specific explanation.

6. **A.** Using Ohm's law, $V/R = I$, so $110V/10$ ohms $= 11$ amps current.

7. **B.** Neutral is always indicated by white, while both black and red can indicate positive. Green or bare wires are used for ground.

8. **A.** An ampmeter measures amps, the unit of measurement that describes current force or flow through a circuit.

9. **D.** Landscape lighting plugs into standard household current of 120V and uses a transformer to drop the voltage to 12V to actually power the LED lights.

10. **C.** A DVOM, or Digital Volt Ohm Meter, is a diagnostic tool and has no ability to control circuits.

11. **D.** Rubber is an insulator, but fragile. Leather helps protect the rubber from damage so that the insulating barrier is maintained.

12. **B**

13. **D.** This depicts a 2-cell battery. (A) represents DC supply, (B) is a fuse , and (C) is a lamp.

14. **A.** (D) is possible but not necessary.

15. **C.** All of the other options are wrong and you should only work on a disabled AC circuit containing no voltage.

16. **C.** Using Watt's law, $I \times V = P$, so $20 \times 120 = 2400$ watts.

Automotive Answers

1. **D.** Relay, switch, and fuse are all electrical parts affecting the radio's function, but a bushing is a mechanical part that connects components in a somewhat flexible way.

2. **B.** (A) defines an alternator, the climate control system regulates climate, and (D) defines a differential.

3. **B.** Two, because a 4-wheel vehicle has two driveshafts, one transferring power to the front wheels, and the other to the rear wheels.

4. **A.** Co-dependent is not a style of suspension. Independent, semi-independent, multi-link and torsion bar are all some of the many types of suspension.

5. **D.** The exhaust manifold collects exhaust from all of the engine cylinders into a single exhaust pipe.

6. **A.** The camshaft opens the intake and exhaust valves, whereas the crankshaft moves the pistons. Camshafts are part of the engine, and NOT directly linked to the cooling or starting systems.

7. **C.** Secondary ignition refers to the high-voltage part of an ignition system needed to form the arc of electricity at the spark plug.

8. **B.** A super-charger is a belt driven air pump used to force air into the intake manifold.

9. **D.** Neither, because a 50/50 mixture of coolant and water lowers the freezing point and raises the boiling point of water.

10. **A.** An idler arm and center link are found only in gearbox systems. Tie rods are found in rack and pinion steering system as well as gearbox systems.

11. **A.** A brake drum is a friction component of the brake system, but the wheel cylinder, master cylinder, and brake calipers are all hydraulic.

12. **B.** The spark plug must be threaded into the engine so the spark can be delivered to the combustion chamber.

13. **C.** 16:1 is higher than the ideal 14.7:1 ratio, indicating too much oxygen, or a "lean" mixture.

Shop Answers

1. **D.** Material choice determines the substances present, and MSDS gives you more information about the hazards, and the NIOSH ratings of respirators help you to make an informed decision.

2. **B.** A center punch will only make a dent, a stepped bit is for metal, and the chuck is a part of the drill itself.

3. **D.** Oxy-acetylene uses only oxygen and acetylene gases. The three other types of welding listed use electricity to create an arc.

4. **C.** The tools listed are all used for metal working.

5. **B**

6. **C**

7. **C.** Where the tiles are used has no effect on how they are cut and a standard tile saw fitted with a disc blade cannot cut curves. Mixing the mortar is an entirely separate operation from cutting the tiles.

8   **B.** Orbital, because it is appropriate for small jobs and detail work. A drum sander has a cylindrical abrasive surface inappropriate for use on a tabletop, and a floor sander would be too big. A bench sander would be impossible to use in this situation.

9. **D.** The hammering action of an impact wrench aids in removing tight bolts. The chisel is a cutting tool. The ratchet and socket can remove bolts, but lack the added benefit of "shaking" tight bolts loose.

10. **A**

11. **A.** A rip saw is used for wood, a utility knife works best with soft material, and a vise is for clamping.

12. **B.** A Japanese saw is specifically for fine cuts in wood, while A, C, and D can all be used to shape metal.

Mechanical Comprehension Answers

1. **C.** Displacement has a magnitude (distance) and a direction.

2. **D.** Acceleration is the change in velocity (+30 m/s) divided by the time interval (2 s), which comes out to be +15 m/s².

3. **C.** The bungee jumper is free-falling and accelerating due to the force of gravity. According to Newton's Second Law, because he is accelerating, he has a net force acting upon him.

4. **A.** Drag is a force of friction caused by the molecules of a fluid colliding against an object moving within the fluid.

5. **B.** Weight is the product of mass and acceleration due to gravity. So, the 30-kg child has a weight of approximately e00 N (W = (30kg)(10 m/s²) = 300 N).

6. **D.** The action force is the firing of the shell. According to Newton's Third Law, the reaction force is the recoil of the cannon.

7. **C.** Arrow A is the upward support force exerted by the floor on the box and opposing the weight. It is the normal force.

8. **C.** While at the top of the hill, the package has potential energy by virtue of its height, but no kinetic energy. According to the principle of conservation of energy, as the ball travels downhill, its kinetic energy increases to maximum, while the potential energy decreases to zero.

9. **C.** The masses are balanced, so the torques must be equal. The force acting on the lever arm of the unknown mass is half that of the 5 kg mass, so the unknown mass must be twice the 5-kg mass or 10 kg.

10. **D.** Work is the product of force (50 N) times the distance over which it is applied (10 m), which is 500 J.

11. **B.** A wheelbarrow is an example of a class 2 lever.

12. **C.** The crossed belt between Pulley A and B will cause Pulley B to turn in the opposite direction of Pulley A. Pulleys C and D will turn in the same direction as Pulley B (i.e. opposite Pulley A). However because Pulley D is smaller, it will turn at a faster rate.

13. **C.** Bicycles use wheels and axles (the wheels and pedals), belts (chains), and gears to change the input force. So, they are compound machines.

14. **A.** The mechanical advantage is the ratio of the output force to the input force. If MA >1, then the output force is greater than the input force.

15. **D.** Pressure is equal to the applied force (10 N) divided by the area (0.1 m²), which is 100 Pa.

16. **D.** The multiplication factor of force in a hydraulic press is the ratio of the area of the second piston to the first. In this case, that ratio is 100. So, the output force will be 100 times the input force.

Assembling Objects Answers

1. C

2. A

3. B

4. A

5. D

6. A

7. C

8. B

9. B

10. D

11. B

12. A

13. C

14. C

15. D

16. A

chapter 21

ASVAB Practice Test 2

General Science Questions

1. A geoduck is a bivalve mollusk, so it has
   A. webbed feet
   B. a backbone
   C. plumage
   D. a shell

2. Which of the following major kingdoms of organisms contains prokaryotes?
   A. Protista
   B. Plantae
   C. Fungi
   D. Bacteria

3. Protists are usually
   A. single-celled organisms that lack membrane-bound organelles
   B. single-celled eukaryotes
   C. multicelled organisms that have membrane-bound organelles
   D. multicelled prokaryotes

4. Carbohydrates are composed of long strings of
   A. lipids
   B. nucleotide bases
   C. sugar molecules
   D. amino acids

5. Where they diverge, two continental plates can form a
   A. mountain range
   B. trench
   C. thick crust
   D. transform boundary

6. Tidal waves are most often caused by
   A. tides
   B. shifting tectonic plates
   C. climate change
   D. meteorological conditions

7. Cirrus clouds are
    A. fluffy and rounded, but flat at the bottom
    B. wispy and high-altitude
    C. low-altitude and flattened
    D. ground-level fog

8. A great deal of ultraviolet radiation is absorbed by the ozone layer, which is located in the
    A. mesosphere
    B. troposphere
    C. exosphere
    D. stratosphere

9. Warm air masses are most likely to form near
    A. the North or South Poles
    B. the equator
    C. large land masses
    D. the jet stream

10. Of the following, the rock type most likely to have formed on the earth's surface is
    A. peridotite
    B. sedimentary rock
    C. intrusive igneous rock
    D. metamorphic rock

11. Two planets do not have a moon, including
    A. Mars
    B. Saturn
    C. Mercury
    D. Jupiter

12. Which of the following sequences of objects is arranged from closest to farthest from Earth?
    A. The sun, the moon, the star Proxima Centauri
    B. The moon, the sun, Neptune
    C. The sun, the star Proxima Centauri, Neptune
    D. Venus, the moon, the sun

13. After the moon, the brightest natural object that can be seen in the night sky is
    A. the North Star
    B. Alpha Centauri
    C. Venus
    D. Jupiter

14. The eye's retina distinguishes different colors of light using its
    A. cones
    B. rods
    C. melanin
    D. axons

15. Certain white blood cells create special proteins that stick to foreign molecules, including those on the surface of invading viruses and bacteria. These proteins are called
    A. myelin sheaths
    B. polymerases
    C. antibodies
    D. reductases

16. In humans, after blood picks up oxygen in the lungs, the first organ it travels to is the
    A. heart
    B. brain
    C. liver
    D. kidneys

17. The equation F = ma shows the relationship between force,
    A. mass, and acceleration
    B. meters, and acceleration
    C. mass, and action
    D. meters, and attenuation

18. Of the following materials, the LEAST suitable electrical insulator is
    A. glass
    B. copper
    C. rubber
    D. air

19. Which of the following is the correct definition of acceleration?
    A. (change in position)/(time)
    B. (change in direction)/(time)
    C. (change in velocity)/(time)
    D. (change in momentum)/(time)

20. When torque is applied to an object, it tends to
    A. move in a straight line
    B. rotate around an axis
    C. accelerate toward the center of rotation
    D. gain mass

21. A liquid with a pH of 3 is
    A. basic
    B. alkaline
    C. acidic
    D. neutral

22. Absolute zero is defined as a temperature of zero in
    A. Celsius
    B. Fahrenheit
    C. Newton
    D. Kelvin

23. Which of the following chemical formulas describes sodium chloride, commonly known as table salt?
    A. $CaCl_2$
    B. $NaCl$
    C. $CaSO_4$
    D. KCl

24. The central nervous system includes the brain and the
    A. heart
    B. skull
    C. spinal cord
    D. muscles

25. The bacterium known as blue-green algae performs photosynthesis, which means it is a
    A. producer
    B. primary consumer
    C. secondary consumer
    D. decomposer

Arithmetic Reasoning Questions

1. A wall measures 8 feet tall by 11 feet long. How many square feet of wallpaper must be used to cover this wall completely?
   A. 19 square feet
   B. 38 square feet
   C. 56 square feet
   D. 88 square feet

2. Manny ran 14 miles one week, 12 miles the next week, and 16 miles the third week. On average, how many miles did Manny run per week?
   A. 10.3 miles
   B. 14.0 miles
   C. 15.1 miles
   D. 42.0 miles

3. A car rental is charged at $15.95 a day plus $0.20 per mile. If a 5-day rental cost $87.15, how many miles was the car driven?
   A. 35.6 miles
   B. 37.0 miles
   C. 41.0 miles
   D. 43.5 miles

4. What is the next number in the sequence: 1500, 300, 60
   A. 0
   B. 12
   C. 30
   D. 1800

5. Randi ran 2 miles in 15 minutes. What was Randi's speed in miles per hour?
   A. 4 mph
   B. 7.5 mph
   C. 8 mph
   D. 30 mph

6. An office supply shipment cost a total of $450.20 and included copy paper which accounted for ¼th the cost of the order. How much was the copy paper?
   A. $112.55
   B. $225.10
   C. $337.65
   D. $415.80

7. At a particular station, gas costs $3.45 per gallon. If it cost $51.75 to fill a tank, how many gallons of gas can the tank hold?
   A. 10
   B. 15
   C. 20
   D. 25

8. A large refrigerator contains 480 pounds of produce. About half of the produce is potatoes and carrots while about a third is tomatoes. The remainder is broccoli. How many pounds of broccoli is in the refrigerator?
   A. 80 pounds
   B. 160 pounds
   C. 240 pounds
   D. 400 pounds

9. In the past, 3 out of every 10 people fail a certain physical test. Out of 2,400 people, how many can be expected to pass the test?
   A. 343
   B. 720
   C. 800
   D. 1680

10. $5\dfrac{1}{4} \div 2\dfrac{4}{5} =$

   A. $1\dfrac{7}{8}$

   B. $2\dfrac{1}{2}$

   C. $7\dfrac{2}{5}$

   D. $10\dfrac{1}{5}$

11. A rectangular garden has an area of 156 square feet including a 1-foot irrigation trench that surrounds the entire garden. If the length of the garden is 13 feet when the trench is included, what is the area of the garden without the trench?
    A. 104 square feet
    B. 132 square feet
    C. 152 square feet
    D. 208 square feet

12. Three roommates plan to split a movie collection containing 152 different titles. Since one roommate is owed money by the other two, he will get to have 80 of the movies. The rest of the collection will be split evenly by the other two. How many movies will each of the remaining roommates get to keep?
    A. 20
    B. 36
    C. 40
    D. 72

13. A father agrees to pay 85% of the down payment on his son's new car once he graduates high school. If the down payment is $1,200, how much will the father contribute?
    A. $102
    B. $180
    C. $1,020
    D. $1,098

14. A scale model of a skyscraper is to be built such that one foot is represented by ¾ inches. If the actual skyscraper is 864 feet tall, how tall will the model be?
    A. 648 inches
    B. 896 inches
    C. 1,152 inches
    D. 2, 592 inches

15. A flight leaves Chicago, IL, at 1:45 p.m. local time and arrives in Los Angeles, CA, at 3:35 p.m. local time. Los Angeles is in the Pacific time zone, which is 2 hours behind the Central time zone where Chicago is located. How long was the flight?
    A. 1 hour 50 minutes
    B. 2 hours 50 minutes
    C. 3 hours 50 minutes
    D. 4 hours 50 minutes

16. A purchase order is made for $45.06 in supplies, $86.12 in equipment, and $12.98 for other items. In total, how much will the order cost?
    A. $108.16
    B. $133.06
    C. $144.16
    D. $154.26

Word Knowledge Questions

This test is about the meanings of words. Each question has an underlined word. You may be asked to decide which one of the four words in the choices is a synonym or most nearly means the same thing as the underlined word. It may ask which one of the four words means the opposite. Some of the underlined words are used in sentences. In this case decide which of the four choices most nearly means the same thing as the underlined word as used in the context of the sentence.

1. Lithe most nearly means
   A. lazy
   B. supple
   C. polite
   D. amusing

2. The meaning was clearly intrinsic.
   A. invented
   B. unintelligible
   C. interesting
   D. inborn

3. Propensity most nearly means
   A. tendency
   B. education
   C. eloquence
   D. expanse

4. Oscar had the prescience to lunge left for the ball.
   A. formula
   B. education
   C. problem
   D. forethought

5. Justin was not being pragmatic about the situation.
   A. enigmatic
   B. serious
   C. practical
   D. profound

6. <u>Obdurate</u> most nearly means
    A. scholarly
    B. unbending
    C. expensive
    D. intricate

7. <u>Sporadic</u> most nearly means
    A. painful
    B. erratic
    C. ironic
    D. restful

8. <u>Bellicose</u> most nearly means
    A. imaginary
    B. brave
    C. hostile
    D. dishonest

9. <u>Auspicious</u> most nearly means
    A. favorable
    B. stressful
    C. playful
    D. sharp

10. <u>Remonstrate</u> most nearly means
    A. complain
    B. excuse
    C. object
    D. bore

11. She was pleased with how <u>intrepid</u> she had remained in spite of the great danger the ship faced.
    A. fragile
    B. cooperative
    C. personable
    D. fearless

12. He was surprised how <u>voluble</u> his little brother had become.
    A. loud
    B. fluent
    C. sentimental
    D. secretive

13. The word most opposite in meaning to <u>bucolic</u> is
    A. practical
    B. straightforward
    C. urban
    D. careful

14. Ted's <u>sojourn</u> lasted much longer than he expected.
    A. morning
    B. examination
    C. rehearsal
    D. stay

15. She felt the others were trying to <u>ostracize</u> her.
    A. defend
    B. exclude
    C. criticize
    D. subdue

16. Not many of them realized that an <u>exigency</u> already existed and someone had to take action.
    A. crisis
    B. escape
    C. solution
    D. excess

17. <u>Ablution</u> most nearly means
    A. forgetfulness
    B. washing
    C. melody
    D. admittance

18. Apprise most nearly means
    A. connect
    B. assign
    C. evaluate
    D. inform

19. Recondite most nearly means
    A. resilient
    B. raffish
    C. obscure
    D. interested

20. Sanguine most nearly means
    A. confident
    B. competitive
    C. clean
    D. interesting

21. Scion most nearly means
    A. flaw
    B. friend
    C. heir
    D. tone

22. They were afraid that Jay was no longer lucid about who he was.
    A. serious
    B. relaxed
    C. effective
    D. clear

23. Pamela was quite circumspect about the situation.
    A. prudent
    B. evasive
    C. curious
    D. secretive

24. The young man worked hard to <u>burnish</u> the coffee table so that it would look good for the party.
    A. damage
    B. rearrange
    C. polish
    D. position

25. Jose always enjoyed the <u>halcyon</u> days of late spring.
    A. warm
    B. tranquil
    C. lengthening
    D. rainy

26. <u>Harbinger</u> most nearly means
    A. girlfriend
    B. complaint
    C. musical
    D. forerunner

27. <u>Lassitude</u> most nearly means
    A. tiredness
    B. melody
    C. complaint
    D. anger

28. <u>Postulate</u> most nearly means
    A. orate
    B. gesture
    C. presume
    D. educate

29. <u>Motley</u> most nearly means
    A. gentle
    B. diverse
    C. obsessive
    D. tired

30. Everyone thought that Gabe's demeanor was very <u>torpid</u>.
    A. inactive
    B. serious
    C. tense
    D. assertive

31. <u>Scurrilous</u> most nearly means
    A. vocal
    B. insulting
    C. poor
    D. exhausted

32. <u>Rescind</u> most nearly means
    A. repeal
    B. complain
    C. inform
    D. urge

33. <u>Inured</u> most nearly means
    A. tested
    B. cleaned
    C. accustomed
    D. secretive

34. <u>Unwonted</u> most nearly means
    A. unnecessary
    B. cheap
    C. defiant
    D. unusual

35. <u>Fruition</u> most nearly means
    A. dedication
    B. accomplishment
    C. consequence
    D. tension

Paragraph Comprehension Questions

1. Beryl Markham was an incredible woman. After learning to fly, she decided she wanted to be the first woman to fly alone across the Atlantic. One person had already flown across the ocean. That was Charles Lindbergh; he flew from the United States to England in 1927. Beryl wanted to go the opposite way, which was a much more difficult feat since the prevailing winds are westerly. At 8 p.m., September 4, 1936, Beryl flew out of London in a Vera Gull single-engine airplane. The trip was not uneventful. Some 20 hours later, she realized her fuel line was frozen so she crash landed in a peat bog on Cape Breton Island, Nova Scotia. She survived the crash. As she got out of the plane, she spied two fishermen, whom she told, "I'm Mrs. Markham. I've just flown from England." Beryl became an instant celebrity as a result of her flight. In New York City, a ticker tape parade was held in her honor.

    Beryl Markham is famous for

    A. flying across the Atlantic in the opposite direction
    B. being honored with a ticker tape parade
    C. crashing in a peat bog
    D. being the first woman to fly solo across the ocean

2. Before the invention of the metric system in the 18th century, a truly accurate and scientific measurement system did not exist. Most units of measure used before the metric system were based on body measurements and, as such, varied from country to country. The idea of basing a unit of measure on a man's finger, palm, or foot began in ancient times. We know from the Bible that King Solomon's temple was measured in "cubits," a unit of measure based on the distance between a man's middle finger and his elbow. The length of a man's foot gave us the unit of measure we call a foot, and this unit was used by the early Romans. In England, it is said that the yard was measured by the length of a king's arm and that the pound as a unit of weight originated from a king's tankard of ale. These stories may not be true. However, we know that body measurements played an important role in shaping the English system of measurement that we use in the United States today.

Which of the following best expresses the main idea of the passage?

A. In ancient times measurements were established by kings and political leaders.
B. Most of the measurement systems used by early societies were based on body measurements.
C. In the old days measurement systems were inaccurate and led to arguments.
D. King Solomon's temple was measured in "cubits."

3. The Medal of Honor, which dates back to 1861 when it was authorized, is this country's highest medal for valor in combat that can be awarded to members of the armed forces. Since its inception more than 3,400 Medals of Honor have been awarded to members of the military services and the Coast Guard.

   The medal is not awarded often and goes only to those who are the bravest of the brave. Take for instance the example of Pvt. Joseph E. Brandle of the 17th Michigan infantry, who was the color bearer, one of the most dangerous and important duties, during a Civil War battle that took place near Lenoir, Tennessee, in 1863. Brandle, who was out front and drawing heavy enemy fire, held the flag high even though he had been wounded twice and lost the sight in one eye. He kept going until he was ordered to the rear by his regimental commander. Brandle is just one example of the kind of bravery the recipients of this medal demonstrate.

   Which of the following statements isn't true?

A. Those who serve in the Coast Guard are not eligible for a Medal of Honor.
B. The Medal of Honor goes only to individuals who display exceptional bravery.
C. The Medal of Honor dates back to the Civil War.
D. Joseph Brandle was a private in the Michigan infantry.

4. People have been debating the pros and cons of buying a newly constructed home over buying an older home for many years. There have been many obvious drawbacks to older houses that are still the same today, like too few and too small closets, and the absence of grounded electrical wiring. The modern family, with home office, computer lines,

faxes, copier/printers, home entertainment systems, gaming platforms and smart phone rechargers can feel challenged, even frustrated, in a home with outdated wiring. Unlined chimneys in older homes can pose a fire threat. And galvanized plumbing can rust and fail, leading to costly repairs. Drafty, single-glazed windows are uncomfortable in the winter months. Kitchens are often small, with not enough storage space.

The author of this passage believes that

A. There is evidence that older homes are unsafe.
B. Galvanized plumbing costs less to install than copper plumbing.
C. Today's families could feel disappointed with the outmoded wiring of an old house.
D. Unlined chimneys can be drafty and uncomfortable.

Questions 5 and 6 are based on the following passage:

South Dakota was the home of the great Sioux Nation. In all, there were about 20,000 Sioux in 7 different tribes throughout the Great Plains. They were nomads riding the plains on horses that were brought to this country by the Spanish in 1519. With horses, they could easily hunt buffalo, and transport their teepees and equipment from place to place. The Sioux were their own masters, roaming freely and coming and going as they pleased. Their lives were based on hunting and gathering foodstuffs and caring for their young. They passed the time too by telling the stories that were the foundation of their civilization. Their central belief was the principle of living in harmony with nature and the environment. Through their relationship with nature and particularly the animals they hunted, the Sioux developed a unique and sophisticated culture.

5. The great Sioux Nation was characterized by
   A. their large numbers
   B. living in harmony with their environment
   C. settling in one place
   D. all of the above

6. Why were the Sioux their own masters?
    A. They rode horses brought to this country by the Spanish.
    B. They used buffalo for many things.
    C. They were able to roam about as they wished.
    D. They were spread across the Great Plains.

7. The Chesapeake Bay Bridge-Tunnel is a four-lane 20-mile-long crossing of the lower Chesapeake Bay. It is the main north-south highway on Virginia's Eastern Shore. The crossing consists of a series of low-level bridges interrupted by two approximately one-mile-long tunnels beneath the Thimble Shoals and Chesapeake navigation channels. Manmade islands, each about 5 acres in size, are located at each end of the two tunnels. There are also high level bridges over two other navigation channels: North Channel Bridge and Fisherman Inlet Bridge. Finally, between North Channel and Fisherman Inlet, the facility crosses at-grade over Fisherman Island, a barrier island which includes the Fisherman Island National Wildlife Refuge. Toll collection facilities are located at each end of the facility.

    Which of the following statements isn't supported by the above passage?

    A. The crossing has five islands.
    B. There are two manmade islands.
    C. Two navigation channels have high level bridges.
    D. The crossing is a toll road.

8. The American Opportunity Tax Credit modifies existing education tax credits. The new credit makes the Hope Credit available to a wider range of taxpayers, including those with higher incomes and those who owe no tax. In addition it adds required course materials to the list of qualifying expenses. The credit can now be claimed for four post-secondary education years instead of two. The maximum annual tax credit is $2,500 per student. The credit is available to anyone with a modified adjusted gross income of $80,000 or less, or $160,000 or less for married couples filing a joint return. The credit is phased out for those with higher incomes.

A married couple who file a joint tax return have an adjusted gross income of $163,500. They have a daughter who is a sophomore at college. They are eligible for a Hope Tax Credit of

A. no credit
B. $2,500
C. $5,000
D. The question can't be answered based on the information contained in the passage.

Questions 9 and 10 are based on the following passage:

While state schools are more affordable than four-year colleges, community colleges are still less expensive. They also tend to have courses geared toward the practical as well as the liberal arts. For people considering sending a child to college, it might be a good idea for them to ask themselves how academically motivated their child is and if their child is ready to be on his or her own. Community colleges are usually more informal than state schools. There are fewer students, and the class size is generally smaller. It certainly represents a more protected atmosphere, since most community college students live at home not on campus. Of course the child may see this as a drawback. State schools are just the opposite. Most state schools require that freshmen live on campus. In general the findings have been that students living on campus do better academically than those who are not. While campus life offers the student a chance to become more independent, it also offers more chances for experimentation. This can be a positive thing or could also make a child more vulnerable.

9. A college-aged student could find a disadvantage in
    A. being motivated
    B. lack of liberal arts courses
    C. having to live at home
    D. smaller class size

10. Over the years, state schools have found that
    A. students avoid practical courses
    B. students like to experiment
    C. students prefer a protected atmosphere
    D. students perform better when living on campus

Questions 11 and 12 are based on the following passage:

Getting pre-approved for a mortgage from your lender helps you in two ways. First, you know how much of a house payment you can afford, and therefore, what selling price is your uppermost limit. Secondly, having a formal pre-approval letter in hand shows sellers that you are serious, and that the deal will not fall through in the end. Your lender will go over your financial picture. She will ask for proof of income (usually the two most recent pay stubs) and get your permission to run a tri-merge credit report. There are three credit reporting agencies—Equifax, Experian and Trans Union. Each one will generate a credit score for you called a FICO score (named after the Fair Isaac Company who originated the formulas for calculating a score, which ranges from the lowest of 350 to the highest of 850).

The middle score is used as your qualifying score in regards to your credit worthiness. Most lenders will want to see a score of at least 660. Based on the information obtained, she will add up all your regular monthly obligations for car payments, student loans and credit card or installment debt. This will be added to the proposed monthly payment for your housing: principal, interest, and mortgage insurance, if applicable, and 1/12 of the property taxes and homeowners insurance (known as PITI). The total is then divided by your gross (before-tax) monthly income which gives a percentage known as the Debt to Income Ratio (DTI). That ratio generally should be no more than 35%.

11. The purpose of running a tri-merge report is
    A. to determine your DTI
    B. to determine your housing payment
    C. to determine your gross monthly income
    D. to determine your credit scores

12. A potential buyer has found a home he likes. Running the numbers, his lender finds that the buyer's proposed DTI would be 49%. The buyer should

    A. try to increase his FICO score
    B. look for a less expensive house
    C. go to another lender
    D. ask for a formal pre-approval letter

Questions 13 through 15 are based on the following passage:

Edgar Degas is one of the world's most famous artists. He was a member of the school of artists known as the Impressionists who began working in a very different style in the second half of the 19th century. They broke with tradition. Instead of painting pictures of rich or famous people, or scenes from history or the Bible, they painted scenes from daily life. They used bright colors, blurred the edges of objects, and used streaks of color, creating a sense of movement and natural light. Degas painted horses, racecourses, and beautifully dressed spectators at these events. He also painted female ballet dancers. He painted people in their homes and gardens, in music halls and in cafes.

Like other Impressionists he experimented with the composition of his pictures. Sometimes it would look as if part of the picture was cut off or cropped at the edges. Sometimes the angle from which the subject was viewed would be very unusual. In his forties Degas' vision became poor. He began to work more as a sculptor because he could feel his work. His bronze statues of ballerinas, horses, and women bathing and dressing seem to freeze a fleeting moment in their activity.

13. One word that best describes the primary theme of the above passage would be

    A. religion
    B. creativity
    C. tradition
    D. fame

14. Degas' paintings have, above all
    A. a feeling of natural light
    B. an unusual perspective
    C. brilliant colors
    D. all of the above

15. The author of the above passage would probably think that
    A. Degas' income suffered as a result of his break with tradition
    B. Degas was able to capture the lives of ordinary people in his art
    C. Impressionist painters paint themes from history
    D. all of the above

Mathematics Questions

1. What is the value of $\sqrt{144}$?
   A. 10
   B. 11
   C. 12
   D. 13

2. Solve for z: $z + 4 = 2z - 4$
   A. 0
   B. 2
   C. 4
   D. 8

3. The legs of a right triangle have lengths 3 feet and 4 feet respectively. Find the area of this triangle in square feet.
   A. 5 square feet
   B. 6 square feet
   C. 10 square feet
   D. 12 square feet

4. Evaluate the following expression for $x = 1, y = 0, z = -3$: $(x + y + z) \div 2$
   A. -2
   B. -1
   C. 1
   D. 2

5. Which of the following is equivalent to $x^2 - 2x - 3$?
   A. $(x - 3)(x + 1)$
   B. $(x + 3)(x - 1)$
   C. $(x - 2)(x - 3)$
   D. $(x + 2)(x + 3)$

6. The length of one side of an equilateral triangle is 3. What is the perimeter of this triangle?
   A. 3
   B. 6
   C. 9
   D. 12

7. Bobby is 2 years older than Karen and the sum of their ages is 42. How old is Bobby?

  A. 18
  B. 20
  C. 22
  D. 24

8. $(x^3 - x) - (x - x^3)$

  A. 0
  B. $-2x$
  C. $x^3 - x$
  D. $2x^3 - 2x$

9. Two six-sided fair die are rolled. What is the probability they both land on an even number?

  A. $\dfrac{1}{36}$

  B. $\dfrac{1}{6}$

  C. $\dfrac{1}{4}$

  D. $\dfrac{1}{3}$

10. Two boats left port, one headed due north and the other headed due east. At 13:00 the ship headed north was exactly 16 miles from port while the ship headed east was exactly 12 miles from port. At 13:00, what was the distance between the two ships?

  A. 4 miles
  B. 10 miles
  C. 20 miles
  D. 28 miles

11. In terms of π, the volume of a 20-foot-tall cylinder is 500π square feet. What is the diameter of this cylinder?

  A. 5 feet
  B. 10 feet
  C. 12.5 feet
  D. 25 feet

12. The semicircle in the diagram below has an area that is exactly ¼ the area of the circle. What is the measure of angle A?

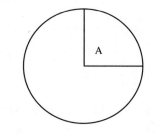

    A. 45°
    B. 90°
    C. 180°
    D. 360°

13. Assuming x is nonzero, divide: $\dfrac{4x^2 - x}{x}$.
    A. 3
    B. $3x$
    C. $4x - 1$
    D. $4x^2 - 1$

14. If $-3 \le x < 2$, which of the following is not a possible value for x?
    A. -3
    B. 0
    C. 1
    D. 2

15. Two complementary angles share the same measure. In degrees, what is the measure of one of these angles?
    A. 30°
    B. 45°
    C. 90°
    D. 180°

16. Solve for x: $\dfrac{2x}{7} = 8$.
    A. 14
    B. 28
    C. 56
    D. 112

Electronics Questions

1. The best type of outlet to use in a bathroom is
    A. wet GCB
    B. junction box
    C. GFCI
    D. single pole

2. The voltage required to run a 30 amp system with ½ ohm resistance would be
    A. 1.5V
    B. 6V
    C. 15V (key)
    D. 60V

3. A momentary, or push-button, switch is represented by
    A.
    B.
    C.
    D.

4. What voltage is required to provide 1000 watts at a current of 5 amps?
    A. 120V
    B. 200V
    C. 240V
    D. There is not enough information to calculate.

5. To operate a low-voltage appliance in a house, you must
    A. Run a parallel electrical system
    B. Use a plug with a built-in transformer
    C. Make sure to use a three-pronged plug
    D. Expect it to work slower

6. Electrical resistance is measured in
    A. Amps
    B. Ohms
    C. Volts
    D. Watts

7. This symbol represents which of the following?

   A. Transformer
   B. Cathode
   C. Ground
   D. Diode

8. On an AC circuit, a green wire would indicate
   A. an aluminum core
   B. the neutral circuit
   C. a grounding wire
   D. Color is not important.

9. In a 12-volt system, what is the minimum current requirement to operate a 60 watt bulb?
   A. 5 amps
   B. 10 amps
   C. 5 ohms
   D. 10 ohms

10. A multimeter is called that because
   A. It can be used to diagnose multiple brands of vehicle.
   B. It can measure multiple attributes of a circuit.
   C. It measures centimeters as well as kilometers.
   D. It controls multiple circuits in a system.

11. This symbol indicates a

   A. transistor
   B. resuscitator
   C. voltage
   D. resistor

12. The difference between a fuse and a breaker is
   A. A fuse can only be used once and a breaker can be reset.
   B. A fuse will fuse together, and a breaker will permanently break.
   C. A breaker is only used with AC, and a fuse is for DC.
   D. They both perform the same function in the exact same way.

13. In a simple 12V circuit containing 4 bulbs with a resistance of 1.5 ohms each, what would be the minimum amp rated fuse?
    A. 1.5 amps
    B. 2 amps
    C. 6 amps
    D. 8 amps

14. A battery can
    A. generate electrical current
    B. store electrical current
    C. convert electrical current
    D. switch electrical current

15. A series parallel circuit has
    A. a group of unconnected circuits installed in a parallel geometry
    B. a series of consumers in a row
    C. portions wired in series linked by multiple pathways
    D. very few applications in modern electronics

16. A high-frequency wave can be said to have
    A. many complete cycles per second
    B. extreme variations in amplitude
    C. a low Hertz rating
    D. none of the above

Automotive Information Questions

1. During which stroke of a four-stroke engine would the valves be closed and the piston be moving upward?
   A. Exhaust
   B. Compression
   C. Power
   D. Both B and C

2. When referring to brakes, ABS stands for
   A. All Braking Shoes
   B. Advanced Braking System
   C. Abort Before Stop
   D. Antilock Braking System

3. Which automotive component is most likely to affect the vehicle's ride height?
   A. Pitman arm
   B. Master cylinder
   C. Sway bar
   D. Spring

4. The alternator in an automotive electrical system is
   A. a circuit protection device
   B. Run by the engine
   C. an electronic control module
   D. responsible for starting the engine

5. As part of the cooling system, which part is responsible for maintaining a constant pressure?
   A. Water pump
   B. Thermostat
   C. Radiator cap
   D. Overflow tank

6. An engine will crank but won't run. What is NOT a likely cause?
   A. Faulty ignition system
   B. Failed fuel pump
   C. Lack of engine compression
   D. Dead battery

7. What attaches the steering gear box to the steering wheel?
   A. Steering column
   B. Connecting rod
   C. Pitman arm
   D. Steering rack

8. This part of the exhaust system's main purpose is emissions control
   A. thermostat
   B. catalytic converter
   C. muffler
   D. exhaust manifold

9. When a vehicle's warning light indicates overheating, you should
   A. Turn up the air conditioner to cool things down and drive to a service station.
   B. Continue to your destination and have the car checked out as soon as possible.
   C. Pull over and stop the engine. Let it cool down and check the coolant level.
   D. Switch to a lower gear so that the engine will turn more slowly and cool down.

10. In a 4-wheel-drive vehicle, how many axles are there?
    A. 1
    B. 2
    C. 3
    D. 4

11. If a vehicle starts using more fuel than normal, all of the following are possible causes except
    A. a leak in the fuel system
    B. a malfunctioning powertrain control module (PCM)
    C. a clogged air filter
    D. a corroded muffler

12. The following systems all utilize hydraulic power to some extent
    A. braking, steering, and automatic transmission
    B. steering, air intake, and ignition
    C. exhaust, powerglide, and fuel delivery system
    D. cooling, electrical, and suspension

Shop Information Questions

1. You are planning to build a mortared rock wall. You'll need
   A. ball peen hammer, trowel, file
   B. plumb bob, impact wrench, mason's hammer
   C. chisel, trowel, goggles
   D. grinder, level, epoxy

2. Your shop foreman sends you to the supply cabinet to get 8 nails to attach ¼" thick trim to a small cabinet. The nails you bring back are
   A. 2d common nails
   B. 4d finishing nails
   C. 6d smooth box
   D. 8d casing

3. When choosing the right welding mask, you should make sure that it
   A. is approved for the type of welding you are doing
   B. lets you see what's going on in the shop
   C. fits well and feels comfortable
   D. all of the above

4. When trying to match a machine screw, you'll need to measure it using
   A. run-out gauge and t-square
   B. level and dial gauge
   C. protractor and caliper
   D. ruler and micrometer

5. You've decided to renovate the porch on your house. The most durable material choices would be
   A. galvanized metal and marine-grade plywood
   B. tin and dimensional lumber
   C. MDF and Hardi-plank
   D. plywood and OSB

6. You realize one shelf is a bit too big to fit properly while assembling a pre-fabricated book case. Luckily, you are able to make it fit perfectly using your
   A. lathe
   B. plane
   C. bow saw
   D. adjustable wrench

7. While removing a bolt with a screwdriver, the driver slips repeatedly on the head. Your next step is to
   A. exert as much downward force as possible
   B. confirm you are using the correct size and style
   C. stabilize the screwdriver with a bucking bar
   D. use a center punch to knock it loose

8. When cutting a curve any of the following saws could be used except
   A. circular saw
   B. coping saw
   C. jigsaw
   D. band saw

9. A main benefit of a pneumatic system in a 10-person shop is
   A. It will be much quieter.
   B. The tools are cheaper.
   C. It is more efficient.
   D. It reduces dust and emissions.

10. Which hammer type is NOT used for striking?
    A. Claw
    B. Ball peen
    C. Masonry
    D. Torque

11. A multipurpose tool capable of great detail is
    A. a flex shaft
    B. a caliper
    C. a rasp
    D. an adjustable sledge

12. When fitting a bolt and nut together,
    A. the bolt can have a smaller pitch than the nut
    B. the nut can have a smaller pitch than the bolt
    C. the nut and bolt must have the same pitch
    D. the nut and bolt pitches are not important

Mechanical Comprehension Questions

1. Which is a displacement?
   A. 100 m/s
   B. 100 m northwest
   C. 100 m
   D. 100 m/s^2

2. Your car goes from + 30 m/s to rest in 2 s. What is its acceleration?
   A. −2 m/s^2
   B. −15 m/s^2
   C. +2 m/s^2
   D. +15 m/s^2

3. A paratrooper reaches terminal velocity where he is free-falling at a constant velocity. Which is true?
   A. The force of gravity is greater than air resistance.
   B. The force of gravity is less than air resistance.
   C. The force of gravity equals air resistance.
   D. There is no gravity acting on him anymore.

4. Which is a force of attraction?
   A. Drag
   B. Gravity
   C. Normal force
   D. Tension

5. Which is the approximate weight of a 100-kg barrel?
   A. 100 N
   B. 200 N
   C. 1,000 N
   D. 5,000 N

6. A 500-kg crate has a weight of 5,000 N. What is the normal force on the crate?
   A. −5,000 N
   B. −100 N
   C. +100 N
   D. +5,000 N

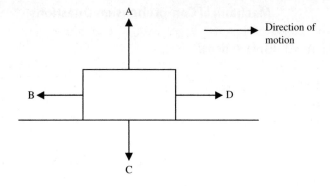

7. A box is moving along the floor as shown in the diagram. Which is represented by arrow C?
   A. Applied force
   B. Weight
   C. Normal force
   D. Friction

8. You push a ball from the bottom of a hill to the top of the hill. Which is true?
   A. The kinetic energy of the ball is zero while its potential energy increases to maximum.
   B. Both the potential energy and kinetic energy of the ball decrease to zero.
   C. The kinetic energy of the ball increases to maximum while its potential energy decreases to zero.
   D. Both the potential and kinetic energy of the ball increase to maximum.

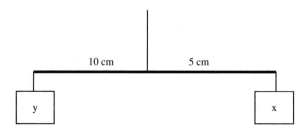

9. Two different masses are balanced from a rod attached to a wire as shown in the diagram. The distances from the center of rotation are shown. What is the ratio of mass y to mass x?

    A. $\dfrac{1}{2}$

    B. 1

    C. $1\dfrac{1}{2}$

    D. 2

10. A man exerts a 50 N force on a bowling ball over a distance of 1 m before releasing it. How much work does he do on the ball?

    A. 5 J

    B. 50 J

    C. 100 J

    D. 150 J

11. In which lever is the direction of the input force opposite that of the output force?

    A. see-saw

    B. wheelbarrow

    C. fishing rod

    D. crowbar

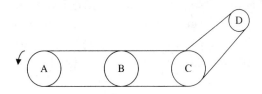

12. A belt-and-pulley system is shown in the diagram. Pulley A is the driving pulley and is spinning in the direction indicated by the arrow. Relative to Pulley A, which is true?

    A. Pulley B will turn in the same direction, but at a slower rate.

    B. Pulley C will turn in the opposite direction, but at a faster rate.

    C. Pulley D will turn in the same direction, but at a faster rate.

    D. All the pulleys will turn in the same direction at the same rate.

13. Which machine is a double lever?
    A. Wedge
    B. Scissors
    C. Baseball bat
    D. Wheelbarrow

14. A machine has 90% efficiency. Which is true?
    A. The output force is 0.9 times the input force.
    B. The output work is greater than the input work.
    C. The input distance is less than the output distance.
    D. The output work is 0.9 times that of the input work.

15. A 70 kg man sits on a 10 kg bicycle. The tires of the bicycle touch the ground with an area of 0.2 m². What is the pressure exerted on the ground by the man and bike?
    A. 1,000 Pa
    B. 2,000 Pa
    C. 4,000 Pa
    D. 8,000 Pa

16. The pistons of a hydraulic press have areas of 1 m² and 100 m². If you press down on the smaller piston with a given force, then how much pressure will be exerted on the second piston?
    A. The same pressure as exerted on the first piston
    B. Twice the pressure as exerted on the first piston
    C. Ten times the pressure exerted on the first piston
    D. One hundred times the pressure exerted on the first piston

Assembling Objects Questions

In each of the following questions, the picture at the left shows a group of parts. Answer choices A–D show objects made from assembled parts. Choose the one that is made from the parts shown at the left.

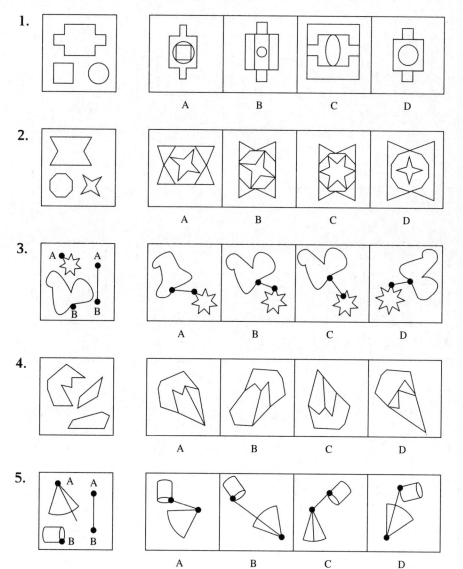

6.

7.

8.

9.

10.

11.

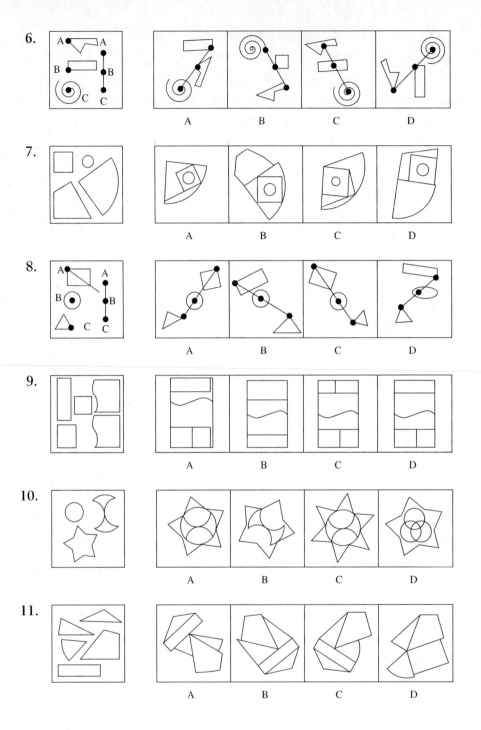

12.

13.

14.

15.

16.

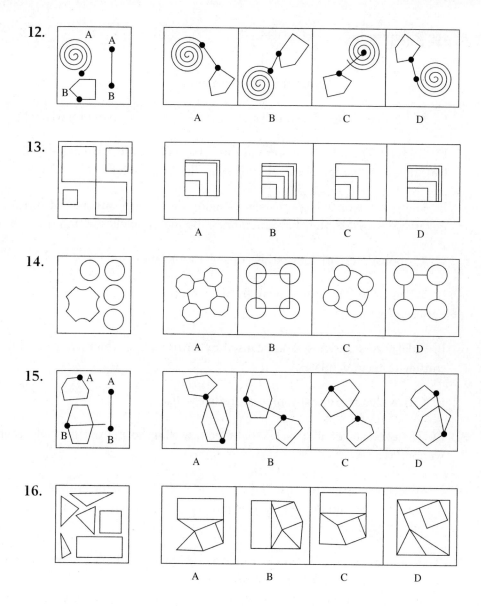

Practice Test 2 Answers

General Science Answers

1. **D.** As bivalve mollusks, geoducks are invertebrates with two hinged shells.

2. **D.** Bacteria. The other kingdoms in this list are all composed of eukaryotic organisms that feature membrane-bound organelles in their cells.

3. **B.** The vast majority of protists are single-celled organisms, and all protists are eukaryotes—that is, they have membrane-bound organelles within their cells.

4. **C.** Carbohydrates are long strings of sugar molecules.

5. **B.** When two plates move away from each other, they can form a deep trench between them.

6. **B.** Tidal waves are most often caused by earthquakes, which are caused by the shifting of tectonic plates.

7. **B.** Cirrus clouds are wispy, high-altitude clouds.

8. **D.** The ozone layer absorbs UV light from within the stratosphere, which grows warmer as a result.

9. **B.** Warm air masses are most likely to form near the equator, both because water abounds at the equator, and because it receives the most direct sunlight year-round, on average.

10. **B.** Sedimentary rocks are made from smaller fragments deposited by water movements and other processes. As a result, they are the most likely to have started forming on the surface. However, extrusive igneous rocks also form on the surface, such as cooling lava from a volcano.

11. **C.** Mercury and Venus are the two planets in our solar system that lack moons.

12. **D.** Regardless of where these objects sit within their orbits at any time, the moon is always closer to Earth than the sun, and Neptune is farther still.

13. **C.** Venus is the second-brightest object in the night sky, after the moon.

14. **A.** Cones are the retinal neurons capable of distinguishing different colors of light. Rods can detect visible light, but they cannot distinguish different colors.

15. **C.** White blood cells called plasma cells make antibodies that bind to specific molecules, generally those that are newcomers.

16. **A.** The heart's left atrium receives oxygen-rich blood from the lungs. From there, it passes to the heart's left ventricle, which sends it through the aorta to the rest of the body.

17. **A.** Mass and acceleration. Force is an influence that changes an object's motion or direction, and it is calculated by multiplying an object's mass by its acceleration.

18. **B.** Copper is a good electrical conductor, so it's the least suitable insulator in this list. By contrast, glass, rubber, and air all inhibit the flow of electricity.

19. **C.** Acceleration is the change in velocity over a period of time.

20. **B.** Torque is a twisting force that tends to cause rotation.

21. **C.** Pure water has a pH of 7, which is neutral. A pH less than 7 is acidic, while a pH higher than 7 is basic. Alkaline is another word for basic.

22. **D.** Zero Kelvin is the theoretical temperature at which no heat can be removed from a system and no particles exhibit movement.

23. **B.** NaCl is the formula for sodium chloride. Na is the symbol for sodium and Cl is the symbol for chlorine.

24. **C.** The brain and spinal cord comprise the central nervous system. They also make up the majority of the total human nervous system.

25. **A.** Producer. Organisms that photosynthesize make their own food from water, carbon dioxide and sunlight.

Arithmetic Answers

1. **D.** This question is asking for the area of the wall which is found by multiplying 8 and 11.

2. **B.** To find the average, add the values and then divide by how many there are: $14 + 12 + 16 = 42$ and $42 \div 3 = 14$.

3. **B.** The daily charge over 5 days was $5 \times 15.95 = 79.75$, leaving a charge of $87.15 - 79.75 = 7.4$ from mileage. Since each mile costs .20 dollars, there must have been $7.4 \div 0.2 = 37$ miles driven.

4. **B.** $1500 \div 5 = 300$ and $300 \div 5 = 60$; therefore, the next number must be $60 \div 5 = 12$.

5. **C.** There are 60 minutes in every hour and $60 \div 15 = 4$. In other words, there are four 15-minutes periods each hour and since Randi ran 2 miles in one of these periods, she must have ran $2 \times 4 = 8$ miles in a full hour.

6. **A.** The copy paper cost $\frac{1}{4} \times 450.20 = 112.55$.

7. **B.** Each gallon contributed $3.45 to the total cost. Therefore, there must be $51.75 \div 3.45 = 15$ total gallons purchased.

8. **A.** Of the shipment, $\frac{1}{2} \times 480 = 240$ pounds are potatoes and carrots while $\frac{1}{3} \times 480 = 160$ pounds are tomatoes. This leaves $480 - 240 - 160 = 80$ pounds of broccoli.

9. **D.** Of the 2,400 people, $\frac{3}{10} \times 2400 = 720$ can be expected to fail leaving 2,400 $- 720 = 1,680$ that can be expected to pass.

10. **A.** $5\frac{1}{4} \div 2\frac{4}{5} = \frac{21}{4} \div \frac{14}{5} = \frac{21}{4} \times \frac{5}{14} = \frac{3}{4} \times \frac{5}{2} = \frac{15}{8} = 1\frac{7}{8}$.

11. **B.** When the trench is included, the area is 156 square feet and the length is 13 feet; therefore, the width is $156 \div 13 = 12$ feet. When the trench is not included, the length and width are both smaller by 1 foot and the new area is $11 \times 12 = 132$ square feet.

12.   **B.** After the roommate who is owed money takes his portion of the movies, there will be 152 − 80 = 72 movies left. These will be split evenly among 2 people, meaning each person gets $\frac{1}{2} \times 72 = 36$ movies.

13.   **C.** The father will contribute 0.85 × 1200 = 1020.

14.   **A.** Each foot is represented by ¾ inches. Therefore, 864 feet will be represented by $864 \times \frac{3}{4} = 648$ inches.

15.   **C.** This can be approached by either converting both times to local L.A. time or both to local Chicago time. If local Chicago time is used, the flight left at 1:45, but arrived at 5:35. This is ten minutes less than 4 hours, i.e., 3 hours and 50 minutes.

16.   **C.** The total will be 45.06 + 86.12 + 12.98 = 144.16.

Word Knowledge Answers

1. **B.** Choice B is correct. Lithe means supple or easily bent. Its origin is from an Old English word. This is the kind of word that needs to be memorized. Make sure to review word lists with definitions.

2. **D.** D is the correct choice. Intrinsic means inborn or natural. The prefix in-, meaning in or within offers some clue. Context clues in the sentence are not a help in figuring out the meaning of this word.

3. **A.** Propensity means tendency or inclination. The word comes from a Latin word that means to be inclined. The other choices are not related to the word. The word propel might be a help in understanding the meaning.

4. **D.** Choice D is correct. Prescience means forethought, knowledge of events or actions before they happen. The prefix pre-, meaning earlier or before, offers you a clue. It is extremely helpful to review the meanings of prefixes and suffixes to help you figure out the meanings of words.

5. **C.** Pragmatic means practical so Choice C is correct. The origin of the word is from the Greek. Since there are no context clues to go by, nor are there obvious affixes that help, this word would need to be memorized. Make sure to review word lists with definitions to prepare for the exam.

6. **B.** Choice B is correct. The adjective obdurate means unbending or hardened against feeling. The root word dur, meaning hard, can give you a clue to the word's meaning as in the expression hardnosed.

7. **B.** Choice B is the correct choice. Sporadic means erratic or intermittent. It comes from a Greek word meaning scattered. This is the type of word that needs to be memorized. Reviewing vocabulary lists with definitions can help you learn more words.

8. **C.** C is the correct choice. Bellicose means hostile. If you are familiar with the word belligerent, it would help you figure out the meaning. The word comes from the Latin word for war. The other choices are not related.

9. **A.** Choice A is correct; auspicious means favorable. You would need to know this word since there is no clear clue. It is very important to review word and definition lists.

10. **C.** Choice C is correct. The verb remonstrate means to object or protest. The word demonstrate comes from the same Latin root. It could help you figure out the meaning.

11. **D.** The adjective intrepid means fearless or brave, so D is the correct choice. You could use context clues to figure out the meaning of this word by placing each of the word choices where intrepid is and see which one makes the most sense.

12. **B.** The correct choice is B. Voluble means fluent or articulate. Unfortunately context clues do not help you understand the meaning of the word.

13. **C.** Choice C is correct. Urban is the opposite of bucolic, which means pastoral or rural. In this case, you need to know the word's meaning.

14. **D.** The noun sojourn means a stay or a temporary period of residence. Context clues do not really help in this instance. Any one of the choices would make sense in the sentence. Make sure to review lists of words with their definitions.

15. **B.** To ostracize someone is to exclude him or her or to banish or blackball that person, especially from a group. The word comes from a Greek word, but there is no easy way to analyze it for its meaning. Context clues do not work here. It needs to be memorized.

16. **A.** Choice A is correct. An exigency is a crisis or a situation that is urgent. Context clues are helpful here. Both choices C and D can be eliminated based on context clues.

17. **B.** An ablution is a washing or cleansing, usually as part of a religious rite. The prefix ab- means away. That is the only clue for this word that is from a Latin word that means the same thing.

18. **D.** The verb apprise means to inform or to give notice to. You will need to memorize words like this one that cannot be analyzed easily.

19. **C.** C is the correct choice. Recondite means obscure or not easily understood. The other choices are not related to the meaning of the word.

20. **A.** Choice A is correct. Sanguine means confident and upbeat. The word comes from the Latin word for blood and can also refer to the color red or someone who has a reddish complexion.

21. **C.** A scion is an heir or a descendant. The other choices are not related. This is a word that needs to be memorized since there is nothing in it that gives clues to the meaning.

22. **D.** Lucid means clear or cogent. The word comes from the Latin for light. It is a good idea to review some of the Latin roots to help you figure out the meaning of words. Context can be of help here as well.

23. **A.** The adjective circumspect means prudent or heedful of a situation. If you analyze the word, you may come up with some clues. Circum is similar to the word circle or around. Spect is related to seeing (spectacles), so it is not hard to figure out the word's meaning. The other choices are not related to the meaning of circumspect.

24. **C.** Choice C is correct. Burnish means to polish or make glossy. Context clues can help here. By placing each word choice where burnish is you can see that polish makes the most sense.

25. **B.** The correct choice is B as halcyon means tranquil or calm and peaceful. The word, which also means a kind of bird, comes from a Greek word for a fabled bird that it was thought calmed the wind and the waves.

26. **D.** Choice D is correct. Harbinger means forerunner, something that indicates or foreshadows something to come. The other choices are not related to the word in meaning.

27. **A.** The noun lassitude means tiredness or lethargy. It comes from a Latin word that means weary.

28. **C.** Choice C is correct; postulate means to presume, or assume as a premise. It is another word that needs to be memorized.

29. **B.** Choice B is correct. The adjective motley means diverse or having great variety. The word comes from the Middle English word mot, meaning speck.

30. **A.** Choice A is correct. Torpid means inactive, even lazy. There is no easy way to figure out the meaning of this word. It needs to be memorized.

31. **B.** Scurrilous means insulting or vulgar, especially in terms of talking. There is nothing that would help you understand the meaning of the word. In fact you might think it was related to the word scurry, but it is not.

32. **A.** Choice A is correct. The verb rescind means to repeal or to make void. The prefix re- meaning over or again should help you figure this word out.

33. **C.** Choice C is correct. Inured means accustomed, especially to something unpleasant. This word does not have much in the way of clues. Remember to review lists of words and their definitions before the examination.

34. **D.** The adjective unwonted means unusual or out of the ordinary. The prefix *un-*, meaning not, is a bit of a clue.

35. **B.** Choice B is correct. Fruition means accomplishment, a realization of something. The base word fruit might suggest the meaning. The fruit is what is created or accomplished by a plant or, if used figuratively, by a person.

Paragraph Comprehension Answers

1. **D.** According to the passage, Markham was the first woman to fly alone across the Atlantic. This is what she was famous for. The other events occurred, but they were not the reason that she was famous.

2. **B.** The second sentence states that early measurements were based on body parts like feet. This is the topic sentence and what the passage is mostly about. Choice A may be true, but it is not what the passage is mostly about. There is nothing in the passage to suggest that choice C is the main idea. Choice D is a detail from the passage, not the main idea.

3. **A.** The passage states that the Medal of Honor is awarded to members of the armed services and the Coast Guard, so Choice A is an incorrect statement. Choice B is clearly correct. Based on the information in the passage, you can figure out that the award dates back to the Civil War. Choice D is also correct.

4. **C.** The author states that modern families, with their computers and equipment, could feel frustrated with old fashioned wiring. Choice A is not correct. This is not what the author says. Choice B may be true, but this is not something that the author talks about. Choice D is also an incorrect choice. The author says that unlined chimneys can pose a fire threat, not that they are drafty and uncomfortable.

5. **B.** According to the passage the Sioux believed in living in harmony with nature and the environment. While there were large numbers of Sioux, this did not characterize them. Choice C is not correct; the Sioux moved from one place to another.

6. **C.** The passage states that the Sioux were their own masters because they could come and go as they pleased, living a nomadic life and answering to nobody. While they did ride horses brought by the Spanish to this country, this does not make them their own masters. Choices B and D are also incorrect.

7. **B.** The passage states that there are manmade islands at each end of the two tunnels, for a total of four, so choice B makes an incorrect statement. Choice A is correct. There are four manmade islands and one barrier island, Fisherman Island. Choices C and D are also correct.

8. **D.** The passage states that the credit is phased out for a married couple filing jointly with an income of over $160,000, but it does not say how much, so the question can't be answered.

9. **C.** The passage states that a child might find it a drawback to community college that he will be living at home, so choice C is correct. Choices A and D would seem to be advantages, not disadvantages. Choice B could be a disadvantage to some students.

10. **D.** The passage states that students who live on campus do better academically, so Choice D is correct. Choice A is not correct; there is no mention that the state schools have found this to be true. The passage notes that choice B occurs, but it is not something that the state schools have found. Choice C is also incorrect.

11. **D.** The passage states that there are three credit reporting agencies—Equifax, Experian and Trans Union. Each one scores consumers with a numerical score that lenders use to determine credit worthiness, so choice D is correct.

12. **B.** The last sentence of the passage states that a borrower's DTI (Debt to Income Ratio) should not be more than 35% of gross monthly income, so choice B is the correct answer.

13. **B.** Degas' creativity is stressed throughout the entire passage, in his use of color, his experimentation, and turning to sculpture when his eyesight became impaired, so B is the correct choice.

14. **D.** All of the statements are supported directly by the passage, making D the correct choice.

15. **B.** The passage stresses that Degas painted ordinary people, in their homes, gardens, music halls and cafes, so choice C is correct. The author does not seem to make a connection between Degas' income and his breaking with tradition so choice A is not correct. Choice C is not correct. The author says that this is not what the Impressionists did.

Mathematical Knowledge Answers

1. **C.** This question is equivalent to asking "what number times itself is 144?" and $12 \times 12 = 144$.

2. **D.** $z + 4 = 2z - 4$

    $4 = z - 4$

    $8 = z$

3. **B.** The area of any triangle is $\frac{1}{2}bh$ where b is the measure of the base and h is the measure of the height. In this case: $A = \frac{1}{2}(3)(4) = 6$.

4. **B.** Plug in the values to the corresponding variables and follow the order of operations: $(1 + 0 - 3) \div 2 = -2 \div 2 = -1$.

5. **A.** To factor this quadratic, find factors of -3 which will add to -2. Those factors are -3 and 1 meaning this quadratic factors to $(x - 3)(x + 1)$.

6. **C.** An equilateral triangle has sides that are all the same length. Therefore, this triangle has sides $3,3,3$ and the perimeter is $3 + 3 + 3 = 9$.

7. **C.** If Karen's age is x then Bobby's is $2x$ and $x + (x + 2) = 42$. Solving this equation results in $x = 20$. Therefore, Bobby's age is 22.

8. **D.** Distribute the negative and add:

    $(x^3 - x) - (x - x^3) =$

    $x^3 - x - x + x^3 =$

    $2x^3 - 2x$

9. **C.** The probability a single die lands on an even number is $\frac{3}{6} = \frac{1}{2}$. Since the rolls are independent, the probability that both land on an even number is

    $\frac{1}{2} \times \frac{1}{2} = \frac{1}{4}$.

10. **C.** The lines representing the paths of both boats form a right triangle with legs of 16 and 12, respectively. The distance between the two ships would be the hypotenuse and can be found using the Pythagorean theorem.

    $16^2 + 12^2 = c^2$

    $256 + 144 = c^2$

    $400 = c^2$

    $20 = c$

11. **B.** The volume of any cylinder is $V = \pi r^2 h$ where r is the radius and h is the height. In this case:

$$V = \pi r^2 \times 20 = 500\pi$$
$$r^2 = 25$$
$$r = 5$$

Since the radius is 5, the diameter must be 10.

12. **B.** The full angle within the circle is $360°$. Therefore, angle A has measure $\frac{1}{4} \times 360 = 90$.

13. **C.** Factor an x from the numerator and cancel it out with the x in the denominator.

$$\frac{x(4x - 1)}{x} = 4x - 1.$$

14. **D.** The inequality states that x can be any value between -3 and 2 including -2, but not including 2.

15. **B.** Complementary angles have a sum of $90°$. Let x represent the shared measure. Then $2x = 90$ and $x = 45$.

16. **B.** Rewrite 8 as a fraction and then cross multiply.

$$\frac{2x}{7} = \frac{8}{1}$$
$$2x = 56$$
$$x = 28$$

Electronics Answers

1. **C.** A GFCI, or Ground Fault Circuit Interrupt, contains a circuit breaker and is designed to reduce the risk of electrocution. Local building codes specify where they should be installed.

2. **C.** Using Ohm's law, $I \times R = V$, or 30 amps $\times$ .5 ohm = 15V.

3. **A.** The other symbols are for different types of switches: B: 2-Way, C: Dual On-off; D: On-Off.

4. **B.** Using Watt's law, $P/V = I$; 1000/5 = 200V

5. **B.** A transformer steps down voltage from household current to low voltage. Many cell phones and portable electronics use these to charge.

6. **B**

7. **D**

8. **C**

9. **A.** Using Watt's law, $P/V = I$; 60/12 = 5. "I" stands for Intensity, or current, which is measured in amps. Ohms are a measure of resistance.

10. **B.** A multimeter can measure circuit attributes such as voltage, resistance, and current flow. (volts, ohms, and amps)

11. **D**

12. **A**

13. **B.** First, find the total resistance in the circuit: $4 \times 1.5 = 6$ ohms. Next, apply Ohm's law: $V/R = I$; 12V/6 = 2 amps.

14. **B**

15. **C**

16. **A**

Automotive Information Answers

1. **B.** While the valves are closed on both the compression and power stroke, it is only during the compression stroke that the piston is moving upward.

2. **D.** ABS stands for antilock braking system which assist with skid control.

3. **D.** Although sway bars and springs are both part of the suspension system, springs determine ride height. A master cylinder is part of the braking system, and a pitman arm is a steering component.

4. **B.** The alternator is a mechanical generator of DC current run by the engine, typically by means of a belt.

5. **C.** Although all of these are components of the cooling system, only the radiator cap regulates pressure.

6. **D.** A dead battery would keep the engine from even cranking over, but the other options would keep an engine from running.

7. **A.** The pitman arm and steering rack are steering components, but are not attached directly to the steering wheel. The connecting rod is part of the engine.

8. **B.** True to its name, the catalytic converter converts hydrocarbons present in the exhaust gases, making it an EPA regulated emission-control device. Mufflers primarily muffle sound, and the exhaust manifold collects exhaust directly from the engine.

9. **C.** Since overheating can cause severe engine damage very quickly, stopping as soon as possible is a good idea, and the coolant should not be checked on a hot engine. To limit engine damage, options A and B are not recommended. Switching to a lower gear won't affect the engine's turning rate, and will not stop overheating.

10. **D.** A 4-wheel vehicle has two driveshafts, one transferring power to the front wheels, and the other to the rear wheels. There are, however, four axles on a 4-wheel-drive vehicle, one to each wheel.

11. **D.** While a corroded muffler would increase noise emissions, it could not increase fuel consumption. All of the other options would increase fuel consumption. A clogged air filter causes the engine to work harder and reduces fuel economy. Since the PCM maintains the fuel mixture ratio it directly affects fuel usage.

12. **A.** Braking, steering, and automatic transmission all use hydraulics to transfer power. Air intake (B) and exhaust (C) process only air, but no liquid. The ignition (B) and electrical systems (D) use electrical current.

Shop Information Answers

1. **C.** The ball peen hammer (A) is used with metal, an impact wrench (B) is used to loosen fasteners, epoxy (D) won't be of any use in a masonry project.

2. **B.** Common nails have too large a head. The 6d (2") and 8d (2.5") nails would both be too long for this application.

3. **D.** Welding operations have different safety requirements, and you should make sure you are adequately protected. Good visibility is important both for quality work and to insure the safety of yourself and others. All safety equipment should fit well, so that it provides maximum benefit, and feel comfortable, so that you actually use it.

4. **D.** The ruler will measure the length of the screw, and the micrometer will measure the diameter.

5. **A.** Both of these are rated for exposure to elements. Tin, MDF, and OSB are not as durable.

6. **B.** A planer removes small amounts of material, usually in the form of shavings.

7. **B.** Since there are so many types and sizes of screwdrivers, it is prudent to confirm you are using the correct driver to match your fastener. Downward force might cause the head of the bolt to wear out or "strip" if you are not using the proper driver. A bucking bar is only used when riveting, and a center punch might damage the bolt's head by gouging it.

8. **A.** The name "circular" refers to the shape of the blade on the circular saw. In fact, it excels at straight, even cuts. Any of the other saws listed can be used to cut curves.

9. **C**

10. **D.** There is a torque hammer, but it is actually a type of drill. All of the other choices are hammers.

11. **A.** Also known as a Dremel, many different attachments can be used with the shaft, from polishing to engraving and carving bits.

12. **C**

Mechanical Comprehension Answers

1. **B.** Displacement has a magnitude (100 m) and a direction (northwest).

2. **B.** Acceleration is the change in velocity (–30 m/s) divided by the time interval (2 s), which comes out to be –15 m/s².

3. **C.** The paratrooper is free-falling at a constant velocity. According to Newton's First Law, there is no net force acting upon him. So, the force of gravity must equal air resistance.

4. **B.** Gravity is a force of attraction between two masses.

5. **C.** Weight is the product of mass and acceleration due to gravity. So, the 100-kg barrel has a weight of approximately 1,000 N (W = (100kg)(10 m/s²) = 1,000 N).

6. **A.** The action force is the weight of the crate (+5,000 N). According to Newton's Third Law, the reaction force is the normal force, which is equal, but opposite to the weight. Therefore, the normal force is –5,000 N.

7. **B.** Arrow C is the downward force exerted by gravity. This force is the crate's weight.

8. **A.** You do work on the ball and increase its potential energy to its maximum. Since the ball is at rest at the top of the hill, then its kinetic energy is zero.

9. **A.** The masses are balanced, so the torques must be equal. The lever arm of mass y is twice that of mass x. Therefore, mass y must be half as massive as mass x.

10. **B.** Work is the product of force (50 N) times the distance over which it is applied (1 m), which is 50 J.

11. **A.** In a class 1 lever, like a see-saw, the direction of the input force is opposite that of the output force.

12. **C.** None of the belts cross, so all of the pulleys turn in the same direction. However, because Pulley D is smaller, it will turn at a faster rate.

13. **B.** Scissors are an example of a double lever.

14. **D.** A real machine has an efficiency (eff), which is the ratio of output work to input work (eff = Wout/Win × 100%). In this case, the ratio of output work to input work is 0.9.

15. **C.** Pressure is equal to the applied force divided by the area (0.2 m²). The man and the bike combined have a mass of 80 kg and, therefore, a weight of 800 N. So, the pressure is 800 N/0.2 m² or 4,000 Pa.

16. **A.** In a hydraulic press, the pressure exerted on one piston is equal to that exerted on the other.

Assembling Objects Answers

1. D

2. B

3. B

4. C

5. B

6. D

7. A

8. C

9. D

10. A

11. C

12. D

13. A

14. D

15. C

16. B

Jobs in Today's Military

The U.S. military is like a giant corporation in many ways. The jobs that exist in most large civilian companies also exist in the military. There are doctors of all specialties, writers, photographers, engineers, mechanics, research scientists, and many other types of jobs.

The benefit of joining the military is that job training for what are often highly specialized careers requiring expensive education and training (for example, engineering and medicine) is provided for free in the military. If you show a particular interest or aptitude for a certain kind of work, it is likely you can find it in one of the military branches.

Jobs in the Army

The official U.S. Army website (http://www.goarmy.com/careers-and-jobs .html) lists the following general job categories:

Administrative Support

Arts and Media

Combat

Computers and Technology

Construction and Engineering

Intelligence and Combat Support

Legal and Law Enforcement

Mechanics

Medical and Emergency

Transportation and Aviation

Jobs in the Navy

The official U.S. Navy website (http://www.navy.com/careers.html) lists the following general job categories:

Arts and Education

Aviation

Business and Legal

Chaplain and Support

Engineering and Applied Science

Healthcare

Information and Technology

Nuclear Energy

Service and Safety

Special Warfare/Special Operations

Jobs in the Air Force

The official U.S. Air Force website (http://www.airforce.com/careers/) lists the following general areas of career interest available to those who join the Air Force:

Aircraft

Arts and Education

Business, Operations, and Administration

Computers and Computer Science

Electronics and Electrics

Emergency Management and Response

Engineering and Applied Science

Facilities

Fuel and Propulsion Systems

Future Technologies

Ground Vehicles

Health and Medicine

Intelligence

Law

Logistics and Transportation

Maintenance and Repair

Natural Science

Space

Special Operations

Weaponry and Materiel

Jobs in the Marine Corps

The official U.S. Marines website (http://www.usmilitary.com/us-marine
-corps-jobs-enlisted-occupations/) lists the following general entry-level categories for new marines:

Combat Specialties

Electronic/Electrical Systems

Engineering, Science, and Technical

Logistics and Supply

Personnel/Base Support

Vehicle and Machinery Mechanics

These general categories included both enlisted and officer-level jobs. New
recruits find their ways into their specialties after basic training, when they
attend advanced individual training (AIT). It is during AIT that recruits learn
what they need to know to start their new jobs. This involves both hands-on
training and classroom training. Often, this classroom training translates into
college credit: in fact, 2,300 colleges and universities recognize some AIT
courses for college credit.

Choosing the Right Job for You

Your job preference is certainly taken into consideration when you join the military; however, your ultimate assignment will depend on your aptitude (as assessed by the ASVAB) and the particular needs of the military at any given time. Recruiters will best be able to answer questions about what the military particularly needs.

Note that not all jobs are open to women. In general, these are combat positions. However, there are many jobs available for women in all branches of the military.

Life After Military Services

Members of the military find that they are given higher levels of responsibility more quickly than many of their civilian counterparts. Young people in the military often find themselves in positions of leadership and great responsibility involving life-and-death situations. Naturally, this leads to strong job prospects after a term of military service is completed. Additionally, since time spent in military service has always been honored by our country, you will find that your time spent in the military will afford you a large measure of respect with potential employers.

When considering what to do after military service is ended, it is often helpful to consider whether you would like to continue in the same line of work you had in the military or pursue an entirely different career. Because of the educational benefits offered to veterans, honorably discharged veterans have many options. The so-called GI Bill (the common name for multiple laws, enacted since 1944, concerning benefits for veterans) provides a wide range of financial assistance for undergraduate, graduate, and vocational training. You can find out more at the official GI Bill website: http://www.gibill.va.gov/.

If you decide that you would like to continue in the line of work that you pursue in the military, a good place to start is the Department of Labor's O*Net Crosswalk website. There you can enter your military occupation code and find suggestions for equivalent or similar civilian jobs. The website can be found at: http://www.onetonline.org/crosswalk/.